Social Identities and Multiple Selves in Foreign Language Education

Also Available from Bloomsbury

Culturally Speaking, 2nd Edition, Helen Spencer-Oatey
Language, Culture and Identity, Philip Riley
Rethinking Idiomaticity, Stefanie Wulff
Second Language Identities, David Block

Social Identities and Multiple Selves in Foreign Language Education

Edited by

Damian J. Rivers and Stephanie Ann Houghton

B L O O M S B U R Y
LONDON • NEW DELHI • NEW YORK • SYDNEY

Bloomsbury Academic
An imprint of Bloomsbury Publishing Plc

50 Bedford Square
London
WC1B 3DP
UK

1385 Broadway
New York
NY 10018
USA

www.bloomsbury.com

First published 2013

British Library Cataloguing-in-Publication Data
A catalogue record for this book is available from the British Library.

ISBN: HB: 978-1-4411-0115-0
ePDF: 978-1-4411-6438-4
ePub: 978-1-4411-6064-5

Library of Congress Cataloging-in-Publication Data
Social identities and multiple selves in foreign language education /
Edited by Damian J. Rivers and Stephanie Ann Houghton.
pages cm
Includes bibliographical references and index.
ISBN 978-1-4411-0115-0 (hardcover : alk. paper) – ISBN 978-1-4411-6438-4 (pdf : alk. paper) – ISBN 978-1-4411-6064-5 1. Language and languages–Study and teaching. I. Rivers, Damian J. II. Houghton, Stephanie, 1969-
P53.S58 2012
418.0071–dc23

2013009055

Typeset by Newgen Imaging Systems Pvt Ltd, Chennai, India
Printed and bound in Great Britain

Contents

List of Illustrations vii

Acknowledgements viii

Notes on Contributors ix

Introduction: Identities in Foreign Language Education
Damian J. Rivers and Stephanie Ann Houghton 1

1 The Institutional and Beyond: On the Identity Displays of Foreign Language Teachers *Jose Aguilar* 13

2 Implications for Identity: Inhabiting the 'Native-Speaker' English Teacher Location in the Japanese Sociocultural Context *Damian J. Rivers* 33

3 Professional Identities Shaped by Resistance to Target Language Only Policies *Brian A. McMillan* 57

4 Language, Culture and Identity: Transcultural Practices and Theoretical Implications *Claudia Kunschak and Felix Girón* 77

5 Social Identifications and Culturally Located Identities: Developing Cultural Understanding through Literature *Melina Porto* 103

6 Reimagining Sociolinguistic Identification in Foreign Language Classroom Communities of Practice *Deborah Cole and Bryan Meadows* 121

7 The Foreign Language Imagined Learning Community: Developing Identity and Increasing Foreign Language Investment *John W. Schwieter* 139

8 Foreign Language Motivation and Social Identity Development *Lou Harvey* 157

9 Emotive Accounts of the Self during an ERASMUS Sojourn Abroad *Sonia Gallucci* 177

10 Setting Standards for Intercultural Communication: Universalism and Identity Change *Stephanie Ann Houghton* 195

References 215

Index 241

List of Illustrations

Figures

6.1	Idealized identity in traditional foreign language classroom	129
6.2	Multimemberships in foreign language classrooms informed by CoP	130
6.3	Reimagining identification in Anytown High School's Japanese languages classroom	133
7.1	Editorial board structure for the magazine project	147
7.2	Editorial stages of scaffolding writing for each essay	147
7.3	Writing development within essays	148
7.4	Writing development between essays	149
9.1	Taxonomy of psychological conditions: Affective lexicon	180

Tables

1.1	An overview of the participants and their teaching context	19
2.1	Demographic overview of the five respondents	39
7.1	Self-ratings of language abilities	146
9.1	Affective lexicon used by the case-study participant	181
10.1	An overview of syllabus design	198
10.2	Definitions of the terms presented to students in Weeks 2 and 4	199
10.3	Statement patterns indicative of student identity development	200
10.4	Data illustrating the statement patterns indicative of student identity development	201

Acknowledgements

We offer our sincere gratitude to all of the contributing authors for their scholarship, investment, perseverance, flexibility and support throughout the duration of this project. We also express our profound thanks to the editorial staff at Continuum and Bloomsbury for their dedicated professionalism and astute guidance.

Damian J. Rivers and Stephanie Ann Houghton
Osaka and Fukuoka, Japan
1 December 2012

Notes on Contributors

Jose Aguilar (Ph.D., Sorbonne Nouvelle-Paris 3 University, France) is a senior lecturer in applied linguistics at Sorbonne Nouvelle-Paris 3 University, in France. His research interests include interaction within institutional contexts, such as classroom situations, foreign language education, especially aspects in relation to language teachers' cognition and beliefs systems, and qualitative research methodology. He is involved in national projects interested in describing the language teachers' savoir faire, and in European research projects that try to answer questions on multilingualism, multiliteracies, the use of information and communication technology in educational contexts, and language teachers' development of professional identities. For more information see (http://aquilario.c.la/).

Deborah Cole (Ph.D., University of Arizona, USA) is an associate professor of linguistics in the Department of English at the University of Texas-Pan American. Her research interests include the ideologies of standardization and variation in institutional discourse and the performance and perception of accent and register in the semiotics of identity. Her ongoing fieldwork in Indonesia gives her a global perspective on diversity and language contact in the United States and informs her approach to pedagogy in classrooms of multilingual students. She currently serves as the programme coordinator and graduate advisor for the MA in ESL programme at her institution.

Sonia Gallucci (Ph.D., University of Birmingham, UK) is lecturer in Italian and Communication across Cultures in the Department of Languages and Cross-Cultural Communication, at Regents College, London. She is also a visiting lecturer at the School of Education, University of Birmingham where she provides dissertation supervision. Gallucci holds a joint MA in Italian Studies, Culture and Communication from the Universities of Warwick and Birmingham, and a BA in Modern Languages and Literatures from the University of Cagliari (Italy), with a specialization in Philology. Her current research focuses on the emotional and social dimensions of university level language learning during a year abroad.

Felicia (Felix) Girón (Ph.D., Cornell University, USA) is an associate professor at Shantou University, China. She holds a BA from Yale University and an MA from Cornell University. Her doctoral research focused on mobility, space and place, diaspora, and the performance of local subjectivity in Shantou. Her current research project investigates Shantou female entrepreneurs' creation of discourse communities and social space. Her pedagogical interests also include cross-disciplinary co-teaching, academic reading and writing for an international interpretative community, and English as a global language.

Lou Harvey holds an MA in English Language and Literature from the University of Edinburgh, an MA in TESOL and an M.Sc. in Educational Research from the University of Manchester, UK. She has taught English as a foreign language and English for academic purposes in Slovakia and in the United Kingdom, and currently teaches on pre-sessional English for academic purposes and the Manchester Leadership Programme at the University of Manchester. She is also a Ph.D. candidate in the Manchester University's School of Education. Her research adopts a Bakhtinian dialogic approach to the English-language learning motivation, identity and agency of international university students based in the United Kingdom.

Stephanie Ann Houghton (Ph.D., Durham University, UK) is an associate professor in Intercultural Communication at Saga University, Japan. She is author of *Intercultural Dialogue in Practice*, co-author of *Developing Criticality through Foreign Language Education* (with Etsuko Yamada), co-editor of *Becoming Intercultural: Inside and Outside the Classroom* (with Yau Tsai) co-editor of *Native-Speakerism in Japan: Intergroup Dynamics in Foreign Language Education* (with Damian J. Rivers) and co-editor of *Developing Critical Cultural Awareness: Managing Stereotypes in Intercultural (Language) Education* (in press, with Yumiko Furumura, Maria Lebedko and Li Song).

Claudia Kunschak (Ph.D., University of Arizona, USA) holds an MA in Translation and Interpreting from the University of Vienna. She has previously taught English, German and Spanish at universities in Austria, Scotland, Spain, the Ukraine and the United States, and most recently served as the executive director of the English Language Center at Shantou University, China. Currently she teaches English and German at different universities in Kyoto, Japan. Her research interests include language variation, multilingualism and foreign/second/additional language teaching and testing. Her pedagogical interests also comprise learner autonomy, task-based learning, computer-assisted language learning and bridging the gap between English for general purposes and English for specific purposes.

Brian A. McMillan (M.Ed., University of Prince Edward Island, Canada) currently finds himself at a crossroads in his career after spending a number of years teaching French immersion in Canada and English as a foreign language at Kanda University of International Studies and Hiroshima Bunkyo Women's University in Japan. His research interests include the role of the first language in second language learning, teacher beliefs and the influence of language policy on teaching practice, forms of collaborative and self-driven professional development which empower teachers as researchers, and issues surrounding academic freedom.

Bryan Meadows (Ph.D., University of Arizona, USA) is an assistant professor of second language acquisition at Fairleigh Dickinson University where he teaches courses in Second Language Teacher Education (SLTE). His main research area is the relationship between nationalism and language education, but his research extends to teacher education, intercultural education, critical discourse analysis and functional linguistics. His research has been published in peer-reviewed journals such as *Critical Discourse Studies, Teaching and Curriculum Dialogue, Critical Inquiry in Language Studies* and *Critical Approaches to Discourse Analysis across Disciplines*, among other venues. Together with a co-author, he recently received the Francis P. Hunkins Distinguished Article Award in Teaching.

Melina Porto (Ph.D., Universidad Nacional de La Plata, Argentina) is a researcher at CONICET (Consejo Nacional de Investigaciones Científicas y Técnicas) in Argentina and a professor of English Language II at UNLP. She holds an MA in English Language Teaching from the University of Essex, UK. In addition to publishing several articles internationally, she is co-author of the *New English Curriculum Design for Primary Schools* in the Province of Buenos Aires, Argentina. She also serves as a member of the *Language Diversity Committee* of the *International Reading Association* and on several other editorial review boards.

Damian J. Rivers (Ph.D., University of Leicester, UK) is an associate professor in the Graduate School of Language and Culture at Osaka University, Japan. His main research interests concern the management of multiple identities in relation to Self and Otherness, the impact of national-level identities upon a variety of foreign language education processes, and social processes underpinning intergroup stereotypes. He has published articles in peer-reviewed journals such as the *ELT Journal*, *International Journal of Intercultural Relations*, *Journal of Higher Education Policy and Management*, *Language Awareness*, *Language and Intercultural Communication*, *System* and *World Englishes*. He is also co-editor of *Native-Speakerism in Japan: Intergroup Dynamics in Foreign Language Education* (2013, Multilingual Matters) and editor of *Resistance to the Known in Foreign Language Education* (in press, Palgrave Macmillan).

John W. Schwieter (Ph.D., Florida State University, USA) is an associate professor of Spanish and linguistics at Wilfrid Laurier University in Waterloo, Ontario, Canada. His research interests include psycholinguistics, bilingualism and second language acquisition. His in-print and forthcoming books include: *Innovative Research and Practices in Second Language Acquisition and Bilingualism* (John Benjamins Publishing), *Studies and Global Perspectives of Second Language Teaching and Learning* (Information Age Publishing), *Cognition and Bilingual Speech: Psycholinguistic aspects of Language Production, Processing, and Inhibitory Control* (Lambert Academic Publishing) and *The Development of Translation Competence: Theories and Methodologies from Cognitive Science* (Cambridge Scholars Publishing). His other studies have appeared in journals such as *Bilingualism: Language and Cognition*, *Diaspora, Indigenous, and Minority Education*, *Language Learning*, *Linguistic Approaches to Bilingualism* and the *Mental Lexicon.*

Introduction: Identities in Foreign Language Education

Damian J. Rivers and Stephanie Ann Houghton

> Sociocultural identities and ideologies are not static, deterministic constructs that EFL teachers and students bring to the classroom and then take away unchanged at the end of a lesson or course . . . rather, in educational practice as in other facets of social life, identities and beliefs are co-constructed, negotiated, and transformed on an ongoing basis by means of language. (Duff and Uchida, 1997: 452)

One can easily observe how, to date, conceptualizations of identity within foreign language education have been addressed and discussed on numerous occasions and in numerous sociocultural contexts (e.g. Block, 2007b; Clarke, 2008; Duff and Uchida, 1997; Edwards, 2009; Higgins, 2011; Kanno, 2003; Kramsch, 2009; Kubota and Lin, 2009; Lantolf and Genung, 2003; Lin, 2008; McMahill, 1997; Mohan et al., 2002; Morgan and Clarke, 2011; Norton and Toohey, 2011; Pavlenko and Blackledge, 2004; Ricento, 2005; Tsui, 2007). However, despite such research interest, it is our view that inadequate attention has been paid to documenting the dynamics of identity development, negotiation and management in specific relation to the concept of 'Otherness' as well as the numerous attitudinal and behavioural overtones created through use of the term 'foreign', despite its position as an integral marker in language acquisition discourse. This neglect has also been noted by Riley (2007: 162) who asserts that the domain of applied linguistics has 'been content to leave foreignness and foreigners to the realm of common sense'. The author further explains how:

> if we look at the expression 'foreign language learning' (or 'teaching', for that matter), we are immediately struck by the fact that whereas two of its constitutive elements – 'language' and 'learning' – have been the objects of intense scrutiny

> and the subjects of vast numbers of publications over the years, the third, 'foreign', has remained relatively unexamined.

Consequently, a number of important aspects related to identity and Otherness in the intercultural interactions of the foreign language education context remain relatively unexplored, yet prime for research given the constant disruption by globalization processes and the often-assumed links between language, culture and identity. With obvious links to Appadurai's (1996) social imaginary framework of 'scapes', this disruption is noted by Kunschak and Girón (this volume) who highlight the way in which '[g]lobal flows merge and disrupt conventional monoliths of space, time and meaning and create new landscapes of knowledge and experience, reset language, reframe culture, and reposition identities.' In other words, the plethora of ways in which identities anchored in dimensions of 'foreignness' impinge upon the possible scopes of interaction situated within foreign language education contexts should be of greater concern to institutions, researchers, teachers and students. Therefore, to address what we see as a prevailing ambivalence towards, and stigmatization of, academic explorations situated around the term 'foreign', observable across numerous national contexts, and from a position which aims to transcend the theoretical boundaries of social psychology and applied linguistics, the chapters within this volume tease out and showcase the intricate mechanisms by which 'identity happens' within the interactional parameters of foreign language education.

When confronted by a concept as vast, enduring and multidimensional as 'identity' one can select among numerous points of departure for investigation and analysis. Throughout this volume, we engage with the notion of social identities (thus emphasizing the significance of context in intergroup identity dynamics) and the associated concept of multiple selves (thus emphasizing the complexity and plurality of the Self-construct). With popular foundations in the late 1970s and the work of Tajfel and Turner (1979), the concept of 'social identity' has been repeatedly theorized through social identity theory, a theoretical stance first developed as a means of understanding the psychological dimensions of intergroup discrimination. Briefly, social identity theory is concerned with individual cognition, attitudes and behaviours manifested and formulated within intergroup situations. Therefore, a particular 'social identity' can be described as an individual's knowledge, and thus self-awareness, that they belong to single or multiple social categories or groups (Hogg and Abrams, 1988). However, and in significant contrast, Stets and Burke (2000: 225) define a 'social group' as 'a set of individuals who hold a common social identification or view themselves as members of the same social category'. This stance immediately points towards processes of categorization and how individuals attribute and perceive similarities and differences between the Self and the Other, and whether such perceived similarities and differences are accepted by other in-group members as being accurate representations of the group.

Stets and Burke (2000: 225) further add that through such processes of social comparison and cycles of evaluation, 'persons who are similar to the self are categorized with the self and are labeled the in-group; persons who differ from the self are categorized as the out-group.' Indeed, it has been extensively documented that '[s]ocial identity theory assigns a central role to the process of categorization which partitions the world into comprehensible units' (Abrams and Hogg, 1990: 2). Of direct relevance to the current volume, the authors also position social identities as a collection of overlapping categories of group membership, noting how one's social identity is most salient when group representations are smoothly integrated into the self-concept of the individual (i.e. without conflict or dissonance produced during or after the categorization process). The subjective categorization mechanisms active within the creation and maintenance of social identities, as well as the resultant division of people into respective in-groups and out-groups is a known basis for group stereotyping, prejudice and discrimination (see Brewer and Pierce, 2005; Reid and Anderson, 2010), and this also extends to intergroup dynamics within foreign language education (see Houghton et al., forthcoming; Rivers, 2011a; Rivers and Ross, forthcoming a, forthcoming b).

Moreover, due to the acknowledgement that some groups are socioculturally imagined to be more powerful and prestigious than others (e.g. the imagined dynamic between 'native speakers' and 'non-native speakers'), the more powerful and prestigious groups, as dominant norm setters, often identify and categorize in a manner designed to maintain the status quo with little attention given to obvious inequalities and inconsistencies. Even when undertaken in relation to one's self-concept, the unscrupulous evaluation of the in-group and degradation of the out-group, although not always an inevitable occurrence (see Kowalski, 2003), usually leads to a positive appraisal of the in-group and negative appraisal of the out-group, and therefore, functions as a primary means of enhancing one's self-esteem and perceived sense of self-worth (Stets and Burke, 2000).

The complexity of such processes is added to through social group 'convergence' and 'divergence' which deals with the cognitive processing and subsequent attitudinal and behavioural responses to certain group memberships that either overlap (to various degrees) or remain distinctly apart, especially when there exists an apparent inconsistency or contradiction in identifying the Self, or being identified by the Other, within two particular categories or groups. For instance, most people could be expected to have no problem in identifying, or being identified as, a 'female' 'teacher' as these two categories are not considered mutually exclusive or conflicting. However, a larger number of people could be expected to find it more problematic to accept that a person could concurrently be an 'active member within the Catholic Church' and also 'openly homosexual'. This second category would thus, in a great many cases, promote a conflict originating from the categorization process and the social identities that certain groups (of those who are socioculturally dominant) prefer, expect or demand in order to legitimize membership or solidify exclusion.

Often influenced by 'the coercive relations of the state' and 'the hegemonic relations of civil society' (Codd et al., 1990: 29), schools, universities and temporal or transferable locations such as school trips, overseas sojourns and international home-stays are cardinal locations for social identity development to take place in relation to foreign language education. For students, exposure to and interaction with various forms of knowledge and information, relationships with diverse peers, and marked associations with a variety of other social groups means that schooling, particularly during adolescence, has been a central context for many previous studies examining social identity and group membership dynamics (see Diehl, 1988; Gini, 2006; Nesdale and Lawson, 2011). From the perspective of teachers, institutions such as schools and universities represent the 'workplace'. These environments provide fertile grounds for employees to 'negotiate and co-construct performances of individual role identities within the wider socio-cultural context of their group, department or company' (Marra and Angouri, 2011: 3), and as such, are of immediate interest in the study of identity development (see Georgakopoulou, 2011).

Whether 'performing roles' associated with 'being a teacher' or 'being a student', and thus assuming certain acceptable identities implicated by the parameters of role and the sociocultural context, of significance concerning the relationship between these two 'groups' is the fact that the majority of interactions between them occur through face-to-face linguistic exchange, regardless of location. As such, it should be known that face-to-face social interaction has been heralded as the 'most immediate site for the construction of social identities of all kinds, for it is there that identity projects are assembled and launched, often through explicit talk about social categories and their associated practices, meanings, and perceived social value' (Bucholtz, 2011: 239). As many of the chapters within this volume demonstrate, face-to-face linguistic interactions are extremely fruitful in terms of the 'identity projects' observable.

Accepting that teachers and students have at their disposal numerous identity options, albeit options that are often regulated by normative assumptions about the role-in-context, it is important to assess the dominant position of 'multiple selves' within the general literature on foreign language education. The notion of multiple selves has been largely advanced through what we deem to be one of the most uncritically accepted notions related to identity – 'the ideal L2 self' – as a central component of recent literature concerning language-learner motivation. At its foundation, 'the ideal L2 self' (Dörnyei, 2005) stands as a modern reworking and combination of Gardner and Lambert's (1972) concept of 'integrativeness' and Markus and Nurius' (1986) notion of 'possible selves'. Recent motivational research into these domains has almost exclusively focused upon the learning of English as foreign language prompting questions to be raised in relation to the validity of the 'imagined communities' in which students are supposedly striving for access to, or inclusion into.

With direct reference to the validity of 'integrative motivation' in a globalized world, Ushioda (2011: 199) argues how a desire to integrate into a target community loses its 'explanatory power' when 'there is no clearly defined target language . . . into which learners of English are motivated to "integrate"' (see also Lamb, 2004). Although we believe that such a position is correct in principle, we also see it as one ignorant to the contextual realities of foreign language-learning situations located in peripheral English-language use countries. In such contexts, the imagined 'native-speaker' English teacher, originating from the Kachruvian inner-circle, still holds immense symbolic cultural and linguistic power, and remains a common figurehead within many foreign language contexts (see Houghton and Rivers, 2013), often accompanied by institutional claims of it being 'best practice' for an *authentic* foreign language learning experience (see McMillan and Rivers, 2011; Rivers, 2010b, 2011e).

Similarly, the notion of the Self as being 'multiple' is also central to theories on intercultural communicative competence (see Byram, 1997) in which Houghton (2007) suggests that identity development is generated primarily through the gradual resolution over time of inner conflict between competing values and 'multiple selves'. However, despite the fact that the fields of language-learner motivation and intercultural communicative competence share overlapping concerns as they address issues related to language development in an increasingly interconnected decentralized world, we see them as currently developing independently of each other, which is problematic as they inadvertently collide.

> While Dörnyei suggests that the exotic nature of encounters with a foreign culture should be emphasized by foreign language teachers who want to stimulate the development of learners' ideal selves, Byram suggests that learner willingness to seek out or take up opportunities to engage with otherness in a relationship of equality, which is an attitudinal component of intercultural communicative competence, should be distinguished from (and implicitly prioritized over) attitudes of seeking out the exotic or of seeking to profit from others. (Houghton, 2012: 155)

It is certainly noteworthy, and as alluded to above, that within many foreign language learning environments 'difference' is sought out and championed more than 'similarity' arguably because of the superior function of knowing difference in the process of self-identity (re)formation and (re)development.

> [Identity] . . . whether exclusively collective, individual or somewhat entangled can only be formed, regulated and maintained through relational processes of social interaction and social comparison. That is, the knowing of oneself is only possible when given the opportunity to compare oneself to, and differentiate oneself from others. (Rivers, 2010b: 102)

Yet, this fixation on difference, championing of the exotic, or 'mindless celebration of difference' (Nicholson, 1990: 41) impacting upon the politics of identity, operates across a multitude of criteria (e.g. gender, race, nationality, language) that are selectively deployed by certain people at certain times and for certain self-serving purposes (consistent with the principles of social identity theory and in-group/out-group categorization).

From the discussion thus far, we can see how the individual should be considered as a complex, dynamic, multiple and systemic construct residing at the hub of an intricate social network of multimodal interpersonal and intergroup interactions. It then follows that the individual identities produced, influenced and entangled with these various forms of interaction owe a significant part of their existence to the immediate environment (or communities) in which the interaction takes place, thus further implicating (beyond the aforementioned processes of categorization) the situated role of power dynamics in identity development. For example, set within a broader discussion championing the rejection of the 'native-speaker' criterion (i.e. the assumed innate bond of power formed between nation–language–individual), Rivers (this volume) demonstrates the impact of the institutional and sociocultural community in shaping the limited identity options available to foreign language teachers in Japan. Similarly, McMillan (this volume) highlights the role of the immediate environment upon an individual teacher-researcher's professional identity development through challenges made to, and conflicts resultant from, questioning the appropriateness of 'expert' reasoning behind the promotion of target language only policies in Canada and Japan. Such examples showcase how within certain contexts or situated communities 'full participation may be denied to novices [or Others in oppressed locations] by powerful practitioners' and that '[c]onstraints on newcomers [or Others in oppressed locations] may be strongest if the latter threaten to "transform" the knowledge and practices of the extant community, since that knowledge is important or "at stake" to the full participants who have invested in it' (Handley et al., 2006: 644, drawing on Carlile, 2004). Dimensions of power dynamics in identity development are also revealed in Schwieter (this volume) who draws attention to the way in which 'definitions of identity may . . . assign importance to the ways in which relationships are socially constructed within specific relationships of power.' Within discussion concerning language-learner motivation, Harvey (this volume) notes how language learners are 'constantly negotiating a range of social identities, while aspiring to participate in a variety of communities at local and global levels with differing degrees of agency and power to accept or resist these identities.' Supporting such a perspective, Gallucci (this volume) indicates how '[r]elations of power are at the heart of poststructuralist thought about discourse' through data obtained from the case-study participant profiled in the chapter who 'constantly challenged being marginalised by Italian native speakers in relative positions of power.'

In more localized educational settings (i.e. the classroom), teacher and student identities (and identity development) can be accessed and analysed in practical ways through, for example, classroom interaction (Aguilar, this volume), students' written work in response to series of tasks aimed at stimulating and tracking identity development in students within predetermined parameters (Houghton, this volume), or students' response to reading materials selected for their cultural content and their potential for developing 'an understanding of Otherness' (Porto, this volume). Moreover, such practical orientation is also able to retain connections to the more theoretical aspects of identity in foreign language education. For example, one of the unifying threads linking chapters within this volume is that focused upon replacing the nation as the primary unit of analysis, as is traditional within foreign language education, with an alternative. And as the chapters within this volume demonstrate there are numerous alternatives available, whether derived through the individual in the analysis of Self and/or Other (Houghton, this volume), the creation of more localized communities of practice (Cole and Meadows, this volume), or the use of imagined learning communities among a small population of students (Schwieter, this volume). In the process of highlighting such alternatives, positive attempts are made to find ways of helping learners and teachers transcend linguistic and cultural boundaries, while successfully managing them*selves* and their identity development.

More detailed analysis of individual chapters can further reveal wide-ranging and discrete identity management and development mechanisms and strategies. For example, Aguilar (this volume) shows how teacher self-disclosure to students during class time embodies 'teachers' self-categorization practices' as they 'show aspects of themselves, and consequently to be perceived by learners in a certain manner'. And Kunschak and Girón (this volume) illustrate various identity-development practices such as resistance and reappropriation in both teachers and students at intermediate and advanced levels of English-language study with advanced students displaying greater critical awareness of language and language use than intermediate students, and with language teachers making a career out of the target language displaying a truce with it despite their apparently advanced levels of critical awareness. Kunschak and Girón's view that 'the ability to become aware of, evaluate and act on cultural differences according to the situation' all form an integral part of transcultural competencies echoed throughout the Intercultural Dialogue Model (Houghton, this volume) with its focus upon self-reflection, critical analysis and evaluation of Self and Other before conscious decision making about identity development takes place. The few examples of identity-development mechanisms highlighted above are by no means exhaustive, but they *do* suggest that identity and identity development need not remain inaccessible concepts considered only in the abstract by researchers; that they can be operationalized practically in various ways also by teachers as they endeavour to equip their students (as well as themselves) to respond constructively to Otherness in the language classroom and language teaching workplace.

As a final word of introduction, we wish to direct readers to our position that while distinctions are often made on the basis of pedagogy between 'second' and 'foreign' language education, for the purpose of this volume we see any potential distinction as being quite irrelevant due to unbounded opportunities for teachers and students in all contexts to communicate across boundaries of various sorts via modern communication technologies. Furthermore, we neither assume nor impose motives for language learning on students primarily upon the basis of their geographical location as the traditional distinction between learning a 'second' language and learning a 'foreign' language has, and continues to do.

Overview of the volume

From a broad conceptual perspective, all of the chapters within this volume deal with, to varying degrees, the central theme of social identity and multiple selves in foreign language education through empirical studies of teacher and student identities. However, from a structural perspective, the volume has been organized in a manner that facilitates theoretical, conceptual, methodological and practical connections between chapters positioned alongside each other. Embracing the notion of 'situated identities' (Zimmerman, 1998: 90) and individual 'performers' (Goffman, 1959: 56), the first chapter (Aguilar) presents a detailed conversation analysis of interactions between foreign language teachers and students of English, French and Spanish within 'traditional classrooms' across a variety of national contexts. Contrary to the view that one's 'capacity to tailor social performance, to draw on specific roles, may sometimes be constrained by the individual's participation in so-called institutional contexts where specialised practices are expected and required' (referencing Schegloff, 1992), the author demonstrates how within teacher-fronted classrooms, 'not only is it possible for all participants, both the teacher and the learners, to negotiate formal aspects of the target language, but also to engage in a complex process of identity construction, attribution, and negotiation.' In addressing the ways in which teachers are able to 'play different identity cards', and in emphasizing the dynamic nature of teacher identities, the author summarizes how essentially responsibility resides with the foreign language teacher 'to negotiate with the learners what is legitimate, possible, impossible, appropriate and inappropriate within the context of the language classroom.'

Continuing the focus on foreign language teacher identities in context (Aguilar), and with specific attention given to the professional or workplace identity implications created by the 'native-speaker' English teacher status label, Chapter 2 (Rivers) shares a selection of narrative stories elicited from five English-language teachers in Japan. The narrative voices shared and the multiple identities formed move the author to conclude that within the confines of the Japanese education system, 'experience amassed . . . seemingly does very little to change perceptions concerning how the "native-speaker" English teacher location can be enduringly restrictive in the workplace, thus in most cases limiting the development of a positive professional identity.' With links to the process of categorization in social identity theory, the author suggests that until there is a significant shift in how people categorized as 'native speakers' of English are perceived by the sociocultural majority, 'the multidimensional identities of the "native-speaker" English teacher will remain under the *fixed* constraints constructed and deployed by others, unable to flourish in a manner that ensures individual, professional, and social identity satisfaction in the workplace and beyond.' Offering an innovative approach to the multiple selves of a single foreign language teacher, Chapter 3 (McMillan) presents a variation of the narrative methodology employed in Chapter 2 (Rivers) through adopting an auto-ethnographical approach to explore the author's own sense of professional identity development throughout his career as a language teacher in Canada (teaching French) and Japan (teaching English). The main thrust of the self-narrative includes the way in which professional beliefs and practices are influenced by multicontextual conflicts with 'target language only' policies and their institutional enforcers. The chapter also addresses the importance of research in validating a role as a professional language teacher-researcher, negotiating the space between teaching French (as a 'non-native speaker') and teaching English (as a 'native speaker'), and the sense of professional satisfaction derived from working collaboratively with 'Others of similarity' (Chang, 2008) as a means of facilitating professional identity satisfaction.

Through multiple focus groups and a microapproach to data analysis, Chapter 4 (Kunschak and Girón) draws upon conceptualizations of transnationalism in exploring the ways in which 'transnational practices emanating from the struggle with language, culture and identity manifest themselves.' The chapter further highlights specific examples of the construction of multiple selves among 'non-native' language teachers and students based in China. In concluding the chapter, the authors assert that '[m]ultiple selves are developed over time and can be created in imitation of, or out of resistance to, perceived target language and culture norms. These multiple selves allow both a critical perspective on one's own community and a successful engagement with the Other culture.' Extending the emphasis on the notion of 'culture', Chapter 5 (Porto), probes cultural understanding through literary texts within the context of Argentina. Although data was collected from a small sample of college students and future teachers and translators of English, this chapter adopts a case-study presentation of data from just one of the participants. As a significant point of departure for the chapter the author explains how 'cultural understanding in reading is often investigated using inappropriate theoretical rationales framed within static and essentialist notions of culture and identity.' From a detailed examination of the data produced by the single reader (known as Tess), the author suggests that the findings point towards 'the need to consider the subtle and varied ways in which comprehension can take place, away from standardized and generalizable interpretations'.

Chapter 6 (Cole and Meadows) develops objection to the nationalist paradigm of foreign language education and its position as 'a major obstacle to foreign language education by preventing it from realizing its core mission of leading students to navigate across borders of culture and language'. In response to this standpoint, the chapter provides an alternative model for 'reimagining identities in foreign language classrooms and suggestions for practical applications to foreign language programmes' on the basis that the 'nation' as a fulcrum of imagined identities should be replaced by the 'community or practice'. With theoretical and practical implications for the previous chapter, Chapter 7 (Schwieter) showcases a practical application of a classroom activity which highlights the importance of learning communities, defined by the author as 'groups of language learners who share common goals and are actively engaged in learning together from each other', in the foreign language classroom. Twenty-four English first language speakers studying Spanish took part in a magazine creation project at a large public university in an English-speaking region of Ontario, Canada. Throughout the chapter and in relation to the data, the author champions the view that learning communities are able to 'underpin a genuine investment in learning' and 'foster the exploration of learners' identities in a second language'.

Shifting from investment to motivation, Chapter 8 (Harvey) details a study into the foreign language-learner motivation and social identity development of three foreign students (from Iraq, Spain, Slovakia) residing in the United Kingdom. The author signals how 'the investigation expands on previous social psychological work in the foreign language motivation field to foreground social identities through the individual voice, experience, perception and agency.' The author further observes through the discourse, produced via interview, how the three students experience a state of constant social identity negotiation accompanied by their aspirations to participate within a variety of communities 'at local and global levels, with differing degrees of agency and power to accept or resist these identities and the wider pressures and influences they face'. Maintaining a focus on students in foreign countries and centralized upon the use of the affective lexicon of a single British participant, Chapter 9 (Gallucci) addresses the role of emotions recalled and experienced during a year abroad as an ERASMUS student in Italy. The author discusses how the 'study brings together perspectives on emotions and identities from the fields of social psychology, pragmatics, applied linguistics and sociolinguistics' and links a cross-disciplinary approach on emotions to a poststructuralist stance on identity. After a thorough analysis of participant discourse, the author concludes how 'through her struggles, she managed not only to recover from an initial phase of loss and to become a competent foreign language speaker, but also to grow as a person and to overcome her emotions when pursuing her linguistic goals.'

The need for both metacognitive and meta-affective awareness and control in identity development are recognized by the teacher-researcher author of Chapter 10 (Houghton), although the value system is considered to play the pivotal role given the focus of the original study (in which this chapter is rooted) upon the management of evaluative processes in the management of prejudice (i.e. prejudgement) (Houghton, 2012). Within this view of identity, a value system is conceptualized as 'a complex, hierarchically organized and unstable system that forms part of a person's broader identity, which contains various interconnected values that include stated values, real, ideal and target values, all of which may be evidenced in, yet sometimes contradict, behaviour and feelings' (Houghton, this volume). It is as contradictions between different parts of students' inner selves arise through structured reflection upon discrete encounters with difference, systematically orchestrated by the teacher following the steps outlined in the Intercultural Dialogue Model (Houghton, 2012; Houghton and Yamada, 2012), that identity development becomes visible in students' written work as they set about reflectively making conscious decisions about whether or not to change in response to their interlocutor(s) over time. This chapter showcases identity development in three English-language students in relation to standard setting in the management of evaluation processes in intercultural communication, and particularly in relation to one of many possible values: universalism.

In pursuing our common desire to move the notion of identity away from theoretical abstraction and towards the lived experiences of foreign language teachers and students, further underpinned by our belief that foreign language education environments are ideal locations for the development of a sophisticated repertoire of discursive strategies for formulating, navigating, expressing and managing identities, the direction of the current volume is cast.

1

The Institutional and Beyond: On the Identity Displays of Foreign Language Teachers

Jose Aguilar

Introduction

This chapter analyses interactions between foreign language (L2) teachers and groups of L2 learners in traditional, L2 classroom settings, where the former acts as an interaction conductor and, to a certain extent, a language model and language provider for the latter. This kind of classroom set-up will be referred to as 'teacher-fronted' throughout the chapter and conversation analysis is adopted to focus on the actions, verbal and other, that L2 teachers display (Richards, 2006). The assumption here is that teachers' observable actions are local materializations of their identities. As will be shown, the observations suggest that teachers sometimes interrupt their 'doing being teachers' within the L2 classroom context, momentarily 'doing being' someone else instead (Mondada, 1999: 28). It is concluded that within the context of such teacher-fronted classrooms, not only is it possible for all participants, both the teacher and the learners, to negotiate formal aspects of the target language, but also to engage in a complex process of identity construction, attribution and negotiation. This chapter focuses on these identity processes from the teachers' point of view.

The difficulties of identifying identity

Research on identity has known both psychological (Lipiansky, 1990; Marc, 2005), and sociological approaches (Goffman, 1959; Gumperz, 1997; Lahire, 1998), whose boundaries are sometimes blurry. The use of conversation analysis for classroom observations is well known and goes back a long way (McHoul, 1978). This method has allowed a closer look at phenomena such as turn-taking organization and repair in classroom settings (McHoul, 1978, 1990; Markee and Kasper, 2004; Seedhouse, 2004). Although the object of study of traditional conversationalists is not *identity* as such, but rather limited, local, observable, materializations of identity, some conversationalists do recognize *identity* as a construct that may fit within a conversation analysis approach (Antaki and Widdicombe, 1998). It is particular instances of behaviour, rather than whole identities, which are addressed, analysed and dealt with here. These behaviours are arguably local, observable, manifestations of something larger, and more difficult to study. In effect, Zimmerman (1998: 90) suggests that *identity* be broken down into three subcategories: the 'discourse identities' that depend on the 'moment-by-moment organization of [an] interaction', the 'situated identities', which 'come into play within the precincts of particular types of situation', and the 'transportable identities', defined as 'potentially relevant in and for any situation and in and for any spate of interaction'. The object of this chapter then is not quite *identity*, but rather the analysis of the 'situated identities' (Zimmerman, 1998: 90) of individual 'performers' (Goffman, 1959: 56) in their capacity as L2 teachers. In other words, it is not the individual who speaks about the individual, but the individual's actions, as read by the analyst.

Identity as social competence: Contexts and boundaries

Functionally, identity allows to *act* within and upon the immediate, particular contexts where people exist socially, to develop a self-image (Markus and Kunda, 1986), to foresee social performance, to recognize, identify and adapt to social circumstances, as well as to draw on specific roles, behaviours and expectations in order to co-construct social life and to make sense out of it (Bucholtz and Hall, 2005; Riley, 2007; Zimmerman, 1998). The individual's lifelong exposure to and absorption of such experiences, as well as the recurrent participation in social contexts and systematic co-construction of action(s) with other fellow-individuals result in an ability to adapt to, identify and recognize social circumstances, as well as to have expectations about these (Edwards, 1994). Not all social contexts are alike. Some human groups have come to recognize specific behaviour and actions as appropriate, or even suitable, for given social situations. This is what Edwards (1994: 212) calls 'scripts'. Scripts give indications of what is possible and expectable in determined social contexts.

According to conversation analysis, an individual's capacity to tailor social performance, to draw on specific roles, may sometimes be constrained by the individual's participation in so-called institutional contexts where specialized practices are expected and required (Schegloff, 1992). In the conversation analysis tradition, aspects of one's identity may be studied as the participants in a social situation orient to specific actions, showing their '(dis)preference' for specific ones (Pomerantz, 1994). These orientations, verbal or other, are indications of how the participants understand their fellow participants' actions, but also how they intend for their fellow participants to make sense of their own actions. This understanding may ultimately be linked with what is arguably most intimate and essential to the individuals, their *Self* (Goffman, 1959). An individual's orientation to a particular action, the display of a given behaviour, informs of the way the individual understands a particular social situation, as well as the place the individual occupies within it.

Identity and language

Language is central to the study of identity (Riley, 2007). Likewise, identity is central to the study of language acquisition (Block, 2007a). Languages are tools for (inter)action and communication. As such, they allow the individuals to construct and act out their identity. According to scholars within a Labovian, variationist sociolinguistic tradition, the analysis of identity construction, expression and negotiation practices may help understand language choices made by the speakers, as well as their behaviour (Gumperz, 1997; Lambert, 2009), whereas scholars closer to conversation analysis regard identity as a partial, local, observable phenomenon (Mondada, 1999), something that is not prior to interaction, but constructed step-by-step, in the heat of social action, partially by virtue of language. In effect, language(s) allow the participants in a social encounter to attribute and claim identities as they interact, and gestures and intonation are other instances of meaning-conveying language-related resources that allow the construction of identities. Among the various categories that participants may attribute or claim, there is (non-)nativeness, which defines a certain relationship with a given language.

Language learning and learner identity

Since the sociocultural turn (Block, 2003; Firth and Wagner, 1997; Lantolf, 1994), some second language acquisition (SLA) researchers have taken an interest in the impact that learning a new language may have on an individual's identity, namely the learners' (Norton and Toohey, 2011; Zuengler, 1989). From a more sociological perspective, Vasquez (1990) and Talburt and Stewart (1999), cited by Block (2003), present accounts of individuals whose experiences as expatriate-learners in foreign countries are incompatible with their self-images. Identity, understood as an implicit process within self and other-categorization practices, is also addressed from a conversation analysis point of view by Mondada (1999), who questions the status of 'foreigner' that is often, and rather automatically, attributed to non-native speakers. According to Mondada (1999), a non-native-speaker's foreignness is not a default identity applicable to those who happen to communicate in, learn, work with or generally use a language different from their mother tongue.

Identity has also been a matter of interest for researchers who study teacher-fronted L2 classrooms. Cicurel (1991) characterizes a group of learners' classroom actions as signs of their coming to terms with an identity that defines, as much as is defined by, an institutional classroom context. Levine (2011) suggests that learners' identities may be enriched by teachers who foster multilingual practices within their classrooms. According to this author, by getting learners to move from a single-code to a multicode choice, one may have an impact on how they regard themselves and their interlocutors as users of other languages. Levine's standpoint is consistent with the multilingual and multicultural educational principles put forth by the Council of Europe (2001).

Teacher identity and professionalism: Teaching as identity work

Just as learning a new language has an impact on identity, teaching a language may also be a matter of coming to terms with one's own identity (Richards, 2006). In effect, identity has been a matter of interest as regards the L2 teachers' education, especially since the development of the so-called 'language teachers' cognition' (Borg, 2009; Woods, 1996). As Freeman (2002) points out, the way L2 teachers are considered has profoundly changed in the past 40 years – at least in Western societies – ever since their identities have come to the fore of educational research, as a result of which teaching has ceased to be regarded as purely behavioural practice. Language teaching is not only a matter of technical knowledge, but also of assumptions and beliefs about how this knowledge may be brought about (Woods, 1996). Language teaching is no longer dissociated from what teachers think and feel about (1) teaching and learning (Aguilar Río, 2011; Cambra Giné, 2003), (2) those with whom they work – teacher fellows and learners – and ultimately (3) themselves, both as teachers and individuals (Williams and Burden, 1997).

The ever increasing complexity of the learning process models produced by SLA research (Ellis, 2008; Larsen-Freeman and Cameron, 2008) has led to significantly more complex characterizations of teaching processes, actions and conditions (Borg, 2009; Cachet, 2009). The L2 teachers' roles multiply as language teaching and learning environments diversify (Bertin et al., 2010; Compton, 2009). Concerning teacher-fronted classrooms, contemporary authors describe L2 teachers as communication and language experts, learning facilitators, contents designers and providers, interaction conductors and cultural mediators (Dupuis et al., 2003; Richards and Rodgers, 1995), who are expected to perform institutional actions such as choosing topics, giving feedback to learners, assigning speech turns in group exchanges, preventing specific learners from taking over (Seedhouse, 2004). This is roughly what an L2 teacher's performance amounts to, within the context of a teacher-fronted classroom situation, if we stick to a mainstream institutional discourse. However, since teaching is not only about possessing certain savoir faire, but also about making sense of them – sometimes on a personal level (see Williams and Burden, 1997) – characterizing L2 teachers' performance is less straightforward and predictable than making a list of their linguistic, pedagogical and professional qualities, precisely because *the L2 teacher* is only a part of what lies within an individual's much larger identity. The teacher-fronted classroom context may be the institutional setting where teachers display aspects of their teacher identity by adjusting their actions to certain expected practices. However, this may not prevent the individuals, who happen to momentarily perform as teachers, from performing as something else. Different teachers may have different understandings of what performing as a teacher means, and this will show in the actions to which they orient in the classroom.

Data and methodology

Research questions

The data presented were produced as part of a Ph.D. dissertation (Aguilar Río, 2010) which featured a central and subsidiary research question:

- By what means and according to which ideas do L2 teachers come to terms with their roles as teachers?
- Is there coherence between L2 teachers' teaching principles and their classroom actions?

The focus was on L2 teachers' observable classroom actions, as well as on their principles, feelings and beliefs about teaching. In order to address these questions, during 2007–8, fieldwork was conducted in four European universities where the dominant official language was taught to young adult learners from Europe, Eastern Europe, the Middle-East, Asia, North, Central and South America. The data produced comprise roundabout 30 hours of teacher-fronted classroom observations, plus open-ended and recall interviews with seven teachers in their mother tongues. On average, each teacher was observed during 6 hours scattered in two to three sessions that took place in the same week, or from one week to the other. Classroom observations always preceded the open-ended interviews.

Participants and contexts

The participants were two female and one male English as a foreign language teachers in Glasgow, Scotland, two female French as a foreign language teachers in Paris, France, and one female and one male Spanish as a foreign language teachers in Andalusia, Spain. The teachers' teaching experience ranged from 34 years – one French as a foreign language teacher in Paris – to 7 years – the female Spanish as a foreign language teacher in Andalusia. The demographics of the participants are shown in Table 1.1.

Procedure

The classroom observations were transcribed in the manner of the conversation analysis methodology (Ten Have, 1999). Upon completion of the classroom transcripts – which ranged from two to twelve months – a recall interview was conducted with six of the seven teachers, during which both the classroom observation transcripts and the original audio/video recorded data were presented to the teachers as stimuli (Pomerantz, 2005). The aim of the recall interviews was twofold: to confirm the validity of the transcripts and to co-construct with the teachers the principles behind their classroom actions. The excerpts presented in this chapter show instances where the teacher or the learners orient to identity-construction discursive practices that comprised self-categorization, self-disclosure, as well as self and other-derision practices. Because of the limited time-scope of these excerpts, it is only possible to observe brief, local, aspects of the teachers' much larger and more complex identities. Since the object of this chapter is the teachers' identity display, only self-derision practices will be considered. These phenomena illustrate identity work performed by the teacher

Table 1.1 An overview of the participants and their teaching context

	Candence (C)	**Richard (R)**	**Janice (J)**	**Marie-Fabienne (MF)**	**Naomi (N)**	**Cristóbal (CD)**	**Marta (MM)**
University context	Glasgow (Scotland)			Sorbonne Nouvelle (France)		Malaga (Spain)	Almeria (Spain)
Language	Academic English		General English	General French		General Spanish	
Experience	30 years (April 2007)	16 years	18 years	34 years (November 2007)	10 years (January 2008)	13 years (April 2008)	7 years (October 2007)
Learners	Middle-East, Northern Africa, Asia		Eastern Europe, Middle-East, Asia, Central and South America	Eastern Europe, Middle-East, Asia, South America	Europe, Eastern Europe, Middle-East, Asia, South America	Europe, Asia, South Africa	Europe, North America
		Young adults			Young adults	Young adults	

beyond the institutional, language-related matters. Each excerpt is preceded by a brief commentary where the commented practices are highlighted. Excerpts from French and Spanish fieldwork have been translated into English and all teachers have been given fictional names in order to respect their anonymity.

Analysis: L2 teachers' self-categorizations

All of the seven teachers displayed categorization practices by means of which they oriented to aspects of their Self. Some teachers' self-categorization practices were explicitly stated. Excerpts 1 and 2 show Janice and Richard, orienting to personal aspects in order to illustrate specific language points ('teacher', 'phobia'). By engaging in processes of self-categorization, they accept being momentarily considered as a certain kind of person in order to facilitate the learners' comprehension – who may likely recognize that Janice is a teacher herself who uses her own role as teacher to illustrate her story, or that Richard's dislike of heights is one possible materialization of 'phobia':

Excerpt 1.1

162 J: pool + this size (.) AND: eh-hmm: (0.2) she's- + she's a teacher

163 of English↑

164 LR: yeah

165 J: like me (0.3) but she: (0.7)

166 <TRAVELS in her CAR↑ + to give LESSONS↑ + in a BANK↑ +

Excerpt 1.2

1 {TS}: what's phobia

2 (0.4)

3 R: AH [OK

4 {AM}: [XXX

5 R: XXX (0.8)

6 FOR example + {I AM} a little-I don't like + HIGH (0.4)

7 for example IN TOKYO I don't like <high buildings:>

8 (0.4)

9 {TS}: °hm-mm°

10 R: yeah↑-I don't like going up [high buildings

Some teachers' self-categorization practices allowed them to detach from contingent identities resulting from interaction in which they participated. In the case of Richard, in Excerpt 1.3, the teacher explicitly stated that these contingent identities did not apply to himself.

Excerpt 1.3

R: [this is OUTSIDE of my
KNOWLEDGE=
AS: =((laugh[ing))
R: [{has anyone been to India}↑
(0.7)

By explicitly stating his ignorance as to the meaning of the symbol on the Indian national flag (lines 43–4), Richard self-categorizes as a non-competent informant, thus as a resourceless participant for the current business – however, he remains the interaction conductor (line 46). Teachers' detachment from the contingent identities was at times implicit, as is the case of Excerpt 1.4, where French teacher Naomi momentarily 'slides' (Cicurel, 2005) from acting as an interaction conductor and facilitator role (line 10) to the denial of the implicit, situated role of 'smoker' (line 14), which her own discourse has made contingent.

Excerpt 1.4

NB: what-can anyone SHOW-ME + I'd rather
show you [{what it is} #a lighter#
AM: [{((soft laughter))}
(0.8)
NB: I can't show you because I'm not carrying one

By explicitly self-categorizing as 'one who is not carrying a lighter', she implicitly self-categorizes as 'one who cannot satisfy the request that has just been made', and implicitly as a 'non-smoker'. Yet, she remains a comprehension facilitator. Teachers' self-categorization practices were also evident when they stated what they were incapable of, or what they did not know prior to the encounter with the group of learners. Janice, in Excerpt 1.5, accepts to momentarily give an image of herself as someone who has preferences and may struggle to have things done her way. As regards French teacher Marie-Fabienne, in Excerpt 1.6, she implicitly agrees to exchange roles with some of the learners, who become for a moment the experts who know what she ignores (Arditty and Vasseur, 1999).

Excerpt 1.5

```
303   J:  ((chuckles)) ALWAYS + yeah↑ but not everybody
          here +
304       {cause} I DON'T LIKE IT + °XXX the carpets°-I don't
          like
305       {it}-and when and when <SOMEBODY COMES to my HOUSE>
          (0.7)
306       it's very DIFFICULT for me [{you know} it's very
          DIFFICULT
307  LR:                             [yeah
308   J:  for me to-PLEA:SE take your shoes very DIFFICULT
```

Excerpt 1.6

```
141     QN:  {they [wax} their: + [their legs↑
142     AF:        [{°wax°}
143     MF:                       [THEY [W:AX
144     QN:                             [they↑ wax=
145     MF:  =WAX↑
146           (0.3)
147     QN:  their {legs}
148     MF:  their legs
149     QN:  °yes°=
150   {IK}:  =it's waxing↑ (0.2) it's like↑
151           (1.5)
152     MF:  OH WELL + I didn't know + <CYCLISTS↑ + THEY:-
             [uh:>
153     QN:  [cyclists
```

Excerpts 1.1 through 1.6 show the teachers' engagement in self-categorization practices. These are coherent with a pedagogical rationale, and thus with an institutional aim, insofar as they serve to clarify language-related matters and facilitate the learners' comprehension. However, the data show instances where the pedagogical function of the teachers' self-categorizations is less clear. This results in more complex and subtle identity work than what has been shown so far.

The teachers' orientation to self-derision

Some instances of the teacher's self-derision were produced as punchlines. In Excerpt 1.7, Spanish teacher Cristóbal orients to laughter by producing a laughable self-categorization that contrasts with LC's preceding turn, which states the social outdoor activities in which the learner has participated (lines 7–9). Cristóbal's feedback does not question the appropriateness of the topic displayed by the learner, yet departs from – or at least does not concentrate on – a concern for language accuracy and explicitly supporting the learners' comprehension – Cristóbal resorts to an insinuation by means of which he self-categorizes as 'one who does not go to the beach'.

Excerpt 1.7

```
7     LC:  uh::: + Friday + I have been: partying:
8     CD:  hm-hmm:
9     LC:  uh: yesterday: + I have gone #to the beach#
           ((lau[ghs))
10    CD:       [((laughs))
11         yes I-I can see some A NICE TAN↑ + [((laughs))
12  {LD}:                                     [((laughs))
13    LC:                                     [{SURE}
14    CD:  I'M PALER BY THE DAY #but# ((laughs)) (0.4)
           ((chuckles))
```

Excerpt 1.8 presents an instance of self-derision by Richard, which seems to support the learners' comprehension. Richard checks the comprehensibility of 'eternal' (line 26), goes on to confirm his satisfaction with the learner's response, and finally suggests an example that is both a punchline to his own question and an instance of self-derision display.

Excerpt 1.8

```
26   R:  what does ETERNAL MEAN↑
27       (0.8)
28  AM:  for ever
29   R:  for ever + yeah + like-sometimes like + my grammar
         lessons
```

Excerpts 1.9 and 1.10 show instances of teachers' implicit self-derision. In Excerpt 1.9, Richard suggests that the reason for such a poor classroom turnout may be that the learners have not felt that his lesson could rival the (rather unexpected) good weather.

Excerpt 1.9

```
6  R:  hmm XXX lots of absents yeah↑ + one two: + three:
       four:
7      five: {°six: seven°} °XXX° (2.5)
8      {>do you THINK< it's because of the sunny DAY↑}
```

9 {KR}: eh #yeah#
10 AM: {((chuckles))}
11 R: YEAH {>they just probably said<} AH:: + Richard's lesson
12 NAH::
13 AS: ((laugh))

As for Cristóbal, it is to be noted that his orientation to self-derision comes as a detour from a language point intervention for which he has chosen himself as an example. The implicit idea here is that Cristóbal, who is usually a 'person', ceases to be one on a Saturday night, when he would practice non-specified Saturday-night activities that would prevent him from being recognized as a person. In either case, the teacher's orientation to self-derision and laughter legitimizes some of the learners' orientation to laughter.

Excerpt 1.10

1 CD: FOR EXAMPLE (1.8)
2 TODAY (1.0)
3 I have seen (1.6)
4 Cristóbal (0.7)
5 guys:: + Cristóbal + is it a person↑ (3.1)
6 not on a Saturday night + no (0.5)
7 #but# [((laughs)) #usually#
8 ED: [((laughs))

The data show cases where self-derision functioned as the highlights – or rather as a punchline of sorts – of one teacher's ongoing turn of a metalinguistic or cultural nature. In Excerpt 1.11, Janice gives an account of her holidays in Spain, which she implicitly depicts as not having met her expectations (lines 88), due to the weather (lines 74–6, 85–6). As Janice implicitly self-categorizes as a victim of bad weather, she accepts that her recounting legitimize laughter among the group (lines 79, 87). Further down, she self-categorizes as a daughter (line 88), who endures her mother's apparent lack of sympathy (lines 88–9). Again, Janice's self-categorization serves to legitimize laughter among learners (line 90). It is to be noted that Janice shifts from self-categorizing in a number of ways, and acting as a facilitator (lines 72, 80–2, 86).

Excerpt 1.11

71 J: ((board)) SOUTH EAST (.) AND: + it was VERY NICE weather in
72 Scotland + it was very nice in Scotland + like this

73 {AF}: hm-mm=
74 J: =and in SPAIN: ((board)) it was: RAINING + [it was: COLD
75 {AF}: [°XXX°
76 J: it was COLD + I had to WEAR {AT NIGHT a} VERY THICK PYJAMA
77 ((board)) PYJA[MAS↑ VERY [THICK A HOT-WATER-BOTTLE +
78 {LR}: [{really↑}
79 {CH}: [((laughs))
80 J: you know this RUBBER [BOTTLE + you put HOT WATER=[{that} you put
81 {LR}: [{yeah}
=[{hmm}
82 J: in the BED + keep you warm + I needed THAT
83 (0.4)
84 LR: {real[ly↑}
85 J: [it was VE::RY COLD: and then it was raining and then there
86 was a THUNDERSTORM BANG BANG BANG {in}the sky [(.)
87 LR: [ouah: ((laughs))
88 J: {and I thought} THIS IS SPAIN and my mother said ((higher pitched
89 voice)) IT'S LOVELY IN SCOTLAND=
90 AS: =((burst of [laughter))

Excerpts 1.7 through 1.11 show the teachers' engagement in self-derision practices. Some of these seemed to support the learners' comprehension, whereas the pedagogical function of others was less clear. The excerpts shown illustrate how teachers may select aspects of their identity in order to exemplify, or simply to trigger a certain emotional effect on learners, which often leads to laughter as a collective practice.

Data discussion

The data presented show several L2 teachers as they interact with groups of language learners in teacher-fronted language classrooms. The language teachers are seen to orient to institutional practices, sometimes of a pedagogic nature, such as correcting, giving feedback, encouraging, selecting the next speaker or facilitating the learners' comprehension by making salient particular language items, checking the learners' comprehension, asking for or giving definitions and explanations. Exemplification has also been identified as a strategy that allowed the teachers to support the learners' comprehension. The data have shown that some teachers oriented to exemplification by drawing on their own personal experiences. By defining such items as elements around which to build local exemplifying actions, the teachers consequently oriented to self-categorization practices, which means that they momentarily showed themselves 'as someone who does (not)' certain practices. The data have shown that self-derision and self-disclosure were embodiments of the teachers' self-categorization practices.

Self-categorization practices and pedagogical functions: Cognition and emotion

In order to illustrate or clarify a potentially problematic L2 item, some teachers made use of whatever language contents were closest to hand – namely their own, personal experiences. It has been suggested that it may be easy for the learners to relate the language awareness activities and processes with the reality of those who inhabit the context of the language classroom – namely the teachers. Relating more or less abstract, metalinguistic aspects of the L2 to be learned, with more concrete, real, situated elements of these very language aspects, may certainly be acquisitionally appropriate and efficient.

Some teachers' self-categorization practices showed a less clear – virtually missing – pedagogical function. Such self-categorization practices have been analysed as local identity-construction processes accomplished by the teachers. Self-derision and self-categorization, taken as instances of the teachers' discursive practices, seem to have opened new interactive sequences that departed from those opened by the language awareness activities in course. In both cases, the learners reacted to the teachers' actions by orienting to laughter, which indicates the momentary prevalence of an emotional dimension over strictly cognitive processes.

Learning and teaching an L2 are both cognitive and emotional business (Imai, 2010; Williams and Burden, 1997). Catering for and addressing the emotional aspects at work in teacher-fronted classrooms are part of the teacher's roles (Dörnyei, 2007). Analysis suggests that the teachers' departure from a strictly institutional discursive order is a way for them to come to terms with their role as emotion regulators. By orienting to self-disclosure and self-derision, the L2 teachers seem to work towards the creation of discursive and identity comfort zones for themselves and for the learners (see Dörnyei, 2007). This idea was confirmed by Richard, as the two following excerpts taken from his open-ended interview suggest: 'I suppose at the back of my mind, as well, you know, is this lesson going to be OK for me, too, yeah, obviously, I think about myself too.'

> I often find, that if I, am not in a very good mood, and I teach, I can be in a better mood afterwards, and I think that's because, I can take on a role, I can take on a role of, hiding my, eh, negativity, so it's not, sometimes teaching can be good for that XXX or, and sometimes it can energise me as well, sometimes it {can have this effect} it can energise me as well, if I'm tired, just the sheer act of, of putting some thought and energy into something can, energise me.

Richard and Cristóbal were among the teachers who affirmed their use of personal experiences as fuel while interacting with the learners. As Richard affirmed during his open-ended interview, his self-awareness helped him to regulate his self-presentation during the encounter with the learners:

> I think it's important, not to reveal, your, all of your self, but to reveal as much of yourself as it's, desirable, for both yourself and the students, so yeah, I try to be who I am, but not all the time.

As regards Cristóbal, he pointed out that the teacher must come across as someone entertaining: 'There is one thing we can't forget, and that is trying to be funny, right . . . you see, lecturing is so easy.' The teachers' orientation to particular discursive practices implies their vision on *how* they conduct the interaction with learners. As Richard put it:

> I try not to be, domineering to the students, I try no [*sic*] to be, I try not to, eh, emphasize any power, really, particular relationships, although of course, I try to maintain the atmosphere of the class, I think it's XXX, perhaps, maybe because my background is in psychology, I'm quite aware that, anxiety, or, nervousness, can interfere with, language learning, in, in, my experiences of learning languages at school would kind of, confirm this, to me, so, eh, that's why I kind of try to take {a kind of an easier approach} with the students, I try to make classroom not, I don't mean a fun place, but a non threatening place.

As regards self-presentation during the encounter with learners, Cristóbal confirmed that his self-categorization practices may be various: 'You are actually their friend, boyfriend, father, you are all of that.' Some of the teachers claimed that their orientation to personal matters must be completely set aside during the encounter with the learners, as was the case with Naomi, who argued that the role of an L2 teacher do not match those of a mother-tongue teacher:

> A French as a foreign language teacher's mission is to stay in the background as much as possible, the teacher must make the learner want to communicate . . . the teacher is a conductor, the teacher tries to create situations that facilitate the learner's willingness to communicate, what we want is for the learner to be autonomous, to be able to communicate.

According to Naomi, an L2 teacher must serve the learners' needs, and that to the extent of ignoring the teacher's own wishes, expectations and desires. This does not mean that the teacher's emotions are not involved in the practice of teaching, bur rather, that the teacher's self-presentation will adopt a certain behaviour, which Naomi described as mothering:

> I think I have a very mothering style, I am a mothering teacher, I like to mother my learners, because I am always worried that they do not understand . . . what is difficult is to find a compromise between being an interaction conductor and this other role of almost mothering, that we sometimes have to play.

Data have shown that the teachers' actions, as they interact with learners in teacher-fronted classroom situations, result from their pedagogical views on teaching, but they may also respond to contingent circumstances co-constructed by all the participants in classroom activities including both teachers and students. Some of the teachers' actions may diverge from the principles they claim.

Limitations of the data presented

Characterizing identity is a cumbersome enterprise. Identity is a hardly observable phenomenon, and its dynamic nature is best characterized along time, within an array of different contexts, as the individual interacts with various interlocutors in a number of situations. Identity develops over time. The local, more or less tangible roles to which an individual's identity may give way sometimes differ within contexts that would seem to be alike – as may be the case of teacher-fronted classrooms. One obvious shortcoming of this paper is the limited scope of the data presented. Plus, the teachers were always observed as they taught the same groups. This means that all conclusions concerning the teaching practices are necessarily limited. In order to account for the teachers' identity materialization and development, larger and richer fieldwork would be required. Case studies, rather than comparative ones as in the data presented, in order to observe single teachers as they teach different groups of learners along time, seem a more appropriate methodological choice for researchers interested in studying teachers' identity.

Conclusion

The participants in the language classroom, the teacher and the learners, show by means of their actions their local understanding of the current situation as they check and adjust to their fellow participants' actions. It is by virtue of this constant, mutual checking, which is accomplished in the situated acts of identity display, that they all negotiate and codefine what is possible and impossible, appropriate and inappropriate in the context of the classroom, and ultimately confirm or review their goals, as well as the means available to achieve these.

The excerpts presented indicate that different teachers have different ways of coming to terms with the institutional roles and functions that they have been assigned in order to facilitate learning. For some teachers, the institutional context of the classroom may also be a place where they orient to activities other than the strict learning facilitation, group conduct, comprehension facilitation and classroom dynamics management, such as self-categorization practices and self-derision. One may wonder what such observed identity-construction related practices may entail L2 learning-wise. Put a different way, what is it to be learned in a teacher-fronted L2 classroom? Is it only, or mainly, a language, a code? Is L2 learning also, or especially, about learning – or, at least, accepting – ways that differ from one's own to conceive of and look at the world, and to inhabit it, which would be partly embodied and expressed by a given language, within a particular community? One likely answer to the question is that it will depend on the learners' needs. However, it may also be argued that expecting L2 teachers to exploit only their technical competences as language and communication experts may be somewhat limiting both for the learners and the teachers themselves. Voices coming from Europe (Council of Europe, 2001; Dupuis et al., 2003) suggest that L2 teachers are also expected to act as educators and mediators among cultures and individuals. It may be the case that in order to accomplish such roles, the L2 teachers' performance calls for more important self-disclosure, for a certain 'investment of the self' (Richards, 2006: 72). In such a case, looking at L2 teachers only as code teachers, or expecting them to only act as such, would certainly be insufficient for learners, limiting for teachers and unrealistic for the institution.

All teachers have been learners. Teachers teach the way they do partly because they have so been taught during their training, but also because they have either become reassured by the teaching ways they have been exposed to, or questioned them, and found new, more convenient ones – either for themselves or for the learners. If we accept that there are 'teaching practices', and if these may come close to the notion of 'professionalism' (Heyworth, 2003: 95), the training for the future L2 teaching professionals should not ignore matters that have to do with the discursive and personal space that teachers occupy within teacher-fronted classrooms. L2 teachers' training programmes should thus spare – and more than that, *devote* – some time to reflect on the facet(s) that teachers construct as pre-service teachers, how these may best be accommodated within the teachers' larger identity, as well as how certain facets, not necessarily L2 teaching related, may develop over time, or be put to the service of the L2 teaching practice. The process of teacher identity construction should not be left unaccompanied; it deserves scaffolding, as is the case of training programmes such as the DELTA (Borg, 2011).

As it has been suggested, language classrooms are contexts where it is expected that learning processes be encouraged and facilitated. In order for L2 classrooms to function as such, L2 teachers are (usually) trained to become aware of (1) whatever complex cognitive and social processes that come into play in teacher-fronted learning situations, (2) learners' differences and needs, (3) as well as specific teaching techniques that will hopefully foster learning. Teachers are also 'persons' (Williams and Burden, 1997: 63): they bring to the classroom their hopes, fears, wishes and preferences – all of which may go beyond the strictly institutional business within the L2 classroom, and yet determine it to a certain extent. The practice of teaching entails the endorsement and renewal of a certain institutional order. This order transpires as participants, namely the teacher, orient to specific functions and roles. Beyond the institutional nature of teaching, the multiplicity and the complexity of the individual L2 teacher's larger identity remain. Teachers may thus develop a certain 'style' (Cicurel, 2005) that learners can identify, relate to, expect or even appreciate. One can affirm without much reservation that the learners' appreciation or a teacher's 'style' may well contribute to facilitate the learning processes. According to Matei and Medgyes (2003: 72) students 'expect teachers to be powerful figures, not only in terms of professional qualifications, abilities and knowledge, but also in terms of personality: students wish to be impressed and entertained, and they appreciate teachers with strong, if not charismatic, personalities.' The data that have been analysed suggest that for teachers to 'play the personality card' may imply for them to assume and exploit aspects of their identity that go beyond their institutional identity work, as much as they complete it. The teachers who exploit their identity within the context of the L2 classroom accept to self-disclose, and consequently to be perceived by learners in a certain manner, which may be a way to cater for all the participants' motivation (Dörnyei, 2007), to detour from being an interaction conductor or comprehension facilitator, to become a rapport manager, to live the space of the classroom in a certain way. Eventually, it is up to every single language teacher to negotiate with the learners what is legitimate, possible, impossible, appropriate and inappropriate within the context of the language classroom. Beyond the institutional expectancies, there will always remain the participants, both the teacher's and the learner's much larger and more complex identities. These will determine the teaching and learning situation. It seems like a good idea not to ignore them, but rather to figure out how to account for them within an institutional teaching–learning context.

Transcription conventions

R, CD, N, J, MF: teacher
EM, FT, AF1, AF2: learners

(0.2): silence measured in tenth of seconds
+: silence shorter than (0.2) seconds
:, :, :::: syllable progressively lengthened
↑: rising intonation
(.): breath intake
((fragment)): analyst's commentary, additional information
[Fragment]
[Fragment]: overlapping turns

/fragment/: phonetic transcription
(fragment): analyst's commentaries, additional information

FRAGMENT: loud utterance
Frag-ment: self-correction or hesitation
{fragment}: analyst is uncertain
°fragment°: whispering
#fragment#: laughter while speaking
XXX: incomprehensible

=: two turns linked without a pause
22: line number
→: observed phenomenon

2

Implications for Identity: Inhabiting the 'Native-Speaker' English Teacher Location in the Japanese Sociocultural Context

Damian J. Rivers

Introduction

This chapter showcases the ways in which narrative accounts and thus identities manifested, are manipulated, restricted and/or empowered by the complexities of the 'native-speaker' English teacher *location* within the Japanese sociocultural context. The study participants are initially bound together by the national context in which they reside, their location as minority members of society (across a variety of criteria), their shared employment in the domain of foreign language education, and most importantly, their institutional categorization as 'native speakers' of English. In turn, the role of categorization is particularly pertinent to the process of identity development as it permits the label of 'native-speaker' English teacher and 'the complex baggage of "nativeness" as it is constructed in the field of English language teaching' (Stanley, 2012: 25), to be conceptualized as a *bounded space* in which one is able to *reside* either voluntarily or otherwise.

As part of the wider narrative inquiry genre of qualitative research (see Bamberg, 2006, 2010; Connelly and Clandinin, 2006; Lieblich et al., 1998; Lyons and LaBoskey, 2002), narrative stories are ideal for explorations seeking richness of representation as storytelling allows one to 'observe how speakers use narratives to display a particular version of self and to understand [how] their everyday worlds' (Simon-Maeda, 2004: 406–7) impact upon identity development. In approaching the broad notion of identity, this chapter is grounded upon a postmodern belief that individuals have the capacity to concurrently enact multiple social identities, and that such identities are primarily formulated through direct social interaction or (dis)interaction with others, as well as through reflections and retrospections on accumulated experience. However, narratives should not be seen simply as 'stories of individuals moving through and reflecting on experiences in isolation. Narratives, by their very nature, are social and relational . . . [and consequently] . . . cannot be separated from the sociocultural and sociohistorical contexts from which they emerged' (Johnson and Golombek, 2002: 5). In giving due consideration to the sociocultural and sociohistorical particulars of context, 'dynamics of power' (Huzzard, 2004) are positioned throughout as being central to the process of identity development.

> Identities are neither fixed nor unified but are about an ongoing process of becoming. Identities are constructed through the differences and exclusions, mediated within disparate and often unequal relationships of power, which largely determine the range of resources – history, values, language, and experiences – available through which individuals and groups experience their relationship to themselves and others. (Giroux, 2003: 100)

It then follows that within intergroup contact situations, the narrative stories of minority group members are especially important as majority group members often utilize in-group bias techniques (see Snyder and Miene, 1994) in order to retain a sense of dominance within the sociocultural hierarchy. These multidimensional techniques are often rationalized as being normative thus sustaining the prejudicial and/or discriminatory treatment of minority group members. For the purpose of conceptualization, the terms 'minority' and 'majority' are used to refer to those individuals and/or groups who *have*, and those individuals and/or groups who *do not have*, an audible voice and/or stakeholder role in the process of shaping normative attitudes, beliefs, behaviours and relationships within a particular sociocultural context. In addition, one must also remain aware of the fact that although:

> [b]oth muted [minority] and dominant [majority] groups generate beliefs or ordering ideas of social reality at the unconscious level . . . dominant groups control the forms or structures in which consciousness can be articulated. Thus muted groups must mediate their beliefs through the allowable forms of dominant structures. Another way of putting this would be to say that all language is the language of the dominant order, and [muted minority groups], if they speak at all, must speak through it. (Showalter, 1988: 346 discussing Edwin Ardener)

On account of this position, one of the primary motives for undertaking this project is to facilitate the conscious empowerment of 'native-speaker' English teachers through provision of a forum in which their otherwise muted voices, locked within the dominant order of the sociocultural majority, can be expressed and explored.

The 'native-speaker' conspiracy

Due to its centrality within this chapter, it is imperative to draw attention to the questionable credibility of the 'native speaker' as a conceptual point of reference. In the first instance, one can turn to theoretical linguists who believed (as some still do) that 'native' language abilities were acquired at birth, and that 'native speakers' were therefore *born* (nature) rather than *made* (nurture) (see Paikeday, 2003 for a fuller discussion of the 'native speaker' as 'linguistic myth'). These principles have long served to restrict the 'native speaker' to the role of experimental yardstick for the linguist (see Kim, 2005 for an example of how linguists use the 'native speaker' as a comparative 'model speaker') and 'the pivot which relates linguistic theory with the facts of language structure and language use' (Ballmer, 1981: 51). In commenting on the dynamics of such relationships, Mey (1981: 73–82) discusses how the 'native speaker' has therefore come to represent 'a shadow, not even of himself [*sic*], but of the real ruler: the linguist', further arguing how the 'native speaker' should be 'treated as a human, not as a figment of some linguist's imagination'.

Detailing a contemporary story of dehumanization within the Japanese sociocultural context, Toh (2013: 183–4) emphasizes how it is vital 'to distinguish between native speaker as the socio-discursive and socio-semiotic construct that it is, and native speakers as the unique individuals (and indeed professionals) encountered in daily life and/or the workplace'. This observation, despite its multicontexual applicability, is given further significance through ideologies and hegemonic discourse of alleged cultural and linguistic capital which have given rise to a social reality in which the imagined has overshadowed, and been historically triumphant in overhauling, the intricate realities of lived experience in relation to matters of intergroup contact, processes of in-group/out-group categorization, and thus identity (see Befu, 2001; Bellah, 1965; Burgess, 2004; Dale, 1986; Liddicoat, 2007; McVeigh, 2002; Maher and Yashiro, 1995; Miller, 1982; Miyoshi, 2010; Rivers, 2010a, 2010b, 2010c, 2011a, 2011b, 2011c, 2013a).

Choosing this as one particular, but not exclusive, starting point in examining the construction and validation of the 'native-speaker' criterion, it can be observed how the concept has infiltrated and been exultantly consumed by the rather vulnerable domain of foreign language education – vulnerability stemming from its traditional role as minion to the more theoretical, and thus prestigious domain of linguistics. The domain of foreign language education has, for the most part, been unable to mount an effective challenge to the appropriateness of referring to linguistic abilities, which are then used to make assumptions concerning teaching ability and professional *authenticity*, as being 'native'. Instead, the domain of foreign language education has found it decidedly easier to embrace and perpetuate the 'native-speaker' criterion on a monumental scale – infecting language teaching pedagogies, institutional policies, student attitudes and teacher recruitment trends on a fundamental level.

Looking first within the Japanese sociocultural context, and converging on teacher recruitment trends, evidence of this *fundamental infection* can be observed within the two dominant foreign language (i.e. English) teaching organizations – JALT (Japan Association of Language Teachers) and JACET (Japan Association of College English Teachers). For example, the guidelines for posting employment advertisements outlined in JALT's *The Language Teacher* publication state: '[t]he editors oppose discriminatory language, policies, and employment practices, in accordance with Japanese and international law. Exclusions or requirements concerning gender, age, race, religion, or country of origin should be avoided in announcements.' Even if overlooking the argument as to whether *discriminatory language* should be inclusive of reference to one's supposed linguistic 'nativity', the marked absence of reference to exclusions made on the basis of *language* is curious considering that: (1) this is a *language* teaching organization, and (2) the list of criteria otherwise deemed to be *off-limits* is quite substantial. Similarly, the position adopted by JACET offers a prime example of organizational ambivalence and avoidance of responsibility in dealing with *all* potential forms of discrimination: 'JACET does not control, supervise, verify, investigate, authenticate or endorse any of the content, communications or representations posted by the advertiser. Should you have any questions, please directly contact the university.' Consequently, the 'native-speaker' criterion is endemic within teacher recruitment advertisements posted through JALT and JACET forums, thereby solidifying its appearance as being *natural* and thus, more difficult to *deconstruct/reconstruct*. Indeed, when looking to *deconstruct/reconstruct* that which is cast as normative, Jacques Derrida (cited in Dick and Kofman, 2005: 64) outlines precisely how 'one of the gestures of deconstruction is to *not naturalize what isn't natural* – to *not assume that what is conditioned by history, institutions, or society is natural*' (emphasis added).

Beyond peripheral English-language use countries, prominent language teaching organizations have been relatively slow in attempting to oppose a continued mainstream subscription to the 'native-speaker' criterion. For instance, it was not until 2003 that the US based TESOL (Teachers of English to Speakers of Other Languages) organization released a position statement which despite not challenging the actual validity of the 'native-speaker' criterion did contribute somewhat to its demythification: '[n]ative speaker proficiency in the target language alone is not a sufficient qualification for such teaching positions; the field of teaching English to speakers of other languages (TESOL) is a professional discipline that requires specialized training' (TESOL, 2003). Likewise, it took BAAL (the British Association for Applied Linguistics) until 2011 to introduce an informal policy refusing to publish teacher recruitment advertisements demanding that candidates meet the 'native-speaker' criterion. After contacting the media officer of the organization on 12 November 2012 to inquire as to whether any formal policy had since been enacted, a written policy was subsequently drafted on 19 November 2012.

Within the draft version of the formal policy it asserts: '[u]se of the term "native speaker" can be seen as discriminating against expert teachers of English for whom English is a second or other language' (cited with permission of the BAAL media officer). It is interesting to note that while the BAAL policy acknowledges that use of the 'native-speaker' criterion *is an act of discrimination* (thus naturally creating *victims* and *perpetrators*), the policy is incorrect in identifying the victim only as someone 'for whom English is a second or other language'. This reflects subscription to a common framework in which the 'native-speaker' criterion is seen to only promote *unidirectional* rather than *multidirectional* acts of discrimination (in this instance during the early stages of the teacher recruitment process). While this is indeed a common juncture for discrimination to manifest in the ways described by the policy, the limited standpoint refuses to account for the multitude of ways in which people labelled as 'native speakers' are also prone to more elaborate or veiled forms of discrimination at both the pre- and post-recruitment stages, thus making them also eligible for legitimate victim status (see Houghton and Rivers, 2013; Rivers, 2012b).

Furnishing the imagination

As one would expect in any situation where certain human beings primarily exist as shadows of the imagination, 'native speakers' of English within the Japanese sociocultural context often endure a turbulent experience in their attempts to navigate the normative labyrinth of inclusion–exclusion, love–hate and acceptance–rejection dynamics. Kiernan (2010: 9) illustrates how 'despite being an attractive location in terms of availability of jobs, often relatively well-paid, accounts of teaching experiences in Japan have sometimes been quite cynical, and professional identity consequently appears problematic.' The *cynicism* dominating this particular sociocultural context can be suggested to originate from McLaren's (1989: 183) observation concerning the manner in which '[t]he dominant culture tries to "fix" the meaning of signs, symbols, and representations to provide a "common" worldview, disguising relations of power and privilege'. Therefore, once categorized as a 'native speaker' of English, freedom to determine the properties and parameters of one's identities becomes encroached upon by a *fixed* framework established and sanctioned by the sociocultural majority. As a consequence, those imagined as 'native speakers' must come to terms with their normalized 'confinement within a narrow ballpark of generalist roles' (Toh, 2013: 189) and the conditional identities which such restrictive roles promote and dictate. For the sociocultural majority, important in such a process is that these roles and identities are not disturbed through entertaining deviations that challenge the *fixed* meanings assigned to the 'native-speaker' location. Within the Japanese sociocultural context, this 'native-speaker' location has been found to be inclusive of elements of culture (Stewart, 2005), gender (Appleby, 2012; Bailey, 2007; Hayes, 2013; Hicks, 2013; Nagatomo, 2012; Simon-Maeda, 2004), language (Houghton and Rivers, 2013; McMillan and Rivers, 2011; Rivers, 2011b, 2011d, 2011e), nationality (Hall, 1998; Masden, 2013; Rivers, 2010a, 2010b; Worthington, 1999) and race (Kubota and Lin, 2006, 2009; Rivers and Ross, forthcoming a, forthcoming b; Simon-Maeda, 2004). Such multifaceted associations create further implications for identity development when considering how the mere presence of a particular group label (i.e. the 'native speaker') is sufficient for the activation of stereotypic information about the group (Lepore and Brown, 1997).

The study

Participants and data collection

During early 2011, a small number of non-Japanese (i.e. foreign) English-language teachers were contacted via email requesting their participation in the current project. The details of the project were outlined and the purpose and future uses of their potential data were made clear. These teachers were working at a number of different Japanese universities (and a conversation school) and were known either directly to the author or indirectly through mutual acquaintances. Although ten complete narratives were received, due to spatial constraints, only five are presented within this chapter (Table 2.1).

Research questions and procedure

After the teachers had agreed to participate in the project, a second email was sent inclusive of a single Lead Research Question (LRQ) as well as a small number of Other Research Questions (ORQs). The LRQ was intended to be specific in guiding the participants to engage with the topics under investigation but was also vague enough to allow them to freely interpret the language used in different ways (e.g. a *minority member of society* could be conceptualized around a variety of criteria). The ORQs were designed to more comprehensively tease out prevailing attitudes and opinions relating to the identity implications of being cast as a 'native speaker' of English in the Japanese sociocultural context. The participants were not required to answer all of the ORQs individually but rather to use them to focus their thoughts towards more fully answering the LRQ.

- **LRQ:** As a minority member of society how do you deem your multiple identities (personal, professional, social) to be manipulated, restricted and/or empowered by the complexities of the real and imagined dimensions of the 'native-speaker' English teacher status label?
- **ORQs:** Do you consider yourself to be a 'native speaker' of English? On what grounds do you primarily define your status as a 'native speaker' of English? When referred to as a 'native speaker' of English by different people how does this make you feel? What are the advantages and disadvantages to being a 'native speaker' of English in Japan? What is your opinion concerning how 'native speakers' of English are socially positioned and

Table 2.1 Demographic overview of the five respondents

Name	Gender	Age	Highest degree	Years in Japan	Nationality	Race	Workplace
Karl	M	32	MA	1	Australian	White	University
Daniel	M	32	MA	4	American	White	University
Tony	M	36	BA	5	Australian	White	Conversation School
Peter	M	35	MA	10	American	White	University
Tina	F	40	MA	13	Australian	White	University

Note: All names shown are pseudonyms.

perceived in Japan? How do you manage the discord (if one exists) between societal expectations dictated by the 'native speaker' of English status label and your own individual sense of being?

After a period of 60 days all teachers had returned between 200 and 1,500 words of insightful narrative and the decision was made to proceed with the data analysis of the 5 selected narratives. The decision as to which narratives to feature in this chapter was based primarily upon practical considerations rather than actual narrative content.

Data analysis and discussion

Within this section, the data is presented in chronological order based on the duration that each participant had been working within Japan. This decision was made on the basis that the current study is not only seeking to identify commonalities between the participants, but also to demonstrate the variety of ways in which multiple identities are constructed *across time* through narrative accounts of experience in a relatively shared sociocultural context. Therefore, experience amassed was seen to be an important aspect of the data collected.

Narrative 1: Karl

> [T]hroughout this year I have felt as though I have landed in a situation whereby my identities are almost expected to be similar to those around me and that the situation I found myself in was the 'accepted' one that I should abide by. The identity I found most affected by my status of a native-speaker teacher was my professional. I was welcomed to my department warmly by way of a couple of nice welcome parties. However, it was not long before I found myself, daily, alone in my office with very little contact with my colleagues at all. I realized that I was excluded from departmental meetings on grounds I was unsure of. In comparison to other institutions at which I had worked, this was unusual to me – to be left absolutely to my own devices, totally unchecked, as well as to be given no input into departmental dialogue. As the year progressed, this situation reached the point where I could say, truthfully, that the number of conversations I had with faculty members could be counted on both hands! I, like the small group of other native-speaking English teachers in the department, ended up spending the year working alone in my own office and with my students, with no collaboration and with no observation. (Emailed response from Karl)

Karl's narrative is particularly valuable as it illustrates what newcomers, or those not familiar with the Japanese education system, may experience when initially socialized into an institutional culture (see Handley et al., 2006), and indeed a national policy of internationalization, structured along entrenched lines of difference and division. Befu (1983, cited in McConnell 2000: 226) draws attention to how 'a foreigner's wishful thinking is that internationalisation obliterates the line between [themselves] and the Japanese, whereas for the Japanese internationalisation compels them to draw a sharper line than ever before between themselves and outsiders.' However, the concept of internationalization within the Japanese sociocultural context is one neither clearly defined nor understood by administrators, academics and/or institutions (see Horio, 1988; Kubota, 2002; Yamazaki, 1986). This intentional ambiguity is maintained as it then permits a *seemingly harmless* and *neoliberal sounding* concept to be operationalized as an expansive mechanism of nation-state resistant to the concept of globalization, the English language, in addition to those people who are seen as *authentic* transmitters of English-speaking cultures (i.e. 'native speakers') – all of which should be handled with caution and kept at an appropriate distance. With direct relevance to Karl's narrative, Miyoshi (2010: 201) discusses how 'Japan's "internationalization" is being revealed as a sham – ceremonial exchange of niceties and pleasantries without critical engagement – played by *both* Japanese and visiting foreign scholars' (emphasis added).

Karl demonstrates awareness of external pressures to conform to a perceived single accepted identity, one believed to be shared by his 'native-speaker' colleagues. Karl attributes his assigned location of 'native speaker' of English as being responsible for impacting upon (i.e. limiting) the potential scope for professional identity development. The parameters of the expected identity are further drawn out and detailed through the symbolic nature of the welcome party and early collegial pleasantries that stand in stark contrast to the daily realities of Karl's workplace existence. Once the regular semester began, collegial contact and any sense of departmental inclusion quickly evaporated and descended into peripheral isolation. Despite being an experienced foreign language teacher, Karl highlights how he had never encountered such a situation before and had certainly not expected such treatment to be normative. The fact that Karl was never told why he was not included in departmental activities confirms that such treatment of 'native speakers' is considered normative and unproblematic in the mind of the university and regular faculty.

The most probable reason for Karl's exclusion from any kind of departmental activity can be attributed to his employment categorization as a '*specially appointed* associate professor' (i.e. the *tokunin* system). In many cases, the *tokunin* system functions as an employment category for foreigners and is reminiscent of its predecessor (which is still used at some universities) the *gaikokujin kyoushi* system (i.e. foreign lecturer) (see Houghton, 2013). However, such obvious forms of discrimination on the basis of nationality are now more insidiously concealed by recasting the main employment criterion from being foreign to being a 'native speaker' of a particular language. Therefore, as *tokunin* positions are almost exclusively reserved for 'native speakers' of languages other than Japanese (as is the case in Karl's institution), developing language proficiency is usually the primary focus of the role (foreign language education) as opposed to engaging in theoretical research (linguistics). Karl's exclusion from regular departmental affairs was therefore inevitable due to his categorization as a 'native speaker' of English and the employment category, or *fixed* parameter existence, to which he was then condemned. Through direct contact with other sources, it was revealed that university funding for Karl's position was, in the first instance, dependent on a 'native speaker' of English being hired, thus contributing to the continuation of the 'native-speaker fallacy' (Phillipson, 1992: 195) and the 'native-speakerist framework' (Rivers, 2013a: 75) which such a fallacy maintains.

> In terms of my personal and social identities, as a result of the isolating nature of my professional position within the institution, essentially created by the conditions attached to being a native-speaker teacher I found that my friends in Japan needed to come from outside of my work. I had to make a concerted effort at this, or risk having a rather lonely year. It was the first time in my academic or professional life I had felt so excluded in a work environment, and very much missed the environment of collegiality I had experienced elsewhere. Overall, I would have to say that throughout my year in Japan I have felt the development of my own identities restricted as a result of what seem to be common institutional practices in Japan. This, in effect, placed the responsibility upon my own shoulders to take action to aid the quick development and construction of the personal and social identities I was going to need to survive the year – as I was not going to get anything more than a desk and a salary at work. (Emailed response from Karl)

Unable to construct a suitable professional identity within the workplace due to the common institutional practices experienced, Karl was particularly proactive outside of work in his attempts to make friends and thus create an environment in which a positive sense of personal and social identity could develop. Despite having no Japanese language ability, Karl was able to network among the expatriate community and became a member of an expatriate football team. This allowed him to *survive the year* and experience some form of meaningful social interaction, inclusion and a medium for positive personal and social identity expression. During his year in Japan, only his professional identity (i.e. identities created and enacted within the specific context of the workplace) appeared to remain thoroughly undernourished, a direct consequence of being categorized, by others, as a 'native speaker' of English and thus employed on terms that normalized his exclusion, isolation and dissatisfaction. Karl's perception of just how disenfranchised his workplace environment made him feel is best summarized in his admission that he believed that he was *not going to get anything more than a desk and a salary at work.*

Narrative 2: Daniel

> The tertiary education institution I work for make me seem like a monolingual and monocultural individual who ought to ironically be able to function as a sort of cultural diplomat for people who look and communicate like I do in English. This has the dual effect of restricting my full participation in academic life here which is largely tasked to people born and raised in the country, and empowering me, because there is so much value placed on the role of English language and its native speakers in the eyes of most people around me. The subtle manipulation, restriction, and empowerment goes both ways though, because as an individual given the sole responsibility of lecturing about English in a wider educational context, I can decide how to lecture and what to lecture about. I take this feeling of agency to mean I too can manipulate the stereotypical images that people here have of me, and restrict others from holding me to those stereotypes. Obviously then the agency that I enact is a sign of empowerment that I display regardless of whether or not I am a minority member of this society. (Emailed response from Daniel)

Daniel begins his narrative with reference to the perceived influence of his institution in dictating his workplace identity, an identity consistent with the imagined 'native speaker' of English as a monolingual and monocultural individual, and thus someone deemed *authentic* enough to function as a foreign language teacher and *cultural token* of their *home* country (see Rivers, 2010b, 2011a). This awareness can be linked to the accepted identity Karl also believed he was under pressure to conform to in his workplace. Daniel further notes the additional institutional expectation of him to perform the role of *cultural diplomat* representing speakers of English with similar physical description (i.e. white), thus reaffirming the racial element within the 'native-speaker' location (see Kubota and McKay, 2009; Rivers and Ross, forthcoming a, forthcoming b; Simon-Maeda, 2004).

Such pressures to perform imagined symbolic roles reflect the 'burden of representation' (Iwabuchi, 2005) demanded in instances of such 'staged authenticity' (MacCannell, 1973). The Japan Exchange and Teaching (JET) Programme (see McConnell, 2000), administered by numerous Japanese governmental ministries serves as one such instance. On the programme's website it dictates that participants from English-speaking countries are to be '*cultural ambassadors* of their home countries, a role that extends beyond the nine to five workday. JET participants must constantly be aware of their behaviour and *should make efforts to adapt to the Japanese culture and work environment*' (Council of Local Authorities for International Relations, 2010, emphasis added). In requesting participants speak and behave not as individuals but as *cultural ambassadors*, the divisive intergroup dynamics of the programme are designed to ensure that the imported participants (or exotic artefacts) remain *authentically* foreign and compliant in the perpetuation of nation-based stereotypes. At the same time, however, programme participants are expected to make sincere gestures towards adapting to the *Japanese* cultural work environment, one that often limits them to a peripheral and entirely temporal existence.

Noticeable within Daniel's narrative is his ability to see how such treatment has the *dual effect of restricting [his] full participation in academic life* and that *subtle manipulation, restriction, and empowerment goes both ways*. In contrast to Karl who viewed his departmental exclusion as being isolating, Daniel takes professional satisfaction in the agency he is afforded through exclusion from regular university affairs. He indicates that this site of agency acts as a forum from which he is able to challenge *the stereotypical images that people here have of [him]*. From this, it can be observed how physical and psychological exclusion from regular collegial involvement has the potential, in certain cases, to promote the cognitive creation of *new spaces of empowerment* in which one is granted freedom to express agency, and thus construct a positive sense of professional identity in an otherwise restrictive workplace. This is consistent with the observations of Lave and Wenger (1991: 36) who note that when 'one moves toward more-intensive participation, peripherality is an empowering position'. However, the potential consequences of attempting to forge a professional identity that does not fit into the imagined cast of representation sanctioned by the sociocultural majority can be severe. Bueno and Caesar (2003: 5) emphasize the stigma attached to being a 'native speaker' of English who wishes to transcend confinement in the imagination of others into a reality marked by academic freedom and the establishment of a self-determined professional identity. Their edited volume opens with the following dedication: '[t]eaching English in Japan is nothing if not an exercise in silence, among people who in many cases do not even dream of some agency by which they might represent themselves.' Indeed, many of the contributing authors who *dared to demonstrate a degree of agency* and speak of their experiences as 'native speakers' of English in the Japanese sociocultural context opted to remain anonymous, thus not only forgoing academic recognition for the publication, but also serving to further empower a status quo prohibiting the voicing of feelings and experiences which do not meet the approval of the sociocultural majority. Nevertheless, as illustrated in Daniel's narrative, while a positive professional identity often develops within the confines of the classroom (i.e. as a foreign language teacher) rather than through involvement and discourse with colleagues (i.e. as a member of an academic community), it has the capacity to withstand potential limitations resultant from being categorized as a minority member of society *beyond* the confines of the workplace.

Narrative 3: Tony

> I don't really identify as a minority member of society or as a Native English Teacher. Teaching is not my chosen profession rather a means to an end. Being a foreigner in Japan who is not fluent in Japanese or someone who wants to join a Japanese company as a full time/life long employee, I teach English because that is basically my only option. I don't have any formal qualifications as a teacher and consider the fact that I was lucky to be born in an English-speaking country and am therefore a native English speaker to be my only selling point. I think I do a good job as an English teacher and my employers seem happy with my work but I in no way, shape or form feel I have the right to call myself a 'teacher'. It would be disrespectful of actual 'teachers'. (Emailed response from Tony)

Tony differs from the other participants in that he works within the conversation school industry as opposed to the university system and is the only participant not to hold a graduate degree. Through his narrative, Tony chooses not to identify himself as either a minority member of society or as a 'native-speaker' English *teacher*. In this case, resisting or denying the label of minority member of society appears to act as a self-defence mechanism intended to maintain a positive sense of self when confronted with categorizations which are psychologically overwhelming due to the negative connotations evoked. Similarly, being a *teacher* is a professional location that Tony deems himself as being unqualified to legitimately claim or *inhabit*. Tony does, though, identify himself as a *foreigner in Japan who is not fluent in Japanese* suggesting that his primary self-identifications are drawn from social positions marked by disempowerment and deficiency.

Tony rejects *teaching* as being a chosen profession but rather a *means to an end* and his *only option*. Tony reveals additional explicit information addressing his sense of deficiency and unwillingness to claim to be a *teacher* in stating that he does not believe he has the *right* to call himself a *teacher* due to his lack of formal teaching qualifications. Making nativist connections between country and language, Tony states how he considers himself *lucky to be born in an English-speaking country* which is equated to being a 'native speaker' of English and as such, a positive selling point within the sociocultural context of Japan. For Tony, subscribing to the 'native-speaker' location appears essential not only as it offers him an employment opportunity, but also in regard to his sense of self-esteem. However, the benefits and empowerment Tony gains on the basis of his 'native' language are continually undermined by professional insecurity as he asserts that claiming the label of teacher would be *disrespectful of actual teachers*. Despite his reluctance to accept the label of teacher, he believes that he does a *good job* as an English *teacher* and that his *employers seem happy* with his work. This stance, again consistent with the nativist agenda, points to the common perception (embraced by both employee and employer) that foreign language teachers are *born* (nature) rather than *made* (nurture) due to their superior 'native' language abilities. Therefore, the narrative is indirectly identifying *teaching* as being a profession that demands formal qualifications (thus on the one hand excluding Tony from claiming access), whereas *foreign language teaching* is cast as being accessible without formal qualifications on condition that the individual is born within an English-speaking country.

> With regards to how I feel about being part of a minority or that there are any expectations upon me or how I am treated, I don't actually think about it at all. If someone has preconceived expectations of me, fair or unfair, that is not something I can control. I think the world has become too preoccupied with labels . . . and has become so over-sensitive that we are turning into, what I can only put so inelegantly as, pussies. I also think that many English speakers/foreigners in Japan have a superiority complex and regard themselves far too highly. These people, in my mind, make the rest of us look bad. (Emailed response from Tony)

Despite a previous refusal to accept the label of minority member of society, in the next section of his narrative, Tony presents a more dismissive position explaining how he does not *actually think about it at all*. This stance is further elaborated on as he conveys his sense of helplessness in the face of preconceived expectations other people may have of him or prejudicial treatment he is then subjected to. While this attitude may well function to protect Tony from challenges that others make to his self-esteem, such attitudes are indicative of insecurity and anxiety concerning his position (accepted or not) as a visible minority group member. As further evidence of the psychological 'need to reaffirm a threatened self' (Steele, 1988: 270), one can look to his statement about what he sees as a general preoccupation people have with labels. Here, Tony asserts how he believes that people in general are becoming oversensitive, or what he refers to as *pussies* (the Oxford Dictionary defines this plural informal North American term as denoting 'a weak, cowardly, or effeminate man'). This gendered instance of *name-calling* is symbolic as in-group affiliations are often established through such *name-calling* acts (particularly within middle-school settings, see Graham and Juvonen, 2002). Further motivation for the outward degradation of others resides in the fact that the *name-caller* is permitted opportunity to demonstrate a self-determined social identity and establish a dominant position in relation to the *name-called*. Thus, *name-calling* practices are especially attractive to individuals who hold insecurities or anxieties about their position within a specific social context or intergroup situation (hence why it is a practice commonly undertaken by 'bullies' who seek to dominate and degrade their 'victims' as a means of enhancing or repairing their own self-esteem).

Indeed, the increasing sense of hostility developing within Tony's narrative is further channelled directly towards other *English speakers/foreigners in Japan* who are accused of having *a superiority complex and [as] regard[ing] themselves far too highly*. While Tony asserts that these people *make the rest of us look bad*, he does not explicitly indicate to whom the inclusive *us* is referring. One can speculate on the evidence presented that it most likely refers to an imagined in-group to which Tony belongs, one in which such attitudes are reinforced and accepted by other group members. Throughout the narrative, it is possible to observe examples of a refusal to accept certain labels, an apparent sense of helplessness in dealing with naming practices and a passive aggressive attitude towards people who question the underlying legitimacy of certain naming practices. It is therefore difficult to mark a clear distinction between personal, professional and social identities, or to observe instances of identity beyond those constructed through outward refusal, denial and/or aggression.

Narrative 4: Peter

> I do consider myself to be a 'native-English speaker' teacher. I believe I am a 'native-English speaker' because that is the language I grew up using in the USA with my peers, family, at school . . . everywhere. I consider myself a teacher because I have been teaching English as a second/foreign language for 10 years and have a M.A in Applied Linguistics/TESOL. How I feel when referred to as a 'native-English speaker' depends on the context. In Japan, at its most basic and general level I feel like a 'privileged outsider'. The main advantage of being a 'native-English speaker' is that I believe I constitute the 'preferred' foreigner. (Emailed response from Peter)

Peter positively identifies as a 'native speaker' of English on the basis that English was the language he *grew up using*. He also identifies as a 'native-speaker' English teacher on the basis of formal qualifications and experience. With an emphasis on the emotions evoked when referred to as a 'native speaker' of English, Peter stresses the role of context adding how within the specific sociocultural context of Japan the label promotes feelings of being a *privileged outsider*. Peter explains how the main advantage of being labelled as a 'native speaker' of English is that it grants him the status of *preferred foreigner* among the Japanese sociocultural majority, thus highlighting a common conflation between first language and nationality/ethnicity (i.e. 'native speakers' of English are not imagined to be *Japanese nationals* but 'foreigners').

> It becomes problematic, though, when someone decides that [they] want to stay and make a career in Japan. I believe that 'native-speaker' teachers are positioned on the periphery of English education in Japan. Used more as tools to illustrate that English and using English to communicate with foreigners is 'fun'. And by extension, foreigners, or 'native-speaker' teachers should be fun. I believe that Japanese students in general have come to expect 'native-English speaker' teachers' classes to be amusing and place more importance on the fun-factor of the lessons than the educational value of the lessons. This makes it difficult for 'native-speaker' teachers to create a professional identity as an 'educator' or 'teacher'. (Emailed response from Peter)

Turning to the perceived disadvantages of being a 'native speaker' of English, Peter outlines a belief that such a location is restrictive in forming a career within Japan, as 'native speakers' of English are positioned on the periphery of English-language education, an observation shared through the narratives of Karl and Daniel. This perspective is further supported by Rivers (2013a: 77) who in discussing the revolving door treatment of 'native-speaker' English teachers within one specific Japanese institution, points to how 'individual teachers are [therefore] forever disenfranchised from an educational system which exploits them as a collective in order to sustain itself' (see Heimlich, 2013 for further discussion detailing the 'revolving door mentality').

Peter is specific in noting how the peripheral existence of 'native speakers' of English concerns them being *used more as tools to illustrate that English and using English to communicate with foreigners is fun*. The reference to the term *tool* is significant as it reflects discourse within Japan's official policy towards English-language education whereby '[t]he view of English as a tool is applied by treating foreigners as resources' (Hashimoto, 2009: 37). As Peter illustrates, this often leads to the 'native speaker' of English being cast as an innate entertainer and consequently this genre of 'performance' (see Goffman, 1959) is what many students and institutions have come to expect. As a site of potential identity conflict, Peter continues to assert how *this makes it difficult for native-speaker teachers to create a professional identity as an educator or teacher*.

> I realize that Japanese people in general expect me to be a 'fresh foreigner' no matter how long I have been in Japan . . . there are times when I am glad I am not Japanese and not expected to dress in dark suit for work every day, or act in obsequious manner to anyone and everyone who may be 'above' me in societal hierarchy. (Emailed response from Peter)

As within the narrative of Daniel, Peter constructs links between identities created in the professional context (i.e. the workplace) and identities imposed or expected in the social context (i.e. beyond the workplace) by noting awareness of a belief that Japanese people in general expect him to be a *fresh foreigner* regardless of length of residence in Japan. This view is consistent with many 'native-speaker' English teacher workplaces in which the idealized foreigner is someone who is fresh (i.e. young) and generally unfamiliar with Japanese cultural or linguistic affairs, thereby facilitating the psychological control of the sociocultural majority when confronted by an historically imagined superior Other (i.e. a white English-speaking American). This can also be seen through internal politics and policies, such as those within Karl's workplace, which 'regulate foreigners' employment in order to firewall Japanese society from a supposed threat of infiltration' (Heimlich, 2013: 171).

At the end of Peter's narrative, he seeks to affirm a positive sense of self in describing how he is *glad* not to be Japanese. As shown within the more extreme example given in Tony's narrative, this common self-enhancement technique (i.e. the degradation or dismissal of the Other) is undertaken in this instance, not through *name-calling*, but rather through describing the Other in a stereotypical manner (in this case the image of a Japanese company employee). That is, and in contrast to Tony, while Peter can observe and acknowledge the stereotypical views which Japanese people may have of him due to his lived experience, he neglects to describe Japanese people in a manner free from similar such stereotypes and inflexible processes of categorization. This demonstrates the slippery slope of how once accepting certain naming practices or imagined locations (in which certain people are therefore expected to reside) it becomes easier to perpetuate, rather than challenge, them in a non-stereotypical manner, even when one is affected unfavourably by their continuation (i.e. the widespread use of the 'native-speaker' criterion within JALT's and JACET's teacher recruitment advertisements).

Narrative 5: Tina

> I have three personalities living in Japan. I have my professional personality at work, my social personality to fit in with Japanese society and my home personality which is not hindered by cultural and social boundaries. All my past jobs have been in the Japanese school system or *eikaiwa* [English conversation]. I did have more freedom in the *eikaiwa* system they wanted me to be a NES foreigner but to also be more 'Japanese' at the same time. That was always a struggle and I always had to be thinking of Japanese constraints so as not to upset the teachers, students, board of education and also parents. (Emailed response from Tina)

Tina is explicit in identifying three distinct personalities within Japan (professional, social and home) and how each serves different functions. Tina states that her social personality is *to fit in with Japanese society*, while her home personality *is not hindered by cultural and social boundaries*. Tina's emphasis on fitting in and conforming to an apparent unquestionable set of Japanese sociocultural norms is also reflected through her narrative concerning her professional personality and experience. In describing her teaching experience in the English conversation system, Tina associates *freedom* with her employer's preference for her to be a 'native-English speaking foreigner', but sees struggle in the coexisting requirement for her to be more Japanese at the same time (the same kind of conflict observed within the official discourse of the JET Programme). In the classroom, Tina seems happy to embrace the 'native-speaker' English teacher location and all the imagined sociocultural features this location demands. However, outside the classroom Tina appears conscious of acting more Japanese as *not to upset the teachers, students, board of education and also parents*. The implication one takes from this is that *acting* like a 'native-speaker' of English outside of the classroom is likely to cause offence to certain stakeholder groups from within the sociocultural majority. Therefore, the 'native-speaker' English teacher's workplace (i.e. within the classroom) is marked as a place in which the identities required for exhibition (i.e. those *fixed* by the sociocultural majority) can be differentiated from those identities required for exhibition beyond the workplace.

> I have learnt to mix a lot of my 'personalities'. At work I am still my joking, outgoing self, especially among my NES colleagues but if I am around my Japanese work colleagues I tend to transform to a mix of my outgoing self but with Japanese social norms and language. To be honest as we are guests in Japan I think all NES teachers should do the same. We cannot expect to live in another country and be the same as we would in our home country. I feel the same about visitors coming to my home country too. I think to have your own cultural norms in the home is great but they should be adapted outside the home in order to live more harmoniously. (Emailed response from Tina)

The second section of Tina's narrative continues the focus on adhering to situational norms and learning to manage her multiple *personalities*. Deemed to be acceptable among her 'native-speaker' English colleagues is Tina's *joking, outgoing self*, but when among Japanese colleagues, Tina describes how she transforms to *a mix of my outgoing self but with Japanese social norms and language*. Tina also explains how *we cannot expect to live in another country and be the same as we would in our home country*. An additional statement concerning Tina's beliefs about social interaction across cultural and national boundaries then follows this. Tina positions herself, and all 'native speakers' of English as being *guests in Japan* who should therefore follow her *mixing of personalities* and efforts towards adaptation to a perceived set of *fixed* Japanese sociocultural norms. This opinion is reflected in, and perhaps originates from, her view on visitors coming to her *home* country of Australia. However, even overlooking Tina's apparent conservative tone in relation to foreigners within her home country, which also seems to demand assimilation to an assumed set of nation-specific sociocultural norms – thus devaluing and refusing to engage with diversity which (in her opinion) should be confined to the home – it is not clear how a *visitor* is defined.

> I really hate seeing teachers that do not abide by Japanese cultural norms at work when it is so easy to do (especially appearance such as hair, dress codes and make up) I don't mean we should all do things only the Japanese way but there should be boundaries in behavior, dress code, gestures and respect. Maybe if more teachers did that then we wouldn't have so many labels! (Emailed response from Tina)

Tina then switches the focus back to the workplace where her apparent conservative social views in regard to diversity and conformity are more explicitly manifested through her professed *hate* of teachers who do not conform to *Japanese cultural norms* in the workplace. The rather aggressive tone adopted by Tina towards other 'native-speaker' English teachers is also reflected in Tony's narrative (i.e. in his reference to other teachers as having a *superiority complex*). Not only does this contradict her earlier position concerning how her employer was *happy* for her to play the 'native-English speaking foreigner' role in the classroom (another similarity with Tony), but also condemns all non-Japanese residents within Japan to an unattainable ideal – integration into a sociocultural context based entirely upon principles of assimilation and the quashing of diversity – an act made almost impossible on the grounds of physical appearance alone – if not on the basis of ethnicity then on the basis of physical appearance as enforced through superficial 'native-speaker' dress-code policies within workplaces which intentionally differentiate 'native-speaker' English teachers from their Japanese colleagues (i.e. consistent with the earlier references to Japan's version of internationalization). For example, Rivers (2013a: 81) discusses how within the English Center (EC) of one Japanese university 'inter-group boundaries designed to authenticate and protect the "native-speaker" English teachers from contamination are maintained through the strict implementation of an EC dress code'. Rivers further draws attention to how:

> [t]he fact that no other department, affiliated research institution or first language defined population has any such dress code enforced works to undermine the actual educational contributions of the EC teachers through reaffirming symbolic links between physical appearance, linguistic authenticity, institutional positioning and role capability within the minds of university management, regular faculty members and students.

Although Tina insists that she is not suggesting that *we should all do things only the Japanese way*, she further explains her belief that if more teachers conformed to Japanese sociocultural norms there would be fewer labels, thus ignoring the fact that not all labels are accurate as well as the human instinct and social management function of naming practices, specifically how individuals must be identified as different (although not necessarily as exotic) for the smooth facilitation of social comparison and group formation.

> The main advantage of being a NES is that there are always jobs available! We can make better money than our Japanese counterparts. However, a disadvantage is that it is too difficult to get tenure or to move up higher in the education system. With regard to how NESs are socially positioned, I think that it depends on where we work and what country we are from. For example, I am viewed more favourably being Australian and white compared to an Indian person who is also classed as a NES. It is such a stereotypical classification system in Japan. I think that now I work in the tertiary system I am positioned higher in society. Talking to Japanese friends and family they said that working in *eikaiwa* is not such a good job as anyone can do it. Teaching at high school or university means that the teacher is more educated and that is important in Japanese society. (Emailed response from Tina)

Tina ends her narrative with a focus on the advantages of being categorized as a 'native speaker' of English – mainly that there are always jobs available (a truism which confirms how there always needs to be an out-group within any sociocultural context, and that the *authentic foreigner* is particularly attractive in domains such as foreign language education). Although, in stating that 'native speakers' of English can make *better money than our Japanese counterparts*, Tina falls victim to a myth which ignores the fact that full-time Japanese teachers in higher education are usually placed on an incremental salary scale and that their bonuses are often given in addition to their basic salary. This can be compared to full-time non-Japanese first-language teachers such as the *tokunin* teachers who usually get a fixed salary and are omitted from the bonus system. Tina is correct in acknowledging the difficulties which non-Japanese 'native-speaker' English teachers face in securing stable employment and breaking the cycle of their temporal existence (as also noted by Peter), but the issue of employment security across all sectors of the national workforce is a concern currently receiving legal legislation designed *in theory* to better protect contracted workers (see Rivers, 2013b).

In shifting to the social positioning of 'native speakers' of English, Tina is able to see the contextual element in determining location and how teaching English as a foreign language is a racialized profession (see Kubota and McKay, 2009; Rivers and Ross, forthcoming a, forthcoming b; Simon-Maeda, 2004). Furthermore, and despite her earlier comments about how visitors and guests should adapt to host country norms, Tina demonstrates awareness that Japanese society operates on what she terms as a *stereotypical classification system*. However, like Peter, she also fails to see how her own attitudes, behaviours and identities directly contribute to the continuation of the status quo, especially through her emphasis on conforming to, rather than challenging, Japanese sociocultural norms and intergroup stereotypes within the foreign language education workplace.

Implications and conclusions

As an individual employed within the Japanese sociocultural context for over a decade my interpretations of the five narratives presented have, consciously and unconsciously, been influenced by my own experience and the identities to which such experience has given rise. However, this should not undermine or detract from the importance of the issues raised throughout this chapter. I am explicit in my own understanding that the interpretations offered do not reflect any absolute or objective truths.

It has been proposed that 'an individual's organization may provide one answer to the question, Who am I?' (Ashforth and Mael, 1989: 22). With this in mind, the five narratives shared have served to illustrate the multidimensionality of the identity construct among a sample of 'native-speaker' English teachers working within the Japanese sociocultural context. The narratives are not only revealing in terms of their content in relation to the sociocultural environment and its particulars, but also in terms of how experience amassed within the system seemingly does very little to change perceptions concerning how the 'native-speaker' English teacher location can be enduringly restrictive in the workplace, thus in the majority of cases limiting the development of a positive professional identity. Accordingly, and with conceptual links to the earlier citation of Showalter (1988: 346 discussing Edwin Ardener), one should note that all identities, no matter how seemingly unrestricted cannot be created without restraint as they must be believable to others, meaning that '[t]he range within which identities can be changed or manipulated is limited both by the systemic logic of these semantic domains and by social convention' (Schlee, 2004: 137).

Consistent with Giroux's (2003: 100) position that, '[i]dentities are constructed through the differences and exclusions, mediated within disparate and often unequal relationships of power', one can argue that many of the identities expressed throughout the five narratives have been so impinged upon by contextual and interpersonal parameters that favour restriction, (dis)involvement and exclusion, that they are predominantly cast through dominant discourse of deficiency. That is, many of the narratives present stories and display identities in response to treatment stemming directly from being imagined as a 'native speaker' of English. In this regard, not only are identities largely being cast and recast along lines of psychological conflict and discontent but more significantly, many of the identities displayed through the narratives are products of teachers knowing *what they are not* (promoting disempowerment as a basis of identity development) rather than *what they are* (promoting empowerment as a basis of identity development).

Central to the identity implications highlighted is the way in which members of the sociocultural majority, and institutions dealing with foreign language education categorize the 'native-speaker' English teacher. As shown within this chapter, intergroup boundaries and the construction of in-groups and out-groups within the workplace are often drawn not upon criteria such as shared professional interests or similar areas of expertise, but rather, differentiations are created and enforced through being identified as a 'native speaker' of a language *other than Japanese*, and thus foreign. In this regard, one can observe how such institutions are contributing to the maintenance of a insular nation-state 'us versus them' mentality. Indeed, Simon-Maeda (2004: 430–1) explains how such a 'convoluted inclusion-exclusion mechanism has resulted in EFL employment policies that reproduce ethnocentric attitudes and sustain a myopic vision of intercultural dialogue that seeks to maintain rather than cross boundaries'. Based on the evidence outlined in this chapter, the implications for the development of a satisfying career within Japan's education system when identified and categorized as a 'native speaker' of English appear relatively bleak despite the 'masquerade of smiley faces and perpetual pleasantness decorating the veneer of "native-speaker" English teaching' (Rivers, 2013a: 75).

What remains in certain institutions is a normative culture of ethnic nepotism (see van den Berghe, 1987) – a kind of xenophobia-laden academic inbreeding of people, ideas and procedures – characterized by a collective lack of motivation, desire or interest in change. However, until change (in the form of re-evaluating the validity of certain categorization practices) is forthcoming, the multidimensional identities of the 'native-speaker' English teacher will remain under the *fixed* constraints constructed and deployed by others, unable to flourish in a manner that ensures individual, professional and social identity satisfaction in the workplace and potentially beyond. One can speculate that this will not only continue to adversely impact upon workplace relations, intercultural contact dynamics and the psychological well-being of individual teachers, but also on the quality of foreign language education offered to the millions of Japanese students interested in improving their English-language proficiency and exploring their own foreign language identity options and locations.

3

Professional Identities Shaped by Resistance to Target Language Only Policies

Brian A. McMillan

Introduction

In this chapter I employ a narrative, auto-ethnographical approach (see Barkhuizen, 2011; Beijaard et al., 2004; Conle, 2000; Polkinghorne, 1988) to explore and document how my sense of professional identity has evolved in the face of Target Language Only (TLO) policies in different teaching contexts throughout my career as a language educator. Following Duff and Uchida's (1997: 452) observation that 'sociocultural identities and ideologies are not static, deterministic constructs that English as a Foreign Language (EFL) teachers and students bring to the classroom', I examine retrospectively how my beliefs and sense of professional identity have been transformed by critical experiences and encounters with 'Others of similarity' (those with similar values and experiences to Self) and 'Others of opposition' (those with values and experiences seemingly irreconcilable to Self) (Chang, 2008) throughout four phases of my teaching career: beginning as a pre-service and novice French immersion teacher in Canada; becoming an Assistant Language Teacher (ALT) of English in junior high schools in Japan; returning to French immersion teaching in Canada and enrolling in a Master's of Education programme; and becoming a university EFL teacher-researcher in Japan.

Teacher-researcher identity can be understood as an *ongoing process* of interpretation and reinterpretation of experiences (Beijaard et al., 2004) or social practices (Foucault, 1984). With this definition in mind, I draw on Coldron and Smith's (1999) framework for describing the conflict between structure (the socially 'given') and agency – specifically, the moral and scientific dimensions of identity:

> The moral dimension consists essentially in the ability to make defensible judgements about the relative value of instructions, practices and structures. . . . [T]he scientific tradition calls for teachers to base their practice on research and to incorporate research into their practice. . . . [T]he importance of this tradition lies in the way that the scientific method is appropriated to legitimate policy decisions, whilst at the same time the same method enables a critical approach to evidence, often in opposition to the same decisions. It also supports a view of teaching as a rational process and teachers as rational agents [while] there may be other, counter-rational processes at work, such as the operation of the unconscious. (Boreham and Gray, 2005: 5)

In exploring my lived experiences, I focus on how my beliefs and practice with respect to the use of the learner's L1 have evolved – first struggling in my attempts to uphold the 'French only' policy as a novice French immersion teacher in Canada, and then beginning a slow process of freeing myself from the powerful myth (see Levine, 2011) of target language (TL) exclusivity as ideal practice, as both a native (English) and non-native (French) speaker teacher of the TL in different contexts. Key to this process of liberation has been my developing identity as a teacher-*researcher*, which has provided me with a strengthened sense of agency and empowerment, as well as a sense of professional responsibility, as I have attempted to challenge TLO policies through research. I also describe my experience as I struggled alongside one of my colleagues to assert our right to freedom of academic inquiry in the face of institutional censorship at a university in Japan.

TLO polices and ideological control in EFL and French immersion

'English only' policies, which have a long history in EFL programmes around the world, have been thoroughly debunked by an extensive body of research published within the past 20 years (e.g. Auerbach, 1993; Butzkamm and Caldwell, 2009; Canagarajah, 1999; Cook, 2005; Levine, 2011; Macaro, 2005; Turnbull and Dailey-O'Cain, 2009). Yet despite the overwhelming support in the literature for the judicious use of the learner's L1, 'English only' policies remain in place in many EFL contexts (see McMillan and Rivers, 2011; Rivers, 2011d, 2011e; Yphantides, 2013). Similarly, 'French only' policies, which have been in effect in Canadian French immersion since the beginning of the programme in 1965, continue to be promoted by government officials and others in positions of authority. For example, although under review at the time of writing, the province of Nova Scotia's *Program Policy for French Second Language Programs* states: 'All teaching in French second language programs shall be in French' (Province of Nova Scotia, 1998: 4), whereas the *Ontario Curriculum for Grade 8 and 9 French Immer*sion states: 'French must be the language of communication in class' (Ontario Ministry of Education and Training, 1999: 4).

TLO policies are resistant to change, in part, because they are legitimized and reinforced by systems of ideological control based upon coercion and consent (Auerbach, 1993; Fairclough, 1989; Rivers, 2011e). Such policies hold coercive power, with teachers often acting to avoid negative consequences that may result from not following 'proven' best practice procedures. At the same time, such policies are also reinforced through consent, as teachers accept them, either consciously or unconsciously, as legitimate. The language used in TLO policy documents, and the way the policies are framed, also play an important role in exercising such ideological control.

Beginnings: Becoming a late French immersion teacher in Canada

French immersion programmes in Canada are designed for non-native speakers of French, with French being the medium of instruction in most school subjects (e.g. math, history, science). There are a variety of French immersion programmes, with the most common being Early Immersion, beginning when students are in kindergarten or grade 1 (age 5–6), Middle Immersion, starting at grade 4 (age 8–9) and Late Immersion, starting in grade 6 or 7 (age 11–12). My journey towards becoming a French immersion teacher began when I started to learn French as a grade 7 student entering late French Immersion (LFI). Although I sometimes felt a little lost in the beginning, not understanding everything that was in my books or that the teacher said, I enjoyed trying to 'figure out' the meaning of things. I naturally made sense of new French words and grammar by making connections with equivalent expressions in English. My LFI teachers spoke French 99 per cent of the time, only switching into English on rare occasions involving student safety or serious misbehaviour. Students tried to speak French when speaking to the teacher, but we usually spoke English (our shared L1) when talking among ourselves, and my teachers never made any special efforts to police our language use. I generally worked hard and participated in class, wanting to get good grades; however, I also developed a love for the language and culture, and a strong desire to connect with the French-speaking people who lived in the exotic and otherwise inaccessible 'other world' that existed within my own country.

I viewed my LFI teachers, who were either native or near-native French speakers, as role models.

Making connections between French and English continued to be an important learning strategy for me throughout the LFI programme. As my proficiency progressed to a more advanced level in high school, my ability to understand and use French without referring to my L1 increased greatly; but as the ideas I wanted to express became more complex, I continued to use my L1 as an important cognitive tool – especially when working on writing assignments, when I would often use translation as a composing strategy, spending hours looking up words and expressions in my French–English dictionary (see Auerbach, 1993).

As an undergraduate, I majored in French at the University of Prince Edward Island, and spent my senior year studying and 'living the language' at l'Université Laval in Quebec City. I then completed my B.Ed. at l'Université Sainte-Anne in Nova Scotia, with a specialization in teaching French as a second language. As a novice LFI teacher, I felt that I had gained a high degree of intercultural communicative competence (e.g. Byram, 1997) in the TL, and this confidence was central to my developing sense of professional identity. While I sometimes worried about making mistakes and being a non-native-speaker teacher, I did not suffer excessively from the 'nagging inferiority complex' (Rajagopalan, 2005: 300) which many non-native-speaker teachers experience. I believed that my advanced French language skills allowed me to serve as an effective model for the use of the TL and that I also provided my students a model as a proficient, successful L2 user; I also felt that I had an advantage over some native French speaker teachers who had limited proficiency in the students' L1, and that I could put myself in *my students' shoes* based on my own experience as a learner in the LFI programme (see Cook, 2005).

Yet despite being confident in my French language skills, I often experienced feelings of inadequacy as a *teacher*, as I felt that my training had not prepared me to be the expert that I wanted to be. I worried that my teaching was not always based on the latest, proven 'best practices'. While I did not fully realize it at the time, one of the most important gaps in my teacher training was that it had basically ignored the role of the learners' L1 in L2 learning, rather than encouraging pre-service teachers to examine the research literature and reflect on the issues. This created a vacuum in what should have been a fundamental area of pre-service and novice teachers' developing personal beliefs (see Macaro, 2001), thus making new French immersion teachers more willing to accept official policies dictating that '[a]ll teaching in French second language programs shall be in French' (Province of Nova Scotia, 1998: 4). I had also been strongly influenced by reading Krashen and Terrell's (1983) *The Natural Approach* in one of my undergraduate courses, which further reinforced for me the powerful 'French only' myth as I began to form a notion of my 'ideal French immersion teacher self' (Markus and Nurius, 1986).

Despite the fact that I had used my own L1 to great benefit as a learner in LFI, the fear that any use of the L1 would undermine the immersion learning process, or that I might be discovered going against what was widely taken for granted as 'best practice' among French immersion stakeholders, caused me to partially forget and distrust what I should have known from my own learning experience. For example, in my first year of teaching, I recall asking my grade 7 LFI students to 'speak French' as they worked together in small groups writing Christmas stories. This was only two or three months after the students had started the LFI programme, and I knew that they could not really communicate well enough in French to be able to collaborate effectively and create a story together without using any English. Most students were very quiet in their groups, unable to express themselves, as I circulated from group to group, suggesting how they could put their ideas into French, encouraging everyone, to 'speak French', sometimes admonishing them for speaking English, sometimes pretending I hadn't heard it. At the beginning of the lesson, I had presented students with a list of vocabulary that they could use in their stories, but I neglected to spend enough time teaching them the transactional phrases that might have allowed them to use more French as they tried to manage the task and work collaboratively. According to my naïve understanding of second language acquisition (SLA) at the time, struggling to speak French while working together in groups, even though most students could only produce a small number of words and phrases, was an important part of the 'natural' learning process: the students would slowly but surely acquire a repertoire of useful phrases, just by being exposed to comprehensible input, via inference (Krashen and Terrell, 1983; see also Macaro, 2005) and negotiation of meaning, just as young children learn their L1. It did not occur to me at the time – since it would have gone against the 'French only' rule – that it would have been more effective to ask students to first discuss their ideas and write their first draft in their L1 (Auerbach, 1993; Behan et al., 1997; see also Swain et al., 2011), and then have them figure out how to write their story in French.

I also remember, in my first few years of teaching LFI, speaking with parents who were worried that their children were struggling in the programme. I tried to reassure them, saying that learning an L2 was a natural process, and that even if students did not have strong academic skills, they would 'pick up' or 'acquire' the language eventually as long as they received enough exposure to it, just as we all had learned our L1. However, as I said this I remember experiencing an inner conflict, wondering if academic ability might actually play a more important role in language learning in a classroom setting. Doubts flashed through my mind: students who were struggling with the language were likely not gaining a clear grasp of the content, or might quit the programme before they could achieve a reasonable level of proficiency. Wouldn't the amount of language that students could naturally, almost effortlessly, 'acquire' be limited, depending on their 'affective filter' or level of motivation, and given the relatively low number of hours of instruction in LFI as compared to the amount of exposure and opportunities for production enjoyed by young L1 learners? I remember that while I was trying to appear to be an 'expert' by sharing my 'deep insights' into L2 learning with those parents, on another level I was not sure that I believed them myself. In a way, it was a 'cover story' (Clandinin and Connelly, 1995), meant to prove my competence and hide uncertainties, but it was what I thought I was supposed to say. In fact, I was repeating the cover story I had been told by other 'experts'.

As the realities of teaching grade 7 LFI began to impose themselves on my ideal image of what I wanted to be as a teacher, I sometimes 'resorted' to using the students' L1, and felt guilty about doing so. However, I quickly began to realize how effective and efficient a few words of English could be in certain situations, enhancing, rather than detracting from, L2 learning. I continued to provide students with large amounts of input in the TL, but the occasional asides I made in English seemed to make the French more comprehensible to more students. Although it seemed to make perfect sense, in the back of my mind I still worried that I was going against accepted 'best practice'.

I taught relatively large grade 7 and 8 classes, with 33 to 36 students, and levels of proficiency and motivation varied greatly, even in the first and second year of the LFI programme. The textbooks we used were sometimes outdated or too difficult, designed for students who were native French speakers, and there was little time during the day to prepare materials and lessons that would have been truly appropriate and engaging for all of my students. I would have benefited from more opportunities to collaborate with colleagues, but the structure of school culture did not favour collaboration, and wanting to maintain my image as a competent professional also made it difficult to admit that I needed help to improve my teaching. Being frequently distracted from teaching by having to deal with classroom management issues further detracted from my sense of being an 'expert' teacher. Although there were many aspects of teaching LFI that

I enjoyed, I felt that I needed a break, or at least a change of scenery, so I decided to move to Japan to teach English as an ALT. I viewed this move as a sort of voluntary demotion, taking a step back in order to move forward in the right direction, or as the French say *reculer pour mieux sauter* (stepping back to take a better jump). I hoped the change would give me an opportunity to escape the stress and feelings of inadequacy that I had felt as an LFI teacher, and that new opportunities for professional development would present themselves in my new setting.

Moving to Japan: Moving from French immersion to EFL teaching

As an ALT working on the Japan Exchange and Teaching (JET) Programme, my responsibilities included team teaching with about a dozen different Japanese English teachers in five different junior high schools. As a former French immersion teacher in Canada with a few years teaching experience, I was more qualified than most other JET Programme ALTs, many of whom had limited or no training and experience in language teaching. While I occasionally mentioned to people that I had worked as a French immersion teacher in Canada, I was generally happy to take on the 'assistant' role and set aside the LFI teacher identity I had worked so hard to develop. However, I was also giving up the identity status I had enjoyed as a non-native-speaker teacher of French with a high level of proficiency in the TL. I found it a little strange to be granted a rather inflated, ceremonial status in Japan simply based on being a 'native speaker' of English (see Rivers, this volume), and sometimes resented the fact that other foreigners who had little or no background in languages or teaching were automatically accorded the same status.

While some of the Japanese English teachers I worked with tended to overuse the L1, most did a good job of conducting lessons mainly in English. I soon realized that it would have been very difficult, if not impossible, for me to conduct lessons without having a team teaching partner who was proficient in Japanese. I started to learn Japanese in order to be able to communicate more effectively with my beginner-level junior high school students, as attempts to negotiate meaning in English often led to communication breakdowns. After a couple of years of studying and practising, I achieved an intermediate level of proficiency in Japanese which, though far from perfect, was very helpful in my teaching (see Barker, 2003).

It was sometimes challenging to adjust to working with teachers who had different teaching styles, but I generally enjoyed team teaching and found it to be a very enriching experience. I enjoyed planning lessons with my Japanese team teaching partners and participated in monthly meetings and workshops where ALTs shared new teaching ideas. However, I still wanted to gain more formal professional training so that I could become more of an 'expert' teacher, confident that I was using the latest, most effective methods. I started a distance MA (TESOL) programme, but after completing a couple of assignments I dropped out, deciding that I would learn more by attending lectures and working directly with classmates and professors in a more traditional programme. I did not just want to do an MA for the qualification; I wanted to be sure that the time and effort I put into doing a master's degree would truly make me a better teacher.

Returning to LFI teaching and pursuing an M.Ed.

After four years in Japan, I returned to teaching LFI at the junior high level in Canada, feeling that my French was slightly rusty, but still quite confident in my language skills. I also felt that I had benefited from my team teaching experience in Japan and that I would be able to use lesson ideas that had worked well with my Japanese students in LFI. Unfortunately, I found myself teaching new subjects for the first time, with little time for planning. The textbooks and other materials provided often needed to be adapted, and I missed being able to plan lessons with other teachers. I used my students' L1 from time to time, but although I could rationalize it to myself, I still felt uncomfortable, knowing that I was breaking the 'French only' rule and wondering how students, parents, school administrators or department officials would react. Again, I soon started to feel *burned out*, knowing that I wasn't truly meeting the needs of all of my students – especially those who were capable of handling more challenging content, and those struggling to keep up with even basic tasks. I felt that I needed to somehow reinvent myself if I was going to continue my career in language teaching.

I decided to leave my LFI position to enrol in the M.Ed. programme at the University of Prince Edward Island. At first, I had little idea of what sort of work I would be required to do, and was a little unsure that I would be capable of doing it, but the programme soon set me on a path to a *professional awakening*. Up to that point, I had only a limited understanding of what it meant to be a teacher-*researcher*, not realizing that becoming a researcher could in fact be the key to my quest for practical and meaningful professional development. Fortunately, one of my professors was doing research on teacher beliefs concerning L1 use, and he suggested I do my thesis on something similar. I hesitated at first, feeling a sort of aversion to the topic. I had a vague idea that there were arguments on both sides of the issue, but I assumed that the experts and the evidence would be in favour of the TLO approach. I worried that I might be wasting my time, as I felt unsure that I would actually learn something that would help me in my day-to-day teaching.

However, when I began to reflect on the conflict between my own positive experiences with L1 use – both as an L2 learner and teacher – and official TLO policies, I realized that the topic might hold the potential to improve my teaching. As I began reviewing the literature on the topic I made what was, for me at the time, an amazing discovery: there was an extensive body of literature on the topic and, by far, the preponderance of research evidence favoured pedagogically principled L1 use. I started to see that the idea that languages are best taught and learned through using a TLO approach was actually just a myth (see Levine, 2011: 9–17), with almost no empirical evidence to support it.

My thesis research led me to closely examine the official 'French only' policy for LFI in the context where I was teaching, an excerpt of which follows:

> Learning must be intensive, yet should not make students feel that they are drowning. From the early stages of the program, the students must be able to understand French and use it to communicate. **It is therefore essential that French be the only language of communication in the classroom.** According to Calvé (1993), learning a second language follows a 'natural law': 'Learning to communicate effectively in a second language, whether it be in a natural environment or in the classroom, requires a massive exposure to the L2 in meaningful contexts and the opportunity to communicate in the target language'. The use of the L1, even occasionally, will prevent students from developing the strategies which will allow them to function exclusively in French in the classroom. (Atlantic Provinces Education Foundation, 1997: 9, my translation, emphasis in the original)

I was eager to read Calvé's (1993) article, expecting that, as the only work cited, it would provide empirical evidence, or at least theoretical support, for the 'French only' policy. I was surprised to read the following at the beginning of Calvé's article:

> In reaction to the rigidity of the audio-oral approach . . . according to which the teacher performed verbal, visual, and gesticular acrobatics and absolutely everything in the classroom had to take place in the L2, those who advocate the communicative approach have generally shown a good deal of flexibility

> concerning the use of the students' L1 in the classroom. In principle, there is surely nothing wrong with occasionally translating a word or expression which students are unable to figure out in other ways, or giving students certain explanations in English before a test or difficult task. (Calvé, 1993: 15–16, my translation)

Not only does Calvé's article not provide evidence supporting the 'French only' policy, but he actually suggests that judicious L1 use is 'harmless, in principle' and can serve several useful functions. For example, he agrees with Harbord (1992) that the L1 can be useful for dealing with the 'inevitable comparisons and transfers that students make, often unconsciously, between the L2 and L1' (Calvé, 1993: 26, my translation). The main point of Calvé's article is that the TL should be the main language of communication and learning in the classroom, and that teachers should guard against overuse of the L1. Calvé's recommendations are consistent with what Macaro (2001: 535) refers to as the optimal position: 'There is some pedagogical value in L1 use. Some aspects of learning may actually be enhanced by the use of the L1.' It seemed to me that the authors of the Atlantic Provinces Education Foundation policy had cherry-picked a short passage from Calvé' s article – containing the loaded word 'natural' – while ignoring its true intent, using the reference in order to make it appear that the 'French only' policy was supported by research. I thought about how it would be highly unlikely that busy LFI teachers would take the time, or even think it necessary, to locate and check the original source material. I knew that when I was a beginning teacher it probably never would have even occurred to me; I would have accepted the policy at face value, assuming that the 'experts' knew a lot more than me.

No doubt the officials who wrote the policy had good intentions, hoping to encourage high(er) levels of French use by mandating that lessons be conducted in 'French only'; however, as I thought about how my teaching, and the work of teachers in classrooms around the country, had been negatively affected – the atmosphere of my classroom and my relationships with students, as I (sometimes) tried to police their language use; how I had felt guilty about using what were in fact legitimate teaching techniques, supported by research, and how my repertoire of possible teaching strategies had been limited by the TLO fallacy – I felt that I, along with many other L2 teachers in Canada and around the world, had been duped.

Several months later, as I approached the end of my thesis journey, I had a conversation with an official from the department of education who was a fervent believer in the 'French only' approach. I had not yet shared the results of my master's research, but he seemed to assume that I stood with him, firmly on the 100 per cent French side of the issue. He complained that some LFI teachers, who obviously did not understand the principles of immersion pedagogy, were using English with their students, and that doing so would undermine the learning process and as a result those students would not learn to function completely in French. I asked how he had been able to make students understand using 'French only' when he taught French immersion (before becoming a department consultant), and he replied that he felt he had a special ability to communicate meaning through using facial expressions and gestures when speaking and reading stories to his *young elementary level students in early French immersion*. He was also a native French speaker, which likely gave him extra confidence in his ability to adapt his language so that students could understand – skills which he may have felt some non-native-speaker teachers were lacking. As I listened, I remember thinking that many 'experts' and officials did not possess any real expertise in this area. He strongly promoted the 'French only' policy, yet evidently was not familiar with the literature on the topic and had no firsthand experience in teaching *late* French immersion. As a grade 1–3 teacher, his lessons would often have been based in the 'here and now' or would have contained words that could be represented with pictures or gestures; he had never tried to convey the meaning of abstract ideas and more complex content to beginner-level learners in grades 7–9. I thought to myself that this official would probably have started using English himself – judiciously, of course, and to the degree that he could, given his limited proficiency in the learners' L1 – if he had had to teach LFI classes for more than a few days. Our conversation reminded me of Chambers' (1992: 67) story of one of the authors of the National Curriculum anti-L1 guidelines in England presenting an example of good practice:

> What surprised me, however, was that he said that this could be done in the mother tongue. You could have knocked me over with a feather. I had been agonizing over my own shortcomings in terms of target language use and here was a member of the Working Party contradicting para 3.18 and saying that the mother tongue was legitimate, even when safety was not in question.

Of course, in my case the department official was not saying that L1 use could be used in a positive and productive way, but I thought about how many 'experts' and officials were not in a position in which they were required to uphold the policies themselves, and might be criticizing teachers when they had not made an effort to truly understand the policies they were promoting – even though they were much better equipped with the resources to do so than teachers; when in fact, making well-informed policy decisions should have been *their job*. I began to understand that by promoting TLO policies, authorities legitimize and reinforce, perhaps unconsciously, their own position of power (see Auerbach, 1993; Rivers, 2013a), while teachers are kept in subordinate positions, unaware that they are struggling to uphold an impossible ideal – one which, in fact, research has demonstrated as being less than ideal in many teaching situations. TLO policies may further serve vested interests when the 'expert' is a native-speaker teacher with limited proficiency in the students' L1, making it even harder for the official to adopt a critical point of view and become aware of the need to re-examine the policy.

I felt personally and professionally insulted by this paternalistic treatment of teachers and became very distrustful of 'experts' and officials who seemed to be more interested in maintaining, rather than improving, the status quo. I came to realize that many 'experts' were actually no more expert than I was, and resented the fact that, with my master's research, I was really doing their job (and not getting paid for it). At the same time, I knew that those in positions of authority would likely continue to resist change, and I worried that my work would be ignored. In a few short months, my identity had shifted from being an aspiring 'insider' expert teacher to that of a more critically minded 'outsider'; yet at the same time, my master's research had been deeply rewarding in terms of professional development. I felt that I had made discoveries that were highly meaningful and practical for me, and that could potentially be helpful to other LFI teachers. I felt a renewed sense of confidence and pride as a professional, knowing that my professional judgement had been correct and that my use of the L1 was completely justifiable, based on research. I came to realize that each teacher holds the key to their own professional empowerment through research and reflective practice. I had finally discovered a path, grounded in research, that could take me to where I wanted to be as a language teacher.

As I approached the end of my master's programme, I needed to find a new job. Although I was feeling somewhat jaded, and unsure of what kind of reaction, if any, my criticism of the 'French only' policy would prompt from government and school officials, I had also grown professionally and felt ready to take on a new challenge. So it seemed that luck was with me when I received an email from an old friend in Japan suggesting that I should apply for a position as an EFL instructor at the university where he was working. I applied, got the job, and began preparing to move back to Japan with my wife and two young daughters.

Working as an EFL teacher-researcher at a private university in Japan

During the initiation for my new job as an EFL teacher-researcher at a university near Tokyo, Japan, I was shocked to learn that the university had a strict 'English only' policy for all classes taught by 'native-speaker' English teachers. Although most students were English majors, they ranged from advanced to beginner levels in terms of proficiency – and, making a bad situation even worse, in my department the students were placed in mixed-ability classes, with the widest possible range of proficiency levels represented in each class. I was now starting to feel that TLO policies were inescapable and although it was rather stressful and disheartening, I did my best to work around the 'English only' policy in my teaching. At the same time, however, I felt that the policy presented a golden opportunity in terms of research. The following year, a friend I had met several years earlier, when we were both ALTs, came to work at the same university, and we decided that we had to act in order to draw attention to the fact that the policy, which had been considered a 'cutting edge' approach when created some 20 years earlier, was now terribly outdated – an example of what *not* to do, according to the best evidence from research. Perhaps the people who first created the 'English only' policy may have felt that trying to eliminate Japanese completely from the classroom was necessary in order to ensure that students would achieve high levels of proficiency in English, but through the years the university had never attempted to measure the effectiveness of the policy. Management (who were all foreign native speakers of English) had no way of knowing how many teachers were attempting to uphold the policy in their classes, or what effect the policy was actually having in those classes where it was being strictly enforced. It seemed that these questions were of little concern, or were considered best left unanswered.

One effect of the 'English only' policy which was clear, without having to do much at all in the way of research, was that it made teaching more 'manageable' for the many recent graduates the university hired directly from the United States, the United Kingdom, Australia, Canada and New Zealand, many of whom spoke little or no Japanese. The policy was also a key selling point for the university, with the PR department recruiting new students by emphasizing that 'English only' classes taught by native-speaker teachers were the best way to learn, exploiting the erroneous belief, widely held in Japan, that 'native speakers are best', regardless of their ability to use or understand the students' L1 (Cook, 2005; see also Barker, 2003; Rajagopalan, 2005).

A point of pride for the university was that its collective of 'native speaker' EFL teachers were *not just teachers*. The management stressed to us that good teachers were also researchers, and we were expected to work at improving our teaching through research. My friend, who was now a colleague, and I believed that we had a responsibility, to our students, to our fellow teachers and to ourselves as teacher-researchers, to take a closer look at the university's 'English only' policy. We decided to start by surveying the native-speaker teachers at the university about their professional beliefs concerning L1 use. However, it soon became obvious that the university administrators felt that the policy was off limits, too important to allow it to be the subject of academic inquiry (see Rivers, 2013a).

Due to lack of space, and because my experiences in this section and the next will be documented in detail in numerous forthcoming papers, I will limit my narrative here to the main points. My research partner and I surveyed 29 (about half) of the native-speaker teachers at the university, and slightly more than half of the participants expressed professional beliefs that were in support of judicious L1 use. When we shared our findings with the director of the EFL programme (a native speaker of English), he said that we could easily be fired for publishing research that was considered damaging to the university's reputation, and that we ought to think about our young families which we needed to support financially. I managed to control my immediate anger, feeling at the same time that we had already 'won' if threats were the only defence the director could offer. I explained that we felt that the policy was causing real problems for students and teachers, especially in beginner, intermediate and mixed-ability classes, and that we were trying to be constructive and help to improve the programme. It struck me that, like the department official I had spoken to in Canada, the director could see no need to make any changes to the 'English only' policy: he only taught one advanced, fourth-year class per week on the theme of Australian movies, and possessed limited Japanese language ability, which, in addition to his position of authority as director, likely made it very difficult for him to empathize with teachers who taught beginner or mixed-level classes, or who could use their Japanese language skills to help students express their ideas or to make lesson content comprehensible to students.

My co-researcher and I were shocked, as we believed – perhaps a bit naively – that open academic inquiry would be respected in a university context, especially after we had been told that we were expected to do research. We worried that we might actually be fired for what was effectively *doing our jobs*, but at the same time being threatened in such an unprofessional manner made us even more determined to publish our results. We first published a watered-down version of the paper (see McMillan et al., 2009) attempting to placate the director and other university officials. We also presented our results at several conferences and gave an in-house workshop (with special permission from the director) in which we shared our research findings and selected papers on the topic with our colleagues at our university, before finally publishing the full results (McMillan and Rivers, 2011). While our research did not bring about an immediate change to the 'English only' policy at the university, we felt that we had at least brought the issue into the open, setting an example for future research at the university in question, and for teachers elsewhere. Another positive outcome was that the attempt by management to censor our work sparked our interest in another research topic, as my research partner and I began to look deeper into (and present domestically and internationally on) issues surrounding academic freedom, abuses of power and our employment rights as L2 teachers in Japan.

Third time lucky: Successful policy change from the bottom up

The university where I first started working, near Tokyo (hereafter University A), had been hired to design and run a new English programme at another Japanese university (University B), and I jumped at the opportunity to transfer to a new job in a new place, hoping to escape the stress of working under the 'English only' policy at University A and the looming threat of being fired for pursuing what was useful, legitimate research. I also moved to University B for the opportunity to continue working with some wonderful teachers who had also been seconded from University A, as we designed the curriculum and lesson materials for the new programme.

According to the agreement between the two universities, University A was to transplant the best features of their own 'very successful' programme, which of course included the 'English only' policy, into the new programme at University B. However, unlike at University A where learners were English majors ranging in proficiency from beginner to advanced levels, the vast majority (approximately 90%) of students at University B were low-proficiency non-English majors. The new EFL programme at University B was beginning its second year when I arrived, and I had heard from other teachers that most of the curriculum from University A had proven to be much too difficult for University B students. I suspected that the 'English only' policy would also prove to be completely inappropriate, and hoped the management at University B would, with a little persuading, come to realize this and perhaps be willing to consider changing the policy.

After being in my new job for a few months and talking informally with a number of teachers, I realized that the 'English only' policy was only really being followed/enforced by a few teachers, and two of those teachers had very limited proficiency in Japanese. Over the next year and a half, the issue came up in staff meetings from time to time, with some teachers arguing that the 'English only' policy was necessary and indeed very useful and others suggesting that the students' L1 could, at times, play a positive role in their lessons. The director at University B (again a foreign native speaker of English) was willing to recognize that teachers may have different approaches, depending on their personal beliefs and level of proficiency in Japanese, as well as their students' willingness and ability to use English, which could be different from one class to the next. While the director showed some flexibility in allowing teachers to decide how the policy would be implemented in their classes, he did not want to change the wording of the policy in the course outlines given to students. Management wanted to keep the policy in its written form, saying it would serve to motivate students to try to use English as much as possible in class, but perhaps also because the policy was seen as a valuable PR marketing tool, and perhaps also out of a need to show loyalty to the mother institution, University A.

Finally, I suggested to the director that we ought to actually rewrite the policy. I argued that a strict 'English only' rule was inappropriate for our students, pointing to the overwhelming support for judicious L1 use in the research literature, and that the policy should reflect what, in reality, was expected of teachers and students. Much to his credit, and unlike the director at University A, the director at University B responded positively, suggesting that teachers discuss making changes to the policy at the next general meeting. At the meeting, there was general agreement that the policy should have a more positive and softer, more humanistic tone, and should be worded in such a way that allowed for flexibility, so that teachers could teach according to their own beliefs and unique situations. Following the meeting, I worked with another teacher, who had previously been in favour of the original 'English only' policy, to draft a new version for the 2011–12 academic year.

After many years of working under, and around, TLO policies, and especially after the way my research partner and I had been threatened by management at University A, this change felt like a small but important victory – for students and other teachers at University B, for the programme, as well as for me as a teacher-*researcher*.

Conclusion

As I have been engaged in the process of developing my professional identity, I have tried to resolve the conflicts I have experienced in connection to the main subidentities which come through in this narrative: native-speaker EFL teacher, non-native-speaker French teacher, aspiring 'expert' teacher and activist researcher. I have always believed that my language teaching philosophy (which is forever evolving) could be applied equally to the teaching of English or French, or perhaps any language; thus I have generally moved with relative ease between being a French immersion teacher and an EFL teacher. As a non-native-speaker teacher of French, I sometimes feel a lack of confidence concerning the gaps in my skills in the target language and know that I need to continue to learn and improve, but at the same time I know that even native-speaker teachers do not know everything, and that, as a proficient 'L2 user' (Cook, 2005), I am a good model for my students. As for my native-speaker teacher subidentity, I feel that some of my greatest strengths, and also my greatest limitations, especially when teaching beginner and intermediate level students, reside in my ability to use my students' L1 and to support them in finding ways to use their L1 productively in their learning. Through being both a native-speaker teacher and non-native-speaker teacher myself, through working with native-speaker teachers and non-native-speaker teachers in Japan and other contexts, and through studying the literature on the topic, I have developed a critical view of the privileged status which is often automatically bestowed on native-speaker teachers (Rajagopalan, 2005) and hope to work to help empower non-native-speaker teachers in a variety of teaching contexts in the future. My goal is to teach in ways that are respectful of my students' own developing multiple identities, valuing the knowledge and creativity they bring to the classroom – whether we use the TL or their L1 – and empowering them to take control of their own learning. One way of doing this is to invite students to reflect on and regulate their own language use (see Auerbach, 1993; Levine, 2011; Rivers, 2011d, 2011e).

My identity as an aspiring 'expert' French immersion teacher was shaken as I struggled to live up to, and then 'quietly' started to work around, the false TLO ideal. As Wenger (1998) suggests, teacher identity can be formed through 'alignment', bringing one's practice in line with that of other community members. I first thought that I had to follow the 'French only' policy in order to be a good teacher, as I imagined other good LFI teachers did. But as I began to experiment with using the students' L1 in different situations, I started to see that I could be a good teacher without limiting myself to using 'French only'. I began to question the effectiveness of the 'French only' policy, making a moral judgement by evaluating what I was being asked to do (Coldron and Smith, 1999). As I began using my students' L1, I believed that I was doing so in ways that made sense and were helpful to them, but I hoped that my use of English would stay in the classroom, between my students and I, as I wasn't sure that I could defend what I was doing. The 'French only' axiom was so strong that I did not trust my own practice (see Auerbach, 1993). I never imagined that I could challenge the 'French only' policy. Teachers' choices are determined by the possibilities they perceive as available (Coldron and Smith, 1999). TLO policies are often framed in official documents in such a way that they appear to be unassailable, produced and promoted by 'experts' and officials in positions of authority, using powerful rhetoric and appropriating the scientific method to legitimate their decisions (Boreham and Gray, 2005). It was only when I became a teacher-*researcher* that I realized that it was possible to question the 'French only' policy in LFI.

As I began my work as a teacher-*researcher*, I realized that 'Others of opposition' (Chang, 2008) with values and experiences very different from my own – for the most part operating anonymously in the shadows – were creating and promoting TLO policies that were ideologically based rather than being products of the scientific tradition (Auerbach, 1993; Coldron and Smith, 1999). Fortunately, as I dissociated myself from those 'Others of opposition', I was able at the same time to strongly identify with many more 'Others of similarity': my professor and master's thesis supervisor, the many scholars whose research was in alignment with my beliefs and practice, LFI teachers who agreed to participate in my own study, my research partner at University A and numerous other colleagues in Japan.

Equipped with this moral and professional support, and the knowledge I had gained through my research, I felt a new sense of agency, empowerment and responsibility to work towards positive change. This sense of agency and responsibility was put to the test when 'Others of opposition' at University A demanded that we censor our research results. As noted by Wenger (1998), 'alignment' achieved through coercion and oppression leads to dissociation and alienation; but while my research partner and I felt very much like 'outsiders' vis-à-vis the management at University A, we knew that we had the scientific tradition on our side and that we had to remain true to our teacher-*researcher* selves. The director and other members of the management team at University A ought to hold themselves to the high standards of integrity and 'openness' suggested by Fenton-Smith and Torpey (2013), who borrow from Kiely (2009: 100): 'the task of improving a programme requires an openness about shortcomings.' Of course, management may claim to be conducting an open and honest programme evaluation, but it is quite another thing to actually do it! In fact, at the university in question, management shamelessly exploits the research publications of teachers for PR purposes, while promoting the institution through 'fabrications' (Ball, 2000, 2003) which are antithetical to an open and honest, research-based approach to teaching, learning, and programme evaluation.

Going forward, I endeavour to make my future teacher-*researcher* self even more committed to the scientific tradition, and to be guided by moral courage in the workplace (Comer and Vega, 2011) as I continue to exercise my academic freedom and act as an agent of resistance and change (Canagarajah, 1999; Rajagopalan, 2005; Rivers, 2013a).

4

Language, Culture and Identity: Transcultural Practices and Theoretical Implications

Claudia Kunschak and Felix Girón

Introduction

Since the late 1960s/early 1970s, language teaching (we refer to language learners rather than 'foreign' or second language learners following current theories of English as an International Language (McKay, 2002), English as a Lingua Franca (Seidlhofer, 2004) and English as an Additional Language (Leung, 2002)) has tried to mediate between cultures and their bearers, moving from cross-cultural to intercultural to multicultural communication. The transcultural approach (Thurlow, 2001) takes this process one step further by giving learners the freedom to move between cultures, feeling equally at home in more than one at a time, and accepting or rejecting individual traits of different cultures based on personal needs and preferences. This move expresses a change in focus towards the individual as a dynamic representative of culture(s), trading language, culture and power in the process of identity formation and reformation. The transcultural approach, which is the pedagogical twin of the anthropological concept of transnationalism (Appadurai, 1996), also challenges the idea of legitimate peripheral participation as coined by Wenger (1998) to deconstruct the community of practice as a gate-keeping network (Milroy, 1980) by investing learners/apprentices with powers of agency, resistance and reappropriation. Simultaneously, a shift in 'foreign' language teaching philosophy, from language as a given canon to language as a means of individual and collective expression and negotiation, identity kit and political tool, supports the exploration of multiple selves created in the process of interaction with the Other – or created among related selves via the Other's language and culture which thereby becomes transformed into Own.

This chapter illustrates such transcultural appropriation through examples of the non-native language selves of teachers and students at a southern Chinese university level English Language Center that embraces the principle of English as an International Language (McKay, 2002). Exploring the transcultural experiences and projections of language learners, the chapter therefore investigates instances of transcultural discourse, resistance to native-speaker hegemony and most importantly, the agency of the individual in a seemingly homogeneous global village. Identity-in-practice and identities of scale (see Lemke, 2008) intersect in multiple ways and are variously accessed by participants according to context, purpose and abilities. At the same time, limitations in Western theories of agency, resistance and transculturalism become apparent and demonstrate the need for a radical reconceptualization of these parameters to accurately portray transcultural philosophies and practices among language learners from different cultures, educational contexts, socio-economic backgrounds and socio-political areas.

Literature review

Globalization as a frame of reference has disrupted theorization of the linkages among language, culture and identity propounded by early linguistic anthropology (Whorf, 1956) and its later critics focusing on stratification, interaction and power (Bourdieu, 1991; Gumperz, 1982; Labov, 1973). Global flows merge and disrupt conventional monoliths of space, time and meaning and create new landscapes of knowledge and experience, reset language, reframe culture and reposition identities. Infoscapes, ethnoscapes and econoscapes (Appadurai, 1996) redefine perceptions, communication, senses of self and place, and even economic choices. Simultaneously communities, interest groups and individual subjects enjoy increasing influence over public opinion, political decisions and social issues.

This interaction between global flows and individual choices has clearly impacted education with specific consequences for teaching and learning English. Resources and communities that were hitherto available only to a limited number of teachers and learners are only a mouse click away, leading to an age of interactive informationalism (Warschauer, 2000). Meanwhile, language programmes are rushing to cater their curricula to today's learners and markets. English for Specific Purposes, English for the Workplace, Business English or Legal English are being offered everywhere, requiring interdiscursivity between professional genres and practice (Bhatia, 2008).

Academic approaches to pedagogy, culture, identity and their interplay have also shifted paradigms in response to today's mobile, shifting, information-rich and globalized China. The learner has become the driving force of curriculum development with the teacher as facilitator, organizer and expert in methodology. Similarly what is being taught and its rationale has varied; English as an International Language (McKay, 2002), English as a Lingua Franca (Seidlhofer, 2004) and English as an Additional Language (Leung, 2002) are just the most widely discussed perspectives. By recontextualizing English and widening its availability as a means of identification, communication and action, current education theory and practice aligns with larger global processes, creating lingoscapes. These shifts in perspective are predicated upon agency-oriented approaches to culture, identity and language.

Our questions about English-language learning and transculturalism among Chinese speakers build upon conceptions of culture, identity and language emphasizing process, openness, performance and contingency while recognizing the effects of power. Culture as a shared text (Geertz, 1973) opened up the possibility of multiple interpretations and was enhanced by work focusing on cultural change (Greenwood, 1989). More recently, researchers highlight the agency of culture creators, and emphasize the instruments and effects of partial sharing, unequal access and power (Appadurai, 1996; Schein, 2000; Scott, 2011). These approaches correlate with an increasing valuation of the relationships among the linguistic, the performative and embodiment (Farquhar, 2002; Swain, 2009).

Understanding the relationship between language learning and transculturalism builds from constructivist, open, contingent and relational approaches to identity recognizing multiplicity and agency while acknowledging constraints. Identity is not entirely chosen and may be affected by unconscious or repeatedly reproduced habits of discourse, thought and bodily practice (Bourdieu, 1991; Said, 2000). Feminists have provided social constructivist critiques destabilizing relations between biology and identity often by interrogating forms of discourse (Butler, 1990; Haraway, 1989; Martin, 2001; Ortner, 1972). Feminist scholars have critiqued the autonomous, coherent individual as masculinist and ideologically bound to patriarchy and capitalism. Such theorists have instead offered a contingent and relational approach to multiple overlapping or even contradictory identities that are frequently partial, mixed and in process (Mohanty, 2003; Moi, 2002; Weir, 1996).

These approaches highlight the potential proliferation of identities created through the transcultural practices and competencies of Chinese people learning and speaking English who seek out and respond to the cultural productions of and interactions with expert English-speaking Others. The language speaker as culture producer negotiates, becomes, leaves behind and transforms identities through power-laden linguistic interactions such as language-learning environments. When the subaltern subject speaks to expert power, one result is the discursive creation and internalization of imposed identity categories (Foucault, 1978). Yet, despite the contradictions and symbolic violence of using the dominant Other's language (Fanon, 1967; Said, 1978), the potential for local and global subaltern to subaltern discourse (Said, 2000; Yang, 1996), the appearance of subaltern discursive resistance (Scott, 1985, 1990) and the appropriation of dominant discourse for Own purposes (Chen, 1995; Comoroff, 1985) encourages awareness of linguistic resistance and a correlated recognition of subaltern agency in Own identity creation. Chinese learners of English create English-language and transcultural selves through the process of speaking as a contingent after-effect of the language learner's speech acts (Butler, 1990) while their silence may act as resistance to particular cultural norms and linguistically evoked selves (Bhabha, 1994).

Linguists have also re-evaluated the interplay among language, culture and identity. While Block (2007) argues for a stronger focus on language learning as socially co-constructed in view of the cognitive bias of much of SLA theory and research, Riley (2007) examines European intercultural encounters from an ethnolinguistic perspective. Lin (2008) and Caldas-Coulthard and Iedema (2008) meanwhile, provide diverse examples of macrosocial structures and resistances that shape processes of identification. These works discuss identity, identification and multiplicity within a globalized world characterized by geographically, culturally and linguistically contested spaces.

Unsurprisingly, language, culture and identity and their interplay have informed new research paradigms in language teaching. While early proponents of cross-cultural communication (Robinson, 1985) emphasized a chasm that people had to cross, intercultural scholars (Byram, 1997) focused on a two-way exchange, a mutual process of learning and transformation. More recently multicultural foreign language teaching (Tornberg, 2004) has emphasized acknowledging diversity in the classroom by opening up true multivocal discussion. The current stage in culture and identity development in the realm of language teaching is taken up by the translingual and transcultural (e.g. MLA, 2007; Thurlow, 2001), which posits the learner as a free agent between several languages and cultures at different points in time or even in synchronicity. Learners thus have multiple possible identities, choosing actively among various registers, genres, dialects or languages available to them.

Research design

Research purpose

This study investigated how transcultural practices emanating from struggles with language, culture and identity manifested themselves in the non-native language selves of teachers and students. In particular, answers to the following research questions were sought:

- Do non-native speakers in an EFL environment demonstrate transcultural competencies? If so, what factors most influence the performance of transcultural competencies?
- How/when and to what extent do non-native speaker's transcultural competencies involve an imagined, remembered or reflected native speaker or Other culture in the formation of multiple selves?
- Does agency and resistance frame transcultural practices and the creation of multiple selves and if so, how?

The research design of the present study compared reported beliefs, attitudes and behaviours regarding language, culture and identity among students and teachers within an English-as-an-International-Language-based curriculum. Among relevant factors, previous intercultural experience and linguistic competence were included from the start, whereas gender emerged as a major factor during data analysis. The project compared both among teachers and students and within groups. Recruitment for participation was strictly on a voluntary basis.

The data collection methodology and instruments used in this qualitative study included a background questionnaire on participants' language-learning history, self-assessment of proficiency and attitudes towards English as well as an unmoderated focus group conducted with each group of stakeholders. Data from the questionnaire were tallied numerically and used as a first indicator of what to expect from the focus groups and secondarily for triangulation purposes. Unmoderated focus groups (participants discussed a predetermined set of questions with only a recording device present) were employed in order to minimize the 'halo effect' of the native-speaker researcher and to elicit data that would depict the process rather than follow preconceived notions about learner identity and multiple selves (see Benwell and Stokoe, 2006). Discussions in the different focus groups produced data ranging from 40 minutes to 100 minutes. The data were then transcribed verbatim and coded for themes and strands as well as language patterns expressing confidence, sharing, agreement, contestation and silence. With this approach, the researchers align themselves with the school of grounded theory (Strauss and Corbin, 1990) where data speak for themselves and open-ended processes allow for serendipity and new discoveries.

Site description

The present study was conducted at a medium-sized public university in Southern China. The English Language Center, established in 2003, provides instruction to all majors, both at the graduate and undergraduate level. Consistent with an agent-centred approach to language, the Center's declared mission is to enhance critical thinking, learner autonomy and communicative competence through student-centred instruction and student-led extracurricular activities. The teaching staff of 50 is composed of Chinese and international faculty at an almost equal proportion. International teachers were from Australia, Austria, Brazil, France, India, Italy, Russia and the United States. Rather than applying the native-speaker criterion, high-level proficiency, international experience and a strong pedagogical foundation were chosen as requirements.

The students are mainly residents of Guangdong province, where the university is located, with a few exceptions coming from other regions of China. English is a required subject and most students have to take four semesters to comply with the language requirement. While some colleges within the university offer content courses in English and employ 'foreign' faculty from all over the world, students from other colleges mainly aspire to pass the national College English Test. The university encourages students to apply for further study abroad and offers exchange programmes in the junior year. It is through the English Enhancement Programme that the English Language Center facilitates English-language teaching and an English-language environment on campus. Students can choose to participate in English-language club activities that provide an opportunity for using their language skills while developing their interpersonal and organizational competencies.

Participants

Participants of the study were recruited from intermediate (n = 9) and advanced (n = 9) students as well as international (n = 3) and Chinese-speaking (n = 6) teachers. Except for the international teachers, who were all female, groups were well balanced in terms of gender and other aspects like seniority or major. The two main distinguishing characteristics were level of proficiency and teacher or student status. Most participants knew each other from before this study; all participated on a voluntary basis.

Potential and limitations of the study

By using two data collection methods – questionnaire and focus group – a multigroup research design, and an unmoderated focus group for eliciting unbiased data, a rich description and multilayered portrayal of language learners, their discourse, beliefs, attitudes and practices have emerged, providing insight into processes and influences of transcultural competencies at various stages of language learning and foreign language identity formation and reformation. While this qualitative approach traces developments and illustrates mechanisms of change in thinking and doing language, culture and identity among participants, findings are of course strongly determined by the specific site, participants and moment in time. Though not replicable in a quantitative sense of the term, the researchers hope to stimulate similar investigations into language learners' sense of self, other and multiple identity-in-practice at other locations throughout Asia subscribing to the EIL/ELF paradigm of language teaching.

Findings

In the following paragraphs, we will present the themes and quotes that emerged from our analysis of the focus group data according to grounded theory (Strauss and Corbin, 1990). For easier reading and evaluation, the data has been grouped into student and teacher data which are then subdivided into intermediate and advanced in the case of students and Chinese-speaking and English-speaking in the case of teachers, focusing on language, cultural identity, resistance and reappropriation, transcultural practices and gender in turn. Comparisons across all four groups will then be made before discussion of the data as a whole in the next section.

Students

Language use

Language use clearly varied according to linguistic competence with more advanced learners being both more capable of and interested in discussing language abstractly in English. The intermediate students preferred to employ simple words and sentence structures with ubiquitous grammar errors.

To express themselves clearly, the intermediate students used Chinese for unfamiliar words or confusing sentences. This group of students mostly concentrated on the mechanics of English (pronunciation, accent and grammar) even when asked about attitudes or identities. Intermediate students correlated change in attitudes over time with their feelings about learning English.

As Excerpt 4.1 shows, for intermediate students, English was tied either to their success at English in comparison with other subjects, their degree of enjoyment or boredom with it, or their identification with the teacher, mostly a 'foreign' one. Advanced students on the other hand, already commented on cultural code words, code-switching and multiple contexts.

Excerpt 4.1: Data illustrating the language use of intermediate and advanced students

Intermediate: 'We love her very much so we love English.'

Advanced: Yeah they were going almost like they were *tongxianghui* (*from same hometown*).'

The advanced students reported using English in a variety of venues including academic, entertainment, career, social life for multiple purposes demonstrating a self-conscious awareness of cultural and identity effects from learning English. All the advanced students were currently motivated to learn English for varied and multiple reasons. The advanced students described their early experience of learning English as an incomprehensible process that depended largely on the use of Chinese phonetics to aide in memorization:

> 'At the very beginning I I [*sic*] I [*sic*] think that many people do think that apple like . . . '
> 'A po.'
> 'Yeah, in Chinese your grandmother.'

The advanced learners recognized their own increased agency and motivation with the development of their English skills. This group demonstrated these skills in a multilayered discussion of transcultural practices such as code-switching and their use of English when talking about topics that were deemed sensitive by Chinese speakers such as swearing and issues of sex and sexuality. With a few exceptions, participation was largely even.

Culture and identity

English-language linguistic competence was the primary variable in how intensely respondents demonstrated links between culture and identity through both discourse content and conversation patterns. Conversation patterns would change as the conversation flowed between more and less controversial topics. The topics eliciting the most controversy were connected to connections among language use, gender and sexuality. The more advanced English speakers discussed links between these concepts abstractly.

The intermediate learners exhibited the most literal understanding of English culture and were the least affected in terms of identity. Intermediate learners viewed English culture largely as English songs and other cultural productions. This group was not interested in English culture in the abstract; they were all forced to learn English and only employed the language for particular necessary tasks.

Learning English did not change intermediate students' identity. They mostly viewed English as a tool rather than an opportunity to show their characters. When they discussed their process of picking an English name, they stated that they seldom pay attention to its meaning. Generally, most students have an English name because they have to, and 'it is easier for the foreigner to remember me.' Having a special English name, however, might produce a minor influence on students' identity. One student's teacher promised to give her a special English name so she went to class half an hour early before the teacher's arrival. Yet, students expect that learning English can change their identity. One student said that if she had a baby, she would teach English as the first language so that her child could master two different languages simultaneously creating a double identity.

As Excerpt 4.2 shows, as far as culturally bounded identities were concerned, intermediate students still mainly related cultural aspects to their teachers, whereas advanced students were able to reflect on the impact of speaking another language and acquiring a new culture on their own identity.

Excerpt 4.2: Data illustrating the culture and identity of intermediate and advanced students

Intermediate: 'And most of time, I think English teacher is more open than the Chinese teacher and their taste is different from the Chinese teachers.'

Advanced: 'If you have two different names, you have two identities.'

For many advanced students, their foreign English teachers most directly represented English culture. The teacher's foreignness was seen as an additional aspect of their identity above and beyond their native-speaker status and this was further linked to language pedagogy. Another group of foreigners, exchange students from Calgary, represented the English-language culture of a younger group. In addition to working hard, the Canadians' penchant for getting drunk and swearing were pinpointed as part of their culture.

While interactions with individual foreigners were described as direct encounters with English-language culture, by far the more long-term English culture influence was credited to interaction with English-language media. The students discussed songs, television shows, the internet and social connectivity software but movies received the closest attention. The advanced learners described American movies' casual approach to swearing and sex as being part of American English culture. A few students felt that English culture was 'too open-minded' in contrast to others' preference for discussing subjects in English that they felt uncomfortable addressing in Chinese. Hollywood heroes served as a personal inspiration for one student while another consciously worked to avoid such influence. Students also discussed the wider influence of Hollywood's representation of the American Dream.

Like the intermediate learners of English, the advanced learners discussed English names as variably significant indexes for identification. Despite the purported casualness of choices for English names, however, for a few changing English name was inconvenient. One student planned to keep the same English name all his life since it was 'so cool' and phonetically similar to his Chinese name. As one of his listeners responded, 'if you have two different names, you have two identities', and the student with the 'real English name' wanted those two identities to merge. A similar synthesizing logic was behind the story of a senior student who had taken part in an international exchange programme and upon his return to campus switched to using only his Chinese name or its pinyin version.

The advanced learners argued over Chinese- and English-language identities. The focus group multiplied Chinese identities through discovery of the diversity deriving from forms of Chinese, home languages and hometowns. Students first associated hometowns or regions with both dialect and identity, but this conflation was then discovered to be erroneous. This diverse, shifting and non-proscriptive relationship between language and identity was infrequently applied to 'English-language culture and identity' since all foreign teachers of English were described as belonging to one 'Western' or 'English-language' culture. Yet, while this category remained fixed, students extensively discussed whether English-language culture was constant, changing or developing.

Advanced learner attitudes towards Chinese appropriations of English-language culture practices revealed the extent and limitations of the cultural relativism students described as being acquired through English-language learning. The advanced students remarked on the deep influence of English-language culture on China and produced examples of reciprocal or mutual influence. Primarily, however, the advanced learners felt that English culture was hegemonic and that reciprocal influence was not equally penetrating. The homogenizing effects resulting from the universalization of the American dream were not seen as positive and there was a verbal consensus from respondents that China was losing its traditions. The advanced students' ambivalent attitude towards negative aspects of 'English' culture also coexisted with a renewed appreciation for Chinese culture motivated by students' study of English.

Resistance and reappropriation

All four groups presented instances of resistance and appropriation although most of these were muted, indirect and never involved direct confrontation with native speakers. Significantly, resistance to native-speaker hegemony and appropriation did not correlate with either English competence or gender.

Intermediate learners expressed intermittent and indirect resistance to native-speaker hegemony and appropriated English for their own purposes largely by dismissing the need for correct grammar or a wide vocabulary. This stance drew from the group's broadly shared assessment of the difficulty of the learning task. For these students, English is a tool and necessary to get jobs. One student mentioned that shopkeepers do not need English to do business with foreigners; instead shopkeepers use simple words or body language. Hence, she argued that she does not need to pay much attention to grammar in oral English. Yet, not all students shared the same resistant attitude towards the presence or evocation of the English native speaker. The conversation included a controversy over whether watching movies in English was necessary due to the availability of Chinese dubbing which one student advocated and another one labelled 'the terrible voice'.

As Excerpt 4.3 shows, concerning the degree of resistance and the potential for reappropriation, intermediate students chose English as a way to imagine access to a different and more attractive environment. Advanced students on the other hand, had developed a critical perspective, both towards the image of English imposed by its bearers and the image of English created by their fellow students.

Excerpt 4.3: Data illustrating the resistance and reappropriation of intermediate and advanced students

Intermediate:	'Maybe if my baby can choose English as the first language, as a mother, I would feel very proud.'
Advanced:	'We don't learn English just for having chat with foreigners.'

Advanced learners' resistance to native-speaker hegemony and appropriation of English were intermittent and contradictory; they debated wariness or ease in front of native speakers, the identity of the English-language interlocutor, reasons for learning English, the limitations of English, the utility of Chinese definitions and the power of English native-speaker teachers. Some students emphasized their desire and great efforts to act politely when speaking with English native speakers as well as their anxiety about not succeeding. Contrastingly, three students wrote that they felt comfortable and casual speaking with English native speakers because oral English was looser, native speakers were kind and these conversations revealed that native speakers made mistakes in grammar too. One student noted that native speakers also make mistakes, particularly in grammar, freeing her to learn and speak English for her own purposes.

Beyond communication with people unable to speak in Chinese, English was described as a tool and as a valuable skill enabling access to a wider selection of media for career and entertainment. As one of the Physics majors wrote in the questionnaire, 'Not long ago, I read an article on a website titled "We don't learn English just for having chat with foreigners". This makes the purposes of English more clear.'

The advanced learners also described English as having limitations; English was discussed as an inadequate medium for delivering the experience and appreciation of Chinese poetry. The advanced learners also tried out Chinese definitions on non-Chinese phenomena while speaking primarily in English. One student dropped a foreign-taught philosophy class because it did not correspond to his definition of the discipline. Another student, recalled that she had met people from Kenya and had assumed that they belonged to the same *tongxianghui* (native place association), a concept she did not try to translate into English. She described her growing awareness of the disjuncture between the Chinese category, the Kenyans' unconcern with shared locality, and her surprise about their lack of concern.

For the advanced learners group, resistance to native-speaker hegemony was often connected to resistance to teacher power. First, English native-speaker teachers were described as helpful tools for pronunciation and listening practice, but not for learning grammar. Second, despite being in the subordinate student position with respect to most of the native speakers encountered (teachers), the advanced students are very active about searching out or avoiding experiences to speak English with native speakers. Third, these interviewees' consensus critiques of English-language curriculum and pedagogy demonstrated a collective agency towards English and learning English.

Transcultural practices

Unlike resistance to native-speaker hegemony and appropriation of English, transcultural practices joined language use and culture/identity in being linked with greater linguistic competence in English and met similarly gendered limitations. Like resistance and appropriation, however, only certain transcultural practices, such as the use of creative communication tactics, met with general focus group approval; other practices, particularly those linked to gender boundaries invited greater discussion, ambivalence or intensity.

Intermediate learners discussed and demonstrated few examples of transcultural practices other than the use of word-by-word translation, body language and the use of English names. When a student felt frustrated when she could not communicate with a foreigner, she employed body language to solve the problem and the others supported this tactic. Similarly, these students expressed pragmatic attitudes about the utility of English generally for career purposes and English names particularly as a method to better interact with foreigners. The students also chose English names linked to both American and Asian cultural references from pop culture stars to approximating their Chinese names.

As Excerpt 4.4 shows, at the intermediate level, transcultural practices mostly remained within the boundaries of code-switching, body language and the choice and use of English names. For advanced students, experience with English language and culture led to a significant change in attitude and values.

Excerpt 4.4: Data illustrating the transcultural practices of intermediate and advanced students

Intermediate: 'My English name is Air. It means Air Jordan. Do you know Air Jordan?' or, 'It's just translated from my Chinese name.'

Advanced: 'The way towards people who have different opinions, different ideas or opinions to you, uh or . . . um . . . so.'
'Yeah I agree with you, it really changed the values.'

Advanced learners' transcultural practices included body language, enjoying English-language cultural products purely for fun, describing their shifting attitudes towards English and its role in their life, acquiring an 'English perspective' and/or an English-language self, a self-aware cultural relativism and code-switching. While all advanced learners evenly affirmed the first three practices, having an 'English perspective' and an English-language self or selves were occasionally critiqued through a consensus-building process. The advanced learners agreed that learning English and enjoying English media, 'really changed the values [*sic*] very much'. The whole group commented on the growth of their openness to Other culture but also argued over limits to this acceptance. Code-switching occurred in many situations (vocabulary confusion, Chinese cultural concepts, abstract or theoretical topics, multilayered 'translation'). Code-switching was also utilized in a male-dominated discussion focused on swear words and sexuality. This gendered split in linguistic performance correlated with gender boundaries derived from a collectively performed Own identity. In addition, advanced learners' play with identities and names usually bumped up against gender boundary maintenance about which the men were the most concerned. These results indicate that there are gendered limitations for the transculturalism of Chinese speakers of English.

Gender

A category the researchers had not initially planned on investigating, gender emerged as one major issue both in conversation topics and in conversation patters. As Excerpt 4.5 shows, intermediate students mentioned gender-related concepts mainly in relation to the English names they chose for themselves. Advanced students commented more on gender-driven behaviour and gender and sexuality as it is displayed in Western media.

Excerpt 4.5: Data illustrating the gender references of intermediate and advanced students

Intermediate: 'But it is a little bit boy's name.
I don't care.
It is more like a female name.
No!
Yes, yes.'
The names don't have gender.
Yes. I am just kidding.

Advanced: 'I have another thing that means that the English culture has influenced me in the way I, in the way I, I think about sex, . . . or something.'

Teachers

Language

Chinese teachers, who for the most part had studied abroad, had had some experience with different, mutually incomprehensible Chinese dialects, and as language professionals were highly aware of language use, described several instances of conscious language choice. On the one hand, they were very comfortable with code-switching as they were used to the phenomenon in their first language. On the other hand, they preferred using English when talking about sensitive topics as it seemed safer and easier for them. Most importantly, however, teachers reported a high level of confidence with their English and a very utilitarian approach, regarding it as a tool and a means for professional advancement.

As Excerpt 4.6 shows, as far as the language per se is concerned, most Chinese teachers expressed a strongly utilitarian approach to its usefulness. International teachers, who were learning Chinese as a local language of communication, were much more ambivalent about their language use.

Excerpt 4.6: Data illustrating the language use of Chinese-speaking and international teachers

Chinese-speaking:	'It's a simple question like you are learning English you got so many opportunities at work, travelling studying in other countries, even immigrating into another country.'
International:	'I am too unconfident to speak it in front of the students.'
	'It's usually pretty simple being able to surprise somebody, to confuse students.'

International teachers, whose level of Chinese was considerably lower than the English proficiency of their Chinese counterparts (their level of Chinese was low intermediate, having spent several years studying the language and living in China), were also acutely aware of their language use. The teachers interviewed chose Chinese for making a point to students, accomplishing daily tasks downtown and blending in. Overall, they reported a much higher level of dissatisfaction with their lack of competence and the reactions they were experiencing. Yet, they developed strategies around it like listening in on students' conversation and letting on they understood, and commented how they were perceived as accented when they went home. Being in a strange environment, they were even more inclined to make use of their transcultural competence – at times resistant and at other times hegemonic.

Culture and identity

In both teacher groups, culture and identity were manifest in the choice, acceptance or rejection of the respective Chinese or English names. For Chinese teachers, their English name helped them escape their Chinese name, added a new domain to their repertoire, or was simply a beautiful sound. That is to say, it either provided an alternate identity or it at least did not limit their identity. International teachers, on the other hand, seemed to focus less on the name itself but on the process of naming. Whether it was the bestowing of the name by their Chinese teacher, choosing a Chinese name for a sister or rebelling against the gate-keeping function of naming, the mere act of choosing or receiving a new name carried considerable meaning for this group. Their attitude to naming was also influenced by their experience with English names among their students. By the same token, international teachers reported a more dynamic approach to the incorporation of cultural aspects tied to naming and terminology. While Chinese teachers contemplated language and culture and meaning from a philosophical perspective, international teachers appropriated a range of cultural stances and practices at certain points in time but not at others.

As Excerpt 4.7 shows, for Chinese and international teachers alike, the language and their name in the respective other language (English or Chinese) was of considerable importance and encompassed a range of practices (self-naming, naming by teacher, naming by family member, renaming).

Excerpt 4.7: Data illustrating the culture and identity of Chinese-speaking and international teachers

Chinese-speaking:	'I mean in Chinese, if we call someone so and so, there must be expectations.'
International:	[choosing a Chinese name for her sisters was] ' . . . like childbirth.'

Resistance and reappropriation

Contrary to the current postulate of post-colonialism, criticizing English and 'Western culture' for being the hegemonic way of communication, data from the Chinese teachers' focus group demonstrate a very discerning use of the language and culture combo for their own purposes. Beyond any ideological considerations of the above nature, Chinese teachers in the focus group decided to use English for a very utilitarian purpose, that is, for career development. At the same time, acquiring familiarity with the language and culture has led some of them to start thinking critically without feeling the need to challenge the hegemony. Teachers have integrated English into their repertoire and feel free to use it without complexes or struggles.

As Excerpt 4.8 shows, Chinese teachers reported an increased level of critical awareness about English language and culture but did not necessarily feel the need or right to challenge the prescribed norms. International teachers on the other hand were more confident about resisting local cultural norms or adapted them to fit their needs.

Excerpt 4.8: Data illustrating the resistance and reappropriation of Chinese-speaking and international teachers

Chinese-speaking:	'Whether you really like it or not, it's not that important . . . you can't challenge it but you can have a critical opinion about certain cultural aspects.'
International:	'For a while I quit doing it because they would always glare at you or grab it from you quickly but then I started doing it again.'

Based on the focus group data, international teachers also developed a wide range of strategies of resistance and appropriation. First, they strongly resist 'inappropriate' English names among students (onomatopoeia, girls' names or no-names). Second, they consider which feature of Chinese culture they could appropriate and integrate into their personal repertoire long term. On the other hand, criticism is levelled against perceived typical bad Chinese behaviour such as not queuing, not accepting principles of privacy and not pulling their weight if a task was assigned. Teachers agreed that they had grown much more comfortable over time to join the fight for a seat or berate people for what they considered inappropriate behaviour.

Transcultural practices

As far as transcultural practices are concerned, Chinese teachers described several that they had developed through contact with their international colleagues. For one thing, they mentioned being able to think both objectively and holistically/intuitively. For another, they appreciated the experience in awkwardness that their international colleagues have accumulated which made professional interaction supportive rather than confrontational. In general, they reported having learned to respect differences and to assume no particular right or wrong but admitted that the culture they were brought up in was a major factor in shaping their beliefs and behaviour. Though not all had travelled abroad, the mere contact with international teachers had helped them develop this kind of awareness.

As Excerpt 4.9 shows, the main idea that became apparent in the discussion among Chinese teachers was a deeper awareness about their own culture and the workings of culture as such. International teachers showed a clear tendency to merge cultural practices from their two cultural realms and to create a specific new transcultural persona.

Excerpt 4.9: Data illustrating the transcultural practices of Chinese-speaking and international teachers

Chinese-speaking:	'I learn to feel that I am a culture thing, I am not born to be like that but I was brought up to be like that.'
International:	'I keep thinking of things that I can add to what I do like hobbies or interests or aspects of Chinese culture that I can take with me that I take for granted here because that could be part of my new personality of somebody who has lived in China.'

International teachers demonstrated a two-way understanding of transcultural practice. On the one hand, they had experienced a new and different culture in situ and developed strategies to successfully adapt and interact with its population. On the other hand, their new life style and value system had caused them to reconsider their previous socialization, sometimes leading to reverse culture shock upon returning home as they realized that their frame of reference had changed drastically. Mostly they enjoyed having multiple lives/selves, spending summers back home and the remainder of the year in China. By incorporating new habits and values while not entirely relinquishing their previous principles, they successfully negotiated life between two cultures.

Gender

Similar to students, Chinese teachers showed a clear gender-driven self-image more traditionally oriented than those displayed by students. Teachers were eager to maintain their gender roles both in naming and in profession. While a female teacher accepted her English name, Yolanda, when she found out that it referred to a flower, a male teacher became uncomfortable when his name, Gabriel, was linked to its female counterpart, Gabrielle, 'you've got to be careful when you stress the word differently, it would be a female's name.' By the same token, a female teacher had accepted studying to become an English teacher as the way to follow her parents' ideas about careers appropriate for women. The only instance countering these examples could be found in a male teacher's declaration that his choice of career might depend on his appreciation for his role model, his mother. As far as gendered conversation patterns were concerned, though the two most assertive speakers across focus groups were males, seniority emerged as an alternative variable as far as length of turn was concerned.

Among Chinese teachers, gender emerged in the choice of major, their interactional pattern but most of all in the choice of name. The group of international teachers that volunteered for the focus group was all female so no gender factor could be observed.

Across-group findings

After the group-by-group representation of the findings according to themes in the previous section, this section will examine across-group commonalities with reference to the initial research questions. While a combination of factors such as level of proficiency or previous international background might influence the beliefs, attitudes or behaviours of a specific individual, a common tendency transcending levels and groups has become visible. This tendency partly confirms our initial assumptions regarding language culture and identity, while indicating some cultural mismatch in some of the theories underlying our framework.

- Do non-native speakers in an ELF/EIL environment demonstrate transcultural competencies? If so, what factors most influence the performance of transcultural competencies?

Transcultural competencies, the ability to become aware of, evaluate and act on cultural differences according to the situation, have been documented in all four groups albeit to a different degree. The competencies include heightened awareness and critical reflection on both own and other language and culture through exposure to media, interaction with native speakers and also their own community of language learners. The decisive characteristic of true transcultural competencies lies in the fact that participants are able to apply them in various ways, towards the other culture, towards their own culture, internally in their understanding of self or better said multiple selves generated in the process and outwardly in their interaction with members of diverse own and other communities such as family, friends, classmates or colleagues.

A combined analysis of the focus group data, the accompanying questionnaires and background information the researchers had access to in their capacity as colleagues or teachers of the participants revealed language competence, seniority and gender as the three main factors influencing the performance of transcultural competencies. Looking at language competence, we can observe an increase in critical awareness and use from the intermediate learners, who just see the language as a required tool and English names as a practical option, to advanced learners, who demonstrate initial stages of resistance and appropriation in the choice of names or their reflection on other culture as presented in the media, and finally the teachers, who undergo a cycle of interaction and reflection with their international colleagues. Seniority emerged both in the teacher and the student groups with the senior members controlling the discussion through longer turns, choice of topics and a clearer stance, overriding at the times the strongest sociolinguistic category, gender. The latter had emerged as a major factor both in the content and interactional patterns among the groups.

- How/when and to what extent do non-native-speaker's transcultural competencies involve an imagined, remembered or reflected native speaker or Other culture in the formation of multiple selves?

Native speakers or other culture constitute a major part in developing multiple selves of language learners yet get appropriated in the process and increasingly so at higher levels of linguistic proficiency. Already at the intermediate level do learners incorporate other language and culture when choosing English names or creating a double identity for an imagined future baby. At the advanced level, students start playing creatively with other culture to transcend the boundaries of their own culture when reappropriating other gender names for their own purposes or resisting the hegemonic English culture when speaking about Hollywood protagonists or the American dream. Teachers with the closest contact to native speakers reflect on their international colleagues' experience of awkwardness in the face in order to develop a more flexible transcultural self.

- Does agency and resistance frame transcultural practices and the creation of multiple selves and if so, how?

Agency and resistance both inform transcultural practices and the creation of multiple selves. Both seem to be independent of proficiency level or gender in shape but not in degree. While intermediate learners express their resistance by dismissing the need for exact grammar or a wide vocabulary, advanced learners are mostly resistant to teacher power. On the teacher side, Chinese teachers though cognizant of a power differential, seem to have come to a pragmatic truce with English hegemony by reappropriating the language and its culture for their own career purposes. Only the international teachers seem to have developed a wide range of resistance strategies. As far as agency is concerned, the three Chinese focus groups display a strong show of agency for learner but this agency is often expressed as collective rather than individual agency which tends to be more pronounced among the international teachers.

Discussion

The four focus groups (1) highlighted transcultural attitudes and behaviours and investigated their conditions of possibility as well as constraining factors, and (2) identified instances of resistance to native-speaker hegemony.

Transcultural attitudes and behaviours were primarily demonstrated through five practices. In this project, the latter four out of these five transcultural practices were most clearly associated with a high level of linguistic competence in English. The first transcultural practice, code-switching was practised by all groups along with the use of body language and word-by-word translation to bridge communication gaps. The second practice utilized by the native Chinese speakers entailed the use of English to provide distance to discuss topics that would otherwise be sensitive in Chinese. The third practice entailed the active utilization and critique of theoretical concepts such as language, culture and identity in transnational situations. Fourth, respondents demonstrated a largely non-politicized cultural relativism with respect to Other culture and reflexivity with respect to own, although with limitations. Fifth, the perceived influence of non-native language culture provided impetus for an enhanced appreciation and awareness of own culture as important and meaningful while also allowing intellectual distance for reflection and critique.

All four groups exhibited experimentation and playfulness regarding transculturalism and non-native language selves with some limitations. This practice was most literally demonstrated by the creation of English or Chinese language identities through naming games but also involved taking on the ideas or customs of the perceived Other culture. While reserving a muted gate-keeping function in the form of 'inappropriate' English names, the international teachers had the fewest reservations about their own identity creation, perhaps because the group was composed entirely of women. Men were less willing to play with gender roles, more willing to talk about sexuality and more willing to act as guardians over the purported sexual transculturalism of women.

In terms of conversational patterns, men and women alike discussed connections among transculturalism, gender, sexuality and profession with a few examples of strong agreement or disagreement. Most often, however, respondents used indirect or ambiguous forms of agreement or disagreement and frequent back channelling that often created the appearance of consensus. Seniority (itself connected to English competence) was more important than gender in terms of dominant conversational patterns. Personality, as anecdotally observed outside of the focus group, also appeared influential although this variable was too difficult to confidently assess within the scope of the research design.

With the possible exception of the expatriate teachers of English, resistance to native-speaker hegemony correlated with linguistic competence and was largely intermittent, unfocused, ambiguous, muted and very rarely self-conscious. Significantly, all three domestic Chinese focus groups presented motivations for learning English unconnected to speech with native speakers. The advanced learners and Chinese teachers who used English to distance themselves from sensitive topics indirectly resisted native-speaker hegemony; such uses were utilized with other Chinese speakers of English and not directed towards native speakers. Yet, these same advanced English learners expressed more enjoyment of English media productions and acknowledged such media's influence on their Chinese- and English-speaking selves. While learners relativized the role of the native speaker and briefly performed it, the position itself was maintained and never directly confronted. Due to anxiety, the most common resistances to native-speaker hegemony were subtle, non-confrontational, occurred outside of the English learning environment and in the absence of native speakers thus arguing for the continued power of native-speaker hegemony.

A transcultural approach focusing on the agency of individuals to move between cultures, to belong in more than one or to individually accept or reject certain traits needs to include a notion of its limitations. Chinese speakers of English and native English speakers learning Chinese demonstrated an uneven ability to accept unusual or potentially negative behaviours when performed by groups not considered 'own' (possibly influenced by power differentials) indicating that no members of these groups felt equally 'at home' in Chinese and English and that acceptance and rejection of specific traits of a particular culture are not entirely based on individual preference. In particular, radical individual agency does not invariably apply to the Chinese non-native English speakers in the study, even though subjects frequently expressed and defended particular views. In contrast to the expatriate foreign teachers, Chinese respondents would defer agency to a claimed identity group, most often 'Chinese'. Reformulating the transcultural and language speaker agency to include a concept of collective identities would better match the discourse of this project's research subjects and dovetail with a more relational approach to culture and identity.

The transcultural as a collective and constrained phenomenon

Testing the transcultural approach, this paper investigated instances of transcultural discourse, resistance to native-speaker hegemony, and most importantly, the agency of the individual in a seemingly homogeneous global village. All four focus groups exhibited transcultural competencies although the number and complexity of such competencies clearly correlated with linguistic competence. Respondents performed as dynamic representatives of culture(s), utilizing multiple linguistic and metalinguistic tactics to trade language, culture and power in the process of identity formation and reformation. Yet, they did so in relation to and highly aware of the practices and reactions of other focus group members. All groups exhibited resistance to native-speaker hegemony in terms of language use and the native speaker's possible status as a language or cultural model for the formation of identities. With the possible exception of the international teachers, however, such resistance to the native-speaker Other was intermittent, often muted, ambivalent and indirect suggesting that native-speaker hegemony continues, despite contestation, even for the most advanced non-native speakers.

Our data emphasizes that a relational and contingent approach to culture, identity and language should consider (at least) linguistic and gendered constraints to radical agency-oriented theories of the transcultural 'individual' language learner.

Despite expressing opinions, the Chinese non-native English speakers in the study often deferred agency to a group, 'the Chinese', rather than claiming such agency as individuals. This variation was in contrast to the markedly individualistic expressive modes that the three expatriate foreign teachers and native English speakers used to describe their relationship to Chinese that included 'slaughtering' the Chinese language. This contrast suggests that radical individualistic theories of language-learner agency may not be universally applicable and may need to be reformulated to include collective and cooperative forms of learner agency.

While non-native language learners gradually experience a freedom to move between cultures as they gain confidence in the language being learned, occasionally feel at home in multiple language/culture complexes, and may choose particular cultural traits according to personal preference, our data indicates that such speakers do so intermittently, ambivalently, and are strongly influenced by the values, practices and discourse of other speakers of the language perceived as Own. Chinese speakers of English and native English speakers learning Chinese demonstrated an uneven ability to accept unusual or potentially negative behaviours when performed by groups not considered 'own' (possibly influenced by power differentials) which indicates that none of these groups felt equally 'at home' in Chinese and English and that acceptance and rejection of specific traits of a particular culture are not entirely based on individual preference. In contrast to Wenger's (1998) work where people strive for access to the hegemonic, the non-native language speakers 'community of practice' refers to the group perceived as Own, and this 'community of practice' acts as a gate-keeping network to enforce Own cultural identity in particular arenas, such as coarseness (cursing), gender and sexuality rather than seeking to acquire native-speaker status.

Methodologically organizing focus groups according to achieved English linguistic competence allowed comparison of the process of identification (Hall, 1995) and thus helped to pinpoint that competence as a salient variable in transculturalism. Our qualitative microanalysis allowed us to discover gender as a salient factor influencing respondents' performance of transcultural competencies and limiting their creation of multiple selves (see Benwell and Stokoe, 2006). Non-moderated focus groups as communities of practice in the contested spaces of foreign language and culture illustrated the processes of gendered identification, negotiation, resistance and agency. Independent of the lens of the researcher, such focus groups provided insight into respondents' collaboratively constructed realities, interactively negotiated opportunities and intersubjective narratives (Block, 2007b). The same groups also demonstrate the gendered borders, limitations and obstacles encountered in the process of creating those realities and opportunities.

The focus groups' data highlight limitations in Western theories of agency, resistance and transculturalism and demonstrate the need for a radical reconceptualization of these parameters to accurately portray transcultural philosophies and practices among language learners from different cultures, educational contexts, socio-economic backgrounds and socio-political areas. Future research should include individual interviews of respondents, a longitudinal aspect, more finely calibrated gradations in English-language competence, a greater sensitivity to articulations with class and should begin with a less radically individualized concept of agency and an awareness of both the possibilities and limitations of the transcultural.

Conclusion

Language, culture and identity interact in different ways in the process of building multiple selves among language learners. These ways depend on the individual background of the language learner such as their level of proficiency in the language, their gender and their seniority or lack thereof in relation to their interlocutors. Multiple selves are developed over time and can be created in imitation of or resistance to perceived target language and culture norms. These multiple selves allow both a critical perspective on one's own community and a successful engagement with the other culture. However, both multiple selves and resistance/appropriation are clearly delimited by the factors mentioned.

Transcultural competencies and the resulting transnational practices have become apparent in the discourse of learners about language, culture and identity. Competencies evolve through increasing command of the language and familiarity with the culture, exposure to other language and culture in class, through media and by interaction with representatives of the other community, and critical reflection on self and other based on a diverse range of sources and contexts. The resulting transnational practices can be actual or virtual/anticipated according to the current scope of transcultural experience of the learner. Culture or nation in this context does not simply refer to one static community of practice but rather a dynamic ensemble of various cultures, nationalities with individuals switching among them without apparent pattern.

What does this mean for language teachers, researchers and policy makers? Since language learners at all levels are not only able to articulate their beliefs and attitudes concerning the language and culture they are learning and act accordingly, but are constantly re-evaluating their stance towards self and other, teachers should take advantage of that fluid repertoire and challenge students to consider and reconsider their own identities in the light of their experience with the language and culture. Researchers should expand the use of non-moderated focus groups if they wish to study the development of multiple selves which is not only influenced by the target personae but also by interaction within one's own community of practice. Policy makers and curriculum developers can take advantage of the current state of flux and variability and support students in their quest for transcultural competencies and multiple selves in order to become confident players in today's globalized market economy, scientific research community and worldwide, political, social and professional networks.

5

Social Identifications and Culturally Located Identities: Developing Cultural Understanding through Literature

Melina Porto

Introduction

In this chapter, I explore cultural understanding through literary texts. In general, cultural understanding in reading is investigated within static and essentialist notions of culture and identity, but in this chapter I describe the multiple and simultaneous social identifications and groupings that played a role in reading in the context of Argentina, namely the social groupings of the home, the community and the country; and the identifications of age, atheism, gender, race and ethnicity. The aim is to show that multiple social identifications simultaneously play an active role in the understanding of text in this specific sociocultural context. The chapter is exploratory and innovative because cultural understanding in reading is almost exclusively investigated with a focus on the notions of schema, cultural background and culturally familiar/unfamiliar prior knowledge. I begin by presenting the concepts of identity and culture upon which this study rests. Within a dynamic conceptualization of culture, identity is seen here as a construction (i.e. as fluid, multiple and hybrid, as a positioning rather than as essence). I continue to briefly describe the investigation within which this chapter is framed and I then describe the case of one reader in this setting, herein referred to as Tess. I conclude by highlighting some implications for reading such as the need to take into account the subtle and varied ways in which comprehension can take place, away from standardized and generalizable interpretations.

Views of culture and identity in this study

A review of the literature indicates that cultural understanding in reading is often investigated using inappropriate theoretical rationales framed within static and essentialist notions of culture and identity. This means that culture becomes a variable within mental representations and is reduced to just one aspect of an individual's identifications: race, ethnicity or nationality, and occasionally religion (Lipson, 1983; Reynolds et al., 1982; Rice, 1980; Steffensen et al., 1979). This isolation of aspects such as race, ethnicity and religion, constitutes a serious weakness in the literature because the studies fail to consider the complex interplay of the multiple and varied aspects of one's individuality (Rosaldo, 1993), or social identifications and groupings (Norton, 2000; Norton and Toohey, 2011; Robinson, 1996; Tajfel, 1982).

Identity issues are important in reading because language is 'a carrier and shaper of individual and group identities' (Guiora, 2005: 185). Just as readers can come to understand themselves in particular ways as a result of a reading experience, each reading experience plays a role in their identifications and positionings in their own society (McCarthey and Moje, 2002; Tsui, 2007).

Owing to the belief that identities are multiple, hybrid, complex, fluid and contradictory (Genetsch, 2007; Norton, 2000; Norton and Toohey, 2011; Rosaldo, 1993), it is always possible to enact more than one such identity in each reading experience, or different ones in different reading acts, depending on the relationships, interactions and identifications in a reader's life that one chooses to foreground (language, religion, ethnicity, gender, social class, etc.), or in other words, the readers' 'integrated cultural identities' (Maloof et al., 2006: 255). In this sense, identities are viewed as social constructions: 'the aspect of "construction" of identity implies that a self-image does not rely on essentialist formulations but is in need of a difference against which it can be defined' (Genetsch, 2007: vi). It is here where the link with the Other, the cultural and the intercultural becomes clear.

Furthermore, this notion of the continuous construction of cultural identity relates to an emphasis on performativity, particularly associated with the work of the philosopher Judith Butler. In this view, identifications are seen as 'rehearsals' in 'temporary identifications' (Butler, 1997: 266). Butler (1988, 2004) also attributes a great deal of importance to agency in identity construction, which means that all individuals can construct their identities differently and at different points in time. The complexity of the issue is apparent – a specific identification can be seen as the construction of various, different and potentially conflicting acts rather than as an essence.

The investigation

The project from which the data in this chapter were collected was carried out at the National University of La Plata in Argentina during 2009–10. The project participants were Argentine college students (nine female, one male), future teachers and translators of English; they were Caucasian, between 21 and 22 years of age, enrolled in the course 'English Language II'. They had CAE level at this stage (Certificate in Advanced English, Cambridge; C1 in the Common European Framework of Reference).

The participants read a passage from the novel *Mi planta de naranja-lima* (*My Sweet Orange Tree*) (Vasconcelos, 1971: 39–43) and performed a number of subsequent tasks. The literary passage selected from *Mi planta de naranja-lima* is set in Brazil and portrays the Christmas celebration of a low-income family narrated from the insider perspective of Zezé (one of the children in the family). Many typical elements of a Brazilian Christmas celebration are present, such as the mention of midnight mass, church bells and fireworks. Zezé describes the bewilderment of the youngest members of the family, disappointed because, unlike those of the higher-income families in town, they are not to receive Christmas presents. The perception of such inequality leads the characters to question some ideas inherent in Christianity such as the belief in the fairness of Jesus. The rationale for the use of unmodified literary narrative texts includes 'the primary authenticity of literary texts' (Carter, 2010: 116), which contributes to the high ecological validity of this project as 'narratives enable an investigation of contextualized language use' (van Hell et al., 2003: 299). The advantages of literature for the development of an understanding of Otherness (Bredella, 2000; Matos, 2005) are also emphasized.

Data were collected in the first language, Spanish, from the following:

- A biographical questionnaire.
- A prior knowledge task in writing about the cultural content of the fragment (prior to seeing the text). The instructions required participants to describe a typical Christmas celebration in Argentina and in Brazil (where the story is set), and to compare and contrast both with a typical Christmas celebration in their own homes.
- An immediate written reflection log (retrospective self-observation) based on the cultural aspects in the text and the comprehension difficulties found (written immediately after reading the text).

- A reading response task, which is a personal response to the text adapted from Ollmann (1996), and is different from the summary, synthesis, essay and recall protocol generally used in the investigation of reading.
- A visual representation task, which is defined here as the visual representation of textual content that includes the combination of words, phrases and/or sentences with visual information in different formats of varying complexity (such as charts, tables, graphs, grids, mind maps, flowcharts, diagrams, drawings, etc.).
- A delayed interview to focus on issues which emerged from my preliminary analysis of the reading response tasks and the visual representations.
- Post-reading reflections based on any aspect of interest to participants, written voluntarily at any time during the following year after the closure of the collection of the previously listed data types. Specifically in the case of Tess reported here, she delivered her afterthoughts to me via email. She put in words her thoughts as they came to her mind, in a sort of stream of consciousness approach, using the 'comments' option in Word. Here, I include them as plain text, each proceeded by the phrase [Post-reading written reflection], inserted exactly in the same place where Tess initially located them.

The participants voluntarily translated all of their tasks into English from Spanish. The incidental revision of their tasks involved by the translations led them to write further reflections on occasions (clarifications, additional interpretations, etc.). The participants produced unsolicited additional comments and reflections for over a year, thus making the project longitudinal in nature. Although in this chapter the focus is upon one reader (Tess), it should be stressed that the interest does not reside in the individual as an individual of particular interest per se, but rather the case shows that any individual reading is determined by a range of identifications with race, ethnicity, gender, social class, religion, language, and the like. The in-depth case-study analysis of this reader shows how the local in the sense of the Argentinean identity is inevitably interrelated with the local in the sense of identifications with other social groups (gender, religion, social class, etc.).

Data presentation: The case of Tess

The biographical questionnaire revealed that Tess was in her early twenties, had entered university in 2007 and had taken my course (English Language II) during the following year. She lived with her parents and an 18-year old brother and identified herself as an atheist. Different from the other participants, she reported having travelled abroad eight times and having visited English-speaking countries. On this basis, Tess could be expected to have had multiples opportunities in the course of her life to experience Otherness.

The data excerpts quoted in this chapter represent varied data types. I have chosen to italicize the evidence for the particular argument or observation I wish to make in each case. As the data were produced in Spanish, for the purpose of convenience English-language translations are also provided.

Tess's reading as a young adult within specific groupings: The country, the community, the home

Considering that Tess's prior knowledge about Christmas celebrations in Brazil and her attitudes towards it were fundamental as they constituted the point of entrance to the text, the prior knowledge task required her to describe her perceptions of a typical Christmas celebration not only in Brazil, where the story is set, but also in Argentina, with the aim of allowing for the process of comparing and contrasting that is seen to characterize cultural understanding (Byram and Morgan, 1994).

Tess's description of a Christmas celebration in Argentina includes stereotypes of what Christmas involves, in particular in reference to her local community. Some examples are the presents, food, Nativity, dancing and visiting relatives. She is drawing from her social grouping identifications at this point, namely her community and country.

> ***En general,*** *creo que* ***la gente*** *se prepara aprovisionándose de cosas, regalos y comida para la celebración de nochebuena.* A veces hay celebraciones previas, como pesebres vivientes, pero *las reuniones más importantes son las del 24 a la noche.* ***La gente suele*** *quedarse festejando hasta al menos 1.30 o más de la madrugada. Los más jóvenes a veces vamos a visitar amigos después de las doce, y también* ***se puede*** *ir a bailar o salir a algún otro lado.* Al día siguiente **suelen** continuar las visitas a parientes, amigos, etc., pero **en general** al mediodía o a la tarde. **Se va a** ver a las personas con las que todavía **no se pudo** estar.
>
> ***In general,*** *I think that* ***people*** *get ready by sourcing things, presents and food for the Christmas Eve celebration.* Sometimes there are previous celebrations, such as Nativity plays, but *the most important reunions take place on 24th night.* ***Usually people*** *stay up to celebrate, at least until 1.30 a.m. or later. Sometimes, we, the youngest ones go and visit people after midnight, and* ***it's also possible*** *to go to*

> *dance or somewhere else.* **Usually**, the next day, visits to relatives continue, but they take place, **in general**, during midday or the afternoon. *We* visit those with whom *we* haven't been yet.
>
> Tess, prior knowledge task

This description is simultaneously tinted by intrusions from her own cultural practices at Christmas, in particular those typical of her age group, such as celebrating till 1.30 a.m. or later. The generalization and naturalization of such practices as universal is signalled by phrases like *en general* (*in general*), *la gente* (*people*) and verbs like *suele* (in bold in the extract). Tess specifically differentiates customs by age when she points out that younger generations like herself tend to go out after midnight (Los más jóvenes a veces *vamos* a visitar amigos después de las doce; Sometimes, *we*, the youngest ones go and visit friends after midnight). The use of the first-person plural (*vamos*; *we*) is evidence of her identification with this age group. Here she is enacting one specific social identification (Byram et al., 2009), namely age.

Immediately before this recognition, however, she generalizes the habit of celebrating till after 1.30 (*La gente suele* quedarse festejando hasta al menos 1.30 o más de la madrugada; *Usually people* stay up to celebrate, at least until 1.30 a.m. or later). In other words, despite some phrases which narrow the focus of her affirmations to certain groups (such as *los más jóvenes*, *the youngest ones*, including herself in this group) and some expressions of frequency (*a veces*, *sometimes*), she does not show awareness of the existence of difference in Christmas traditions within Argentina among different age groups, for instance. Furthermore, she uses her own cultural practices in the home as the basis for her description of cultural practices in Argentina as a whole, something that she herself later acknowledges. What we see here, therefore, is her identification with different groupings such as the home, the community and the country (Norton, 2000). The reference to Nativity (*pesebres vivientes*) is an instance of Tess's religious identification, which is discussed in the next section.

When prompted by one specific question in the prior knowledge task to describe the Christmas celebrations within her family circle (i.e. the home in Norton's (2000) terms), Tess does not add anything and in fact points out that she had resorted to her own personal experience to write the previous account (como si me hubiera basado en *mi experiencia personal* para hablar de la *generalidad*; as if I had based on *my personal experience* to talk about *generalities*). In what can be seen as an apparent contradiction, it is important to point out that in this account, she does show awareness of the existence of cultural differences among the different provinces within Argentina regarding rituals surrounding Christmas, something that reveals the influence of community groupings.

> Creo que *los festejos en mi casa son prácticamente como los que describí antes, como si me hubiera basado en mi experiencia personal para hablar de la generalidad. Y es muy probable que en otras provincias del país los festejos sean totalmente distintos.*
>
> I think that *the celebrations at home are basically as I described them before, as if I had based on my personal experience to talk about generalities. It's very likely that celebrations are very different in other provinces of the country.*
>
> Tess, prior knowledge task

The data in this section reveal the strong influence of social groupings in Tess's thoughts, ranging from the home (Creo que los festejos *en mi casa* son prácticamente como los que describí antes, como si me hubiera basado *en mi experiencia personal* para hablar de la generalidad; I think that the celebrations *at home* are basically as I described them before, as if I had based on *my personal experience* to talk about generalities), the community (her own and others; como si me hubiera basado en mi *experiencia personal* para hablar de la generalidad. Y es muy probable que *en otras provincias del país* los festejos sean totalmente distintos; as if I had based on my *personal experience* to talk about generalities. It's very likely that celebrations are very different *in other provinces of the country*) and the country as a whole (*en general, la gente suele*; *in general, usually people*).

Tess's reading as an atheist

Tess claimed in the prior knowledge task that she did not specifically know about Christmas celebrations in Brazil. She made the assumption that religion plays a key role because in her view 'Catholicism is even more ingrained' [in Brazil than in Argentina] (el catolicismo está todavía más arraigado). This comparison with her country is interesting, considering that she had manifested her lack of knowledge regarding this celebration in Brazil and taking into account the fact that she is an atheist. Put differently, she highlights here one of her social identifications, namely as an atheist (Ysseldyk et al., 2010) (the same applies to the reference to Nativity previously mentioned). Even though being an atheist does not exclude religious knowledge, Tess shows no evidence of being in a knowledgeable position to affirm that 'Catholicism is even more ingrained' in Brazil than in Argentina. Despite her tendency to generalize in this way, in particular through the use of the present tense (el catolicismo *está* todavía más arraigado; Catholicism *is* even more ingrained), she simultaneously shows tentativeness in all her statements about religiosity through verbs like *supongo* (*assume*) and modality like *debe* (*must*) to make a deduction (el aspecto religioso *debe* jugar el papel primordial; I assume that the religious aspect *must* play the main role).

> No sé exactamente cómo son todas las costumbres en Brasil para Navidad. Sé que por ejemplo, les gusta festejar en la playa si están en la costa, y que los fuegos artificiales son espectaculares. *Creo también que el catolicismo está todavía más arraigado y supongo que el aspecto religioso debe jugar el papel primordial.*
>
> I don't know exactly what the customs are in Brazil for Christmas. For instance, I know that they enjoy celebrating on the beach if they are on the coast, and the fireworks are spectacular. *Besides, I think that Catholicism is even more engrained, and I assume that the religious aspect must play the main role.*
>
> Tess, prior knowledge task

In the immediate reflection log, where Tess reflects on the cultural difficulties posed by the text immediately after reading it, it is possible to observe a link between Zezé's act of placing his trainers on the other side of the door in the hope that he would receive a present for Christmas and the religious festivity of the 'Three Wise Men' in Argentina. This is an example of the resort to prior and familiar knowledge about religion for interpreting Otherness within an ongoing process of comparing and contrasting. While the text describes a Christmas celebration, placing the trainers on the door is something that children do for the festivity of the 'Three Wise Men' in Argentina. Here, Tess is enacting her social identification of atheism to understand the fragment (Ysseldyk et al., 2010). She brings to the surface her knowledge of religious festivities in the country by comparing and contrasting the cultural practices present in the text and in her own culture: *por comparación con nuestra propia cultura* podemos inferir lo no dicho o reconstruir cómo es la celebración de la navidad que se narra . . . podemos inferir que los niños tienen que dejar sus zapatos para que le dejen los regalos. *Aunque no hacemos acá lo mismo, podemos entenderlo porque tenemos esa costumbre en el día de Reyes*; *by comparison with our own culture*, we can infer what is not said or reconstruct the Christmas celebration that is described . . . we can infer that the children have to leave their shoes around to get gifts. *Although we don't do the same here, we can understand this because we have that very custom on the Twelfth Night.* This foregrounding of the religious in the comparison with the Three Wise Men is interesting because even though Tess identifies herself as an atheist in the biographical questionnaire, she simultaneously acknowledges that she engages and participates in this religious festivity through her use of first-person plural pronouns and references (*nuestra, hacemos, podemos, tenemos*; *our, we*, in bold in the extract).

> Creo que las dificultades que tuve para comprender el texto fueron principalmente por el contenido de la historia y no tanto desde el punto de vista cultural. Me parece que con los elementos que da el texto y *por comparación con* ***nuestra*** *propia cultura* podemos inferir lo no dicho o reconstruir cómo es la celebración de la navidad que se narra. [Post-reading written reflection 1: Lo no dicho sería el 'background' de información que el autor puede dar por supuesto, por considerarlo parte del conocimiento compartido con el lector.] Por ejemplo, se puede deducir que la 'rabanada' es una comida y no hace falta saber el significado más preciso para comprender el texto. O podemos inferir que los niños tienen que dejar sus zapatos para que le dejen los regalos. *Aunque no* ***hacemos*** *acá lo mismo,* ***podemos*** *entenderlo porque* ***tenemos*** *esa costumbre en el día de Reyes. Seguramente para lectores de otros orígenes el texto resultaría mucho más difícil.* [Post-reading written reflection 2: Si pensamos que hay una historia común entre las culturas latinoamericanas y muchas tradiciones católicas comunes, lo cual nos acerca al texto y probablemente no sería así para otros pueblos.]
>
> I think the difficulties I had to understand the text were caused mainly by the content of the story and not by cultural issues. I believe that, with the elements that the text provides and *by comparison with* ***our*** *own culture*, we can infer what is not said or reconstruct the Christmas celebration that is described. [See post-reading written reflection 1 below, inserted at this point by Tess four months after data collection.] For example, we can deduce that 'rabanada' is a meal and there is no need to know its precise meaning to understand the text. Or we can infer that the children have to leave their shoes around to get gifts. *Although* ***we*** *don't do the same here,* ***we*** *can understand this because* ***we*** *have that very custom on the Twelfth Night. Surely for readers from other origins the text would turn out to be much more difficult.* [See post-reading written reflection 2 below, inserted at this point by Tess four months after data collection.]
>
> Tess, reflection log

Post-reading written reflection 1: What is not said would be the 'background' of information that the author can take for granted, considering it part of the knowledge that is shared with the reader.

Post-reading written reflection 2: If we consider that there is a shared story among Latin American cultures and very many Catholic traditions in common,

> which brings us closer to the text and would probably not be the case for other peoples.

Although I am discussing Tess's religious identification here, it is important to highlight the interrelationship of the different groupings mentioned in the previous section, namely the home, the community and the country (*nuestra propia cultura, acá*; *our own culture, here*). This points to the impossibility to isolate identifications rigidly, something I will return to later.

In the reading response task that Tess produced after reading the text, she does not refer to Christmas by using the word Christmas itself. She uses a generalization like 'una de las celebraciones religiosas del país' (one of the religious celebrations of the country), tied to a brief description of which one it was, from a religious standpoint (el nacimiento del hijo de Dios; the birth of the son of God). Noteworthy here is precisely the religious standpoint in her definition of Christmas, when she expresses in the biographical questionnaire that she is an atheist. This may be connected with her belief, as stated in the prior knowledge task, that the religious aspect is very much ingrained in Brazilian society. This seems to reveal the foregrounding of her social identification of atheism (or 'irreligion' following Ysseldyk et al., 2010: 65) as well as her ability to decentre (i.e. to see Christmas from a perspective which was not her own, in this case the religious). This ability is a characteristic of cultural understanding (Byram, 1997; Byram and Morgan, 1994). At the same time, it is possible that there is something stereotyped from a cultural standpoint in Tess's assumption that the religious connotation can be generalized to the Brazilians as a national group.

> El texto que se presenta es un fragmento de una novela brasileña, en el que se retrata cómo vive una familia pobre *una de las celebraciones religiosas del país: el nacimiento del hijo de Dios.* El pasaje se centra en cómo esa fiesta que es para muchos un motivo de alegría refleja también la situación penosa y la miseria en que viven muchos habitantes. Por un lado, la narración nos muestra que los adultos de la familia viven la jornada con tristeza y resignación; por otra parte, se presenta la sensación de impotencia que se genera en otros personajes por el marcado contraste entre ricos y pobres. [Post-reading written reflection: Por una situación de injusticia.] La familia no tiene dinero ni para hacer algún obsequio a los más pequeños, como se acostumbra, e intenta explicar la falta culpando al niño, como si fuera un castigo por haber sido malo. En tanto, las familias más ricas comparten comidas muy abundantes y festejan con fuegos artificiales. Todo este lujo resulta incomprensible para el protagonista, que no

puede compatibilizar las enseñanzas religiosas y el origen humilde del niño Dios con la ostentación y con la marcada diferencia que hay entre un hogar y otro. El chico es el único que parece conservar, sin embargo, la esperanza de que la situación mejore. Esta esperanza se manifiesta como el deseo de recibir un regalo *en esa navidad*.

The text consists of a fragment from a Brazilian novel, which depicts how a poor family experiences *one of the religious celebrations of the country: the birth of the son of God*. The excerpt focuses on how that party, which is a happy moment for many, also show the sad situation and destitution in which many inhabitants live. On one hand, the narrative shows us that the adults in the family move through the day with sadness and resignation; on the other hand, we can get the feeling of frustration that is aroused in other characters by the sharp contrast between the rich and the poor. [Post-reading written reflection: Because of an unjust situation.] The family hasn't got money event to buy a present for the little ones, as the custom goes, and they try to explain this lack by blaming it on the child, as if it were some sort of punishment for having been bad. At the same time, the rich families share lavish meals and celebrate with fireworks. Such luxury is incomprehensible to the protagonist, who cannot reconcile the religious teachings and the humble origins of baby Jesus with such ostentation or with the sharp difference that existed between one home and the other. However, the boy is the only one who seems to cling to the hope that the situation could improve. This hope is present in his desire to get a gift *that Christmas night*.

Tess, reading response task

Race and ethnic identifications: Tess's reading as a white, Latin American individual

In her post-reading written reflections based on her immediate reflection log, Tess refers to the existence of a common Latin American heritage, and to the close connection between this heritage and many shared Catholic traditions among Latin American peoples – a connection that in her opinion facilitated her comprehension of this text (Si **pensamos** que hay una *historia común entre las culturas latinoamericanas y muchas tradiciones católicas comunes, lo cual* ***nos*** *acerca al texto y probablemente no sería así para otros pueblos*; If **we** consider that *there is a shared story among Latin American cultures and very many Catholic traditions in common, which brings* ***us*** *closer to the text and would probably not be the case for other peoples*).

> Creo que las dificultades que tuve para comprender el texto fueron principalmente por el contenido de la historia y no tanto desde el punto de vista cultural. Me parece que con los elementos que da el texto y *por comparación con **nuestra** propia cultura* podemos inferir lo no dicho o reconstruir cómo es la celebración de la navidad que se narra. [Post-reading written reflection 1: Lo no dicho sería el 'background' de información que el autor puede dar por supuesto, por considerarlo parte del conocimiento compartido con el lector]. Por ejemplo, se puede deducir que la 'rabanada' es una comida y no hace falta saber el significado más preciso para comprender el texto. O podemos inferir que los niños tienen que dejar sus zapatos para que le dejen los regalos. *Aunque no **hacemos** acá lo mismo, **podemos entenderlo** porque **tenemos** esa costumbre en el día de Reyes. Seguramente para lectores de otros orígenes el texto resultaría mucho más difícil.* [Post-reading written reflection 2: Si **pensamos** que hay una historia común entre las culturas latinoamericanas y muchas tradiciones católicas comunes, lo cual **nos** acerca al texto y probablemente no sería así para otros pueblos.]
>
> I think the difficulties I had to understand the text were caused mainly by the content of the story and not by cultural issues. I believe that, with the elements that the text provides and *by comparison with **our** own culture*, we can infer what is not said or reconstruct the Christmas celebration that is described. [See post-reading written reflection 1 below, inserted at this point by Tess four months after data collection.] For example, we can deduce that 'rabanada' is a meal and there is no need to know its precise meaning to understand the text. Or we can infer that the children have to leave their shoes around to get gifts. *Although **we** don't do the same here, **we** can understand this because **we** have that very custom on the Twelfth Night. Surely for readers from other origins the text would turn out to be much more difficult.* [See post-reading written reflection 2 below, inserted at this point by Tess four months after data collection.]
>
> Tess, reflection log

> Post-reading written reflection 1: What is not said would be the 'background' of information that the author can take for granted, considering it part of the knowledge that is shared with the reader.
>
> Post-reading written reflection 2: If we consider that there is a shared story among Latin American cultures and very many Catholic traditions in common, which brings us closer to the text and would probably not be the case for other peoples.

The post-reading written reflection 2 draws attention to her identity as a Latin American person, beyond her national identity as an Argentinean. She had previously foregrounded her national identity in the immediate reflection log itself as she had reflected upon the centrality of the festivity of 'Three Wise Men' in Argentina (Aunque no **hacemos** acá lo mismo, **podemos** entenderlo porque ***tenemos*** *esa costumbre en el día de Reyes*; Although **we** don't do the same here, **we** can understand this because ***we*** *have that very custom on the Twelfth Night*). The use of first-person plural references (in bold in the extract) is evidence of the fact that she is enacting her social identification as an Argentinean to interpret the fragment. She also remarks that readers from other origins (i.e. not from Latin America) would probably find the text more distant in this respect. Worth noticing is the prominence that she attributes to her identification as a Latin American person for the interpretation of the placing of the trainers on the other side of the door. Implied here as well is the distinction between race as a socially constructed category and ethnic identifications based on cultural practices and identity (Byram et al., 2009).

Gender identification reflected in Tess's linguistic choices

A myriad of research has been carried out on language use and gender. Central to my purpose in this final section is the notion that written discourse may contain linguistic markers by which writers convey their multiple identifications, including gender (biological sex) and gender role orientation (gender role schema). Winn and Rubin (2001: 396–7) show how:

> [e]arly studies of gender and language . . . associate female speakers with features that hedge or blunt assertions (e.g., 'maybe,' 'sort of,' 'I guess') and avoid conflict with listeners by the use of politeness formulas (e.g., 'if you don't mind' or the use of question forms rather than bald requests). Other 'markers' commonly associated with female language include the use of double-sided arguments (e.g., 'It was probably Shakespeare's sister, but then again, some people believe it was Marlowe'), expressions of uncertainty (e.g., 'I don't know, but . . .'), and the use of certain vocabulary likely to be judged as trivial (e.g., fine grained color terms such as *fuchsia*).

Beyond the specificity of findings in this field, one underlying conclusion seems to be that the social identifications expressed through language belong to a continuum (rather than being susceptible of being manifested in dichotomies such as male–female), vary significantly with the elements of the communicative situation (i.e. the context in which language is used) (Winn and Rubin, 2001) and consequently are not culturally generalizable. Furthermore, gender typicality in writing can be difficult to establish, considering that more recent research has revealed that men's and women's language is more similar than different and that apparent differences tend to be context specific (Winn and Rubin, 2001). Finally, considering that semantically encoded meaning does not equal pragmatically realized meaning (Widdowson, 1984), it is impossible to 'read off significance from text as if it were a simple projection from textual features' (Widdowson, 2000: 19).

Despite the notion of a continuum, the determining influence of the context, and the notion of '*functional fallacy*' (i.e. 'the assumption that semantic signification is directly projected as pragmatic significance in language use') (Widdowson, 2004: 96), many empirical studies investigating gender in discourse have revealed that certain language features have been traditionally associated with female writing. Winn and Rubin (2001: 398–9) report research findings that have:

> revealed a series of written language features that have traditionally been linked with gender, including markers of excitability (e.g., the use of underlining or exclamation points), nonessentials (e.g., dashes and parentheses), connectives (a combination of illustrators, illatives, adversatives, causals, additives, temporals, and conditionals), and hedges (e.g. a combination of intensifiers, deintensifiers, proximals, modal adjuncts, perceptual verbs and auxiliaries of possibility, audience acknowledgements, first-person markers, enumerations, and sentence length/verbosity).

In general, the markers of non-essential information (dashes, parentheses) can be seen as signalling digression from and/or the embellishment of a text, while markers of excitability (exclamation points, underlining) may signal high emotionality and may also be used to embellish the text. Hedges may signal the writer's tentativeness or lack of assertiveness towards propositional content. Furthermore, the use of first-person pronouns in conjunction with verbs of perception, affect or cognition (I guess/feel/suppose/imagine . . .) signals tentativeness or subjectivity (Winn and Rubin, 2001).

Despite the caveats mentioned, and based on Winn and Rubin (2001), it is possible to say that the immediate reflection log shows instances of language use which might be seen as a characteristic of gender enactment in writing. For example, through the use of tentative language (*me parece que, resultaría; I think, the text would turn out to be*), speculations and deductions (*podemos inferir, se puede deducir que; we can infer, we can deduce*), modality (*resultaría, si . . .; would turn out to, if . . .*), hedging devices (*principalmente, seguramente, probablemente; mainly, surely, probably*), denials (*no tanto, lo no dicho, no hacemos, no sería así; not, what is not said, we don't do that here, would not be the case*), first-person references with verbs of cognition (*creo que; I believe that*) and the tendency to present more than one side, aspect or perspective of a topic (i.e. double-sided or multiple-sided views) (*principalmente por . . . y no tanto desde el punto de vista cultural; podemos inferir lo no dicho o reconstruir . . .; o podemos inferior que . . . aunque . . .; mainly by . . . and not by cultural issues; we can infer what is not said or reconstruct . . .; Or we can infer that . . . although . . .*). As an experienced and knowledgeable user of the language, Tess manipulates linguistic choices in order to appear more or less assertive, more or less tentative, at different points in her tasks.

> **Creo que** las dificultades que tuve para comprender el texto fueron **principalmente** por el contenido de la historia y **no tanto** desde el punto de vista cultural. **Me parece que** con los elementos que da el texto y por comparación con nuestra propia cultura **podemos inferir lo no dicho o** reconstruir cómo es la celebración de la navidad que se narra. [Post-reading written reflection 1: Lo **no** dicho sería el 'background' de información que el autor puede dar por supuesto, por considerarlo parte del conocimiento compartido con el lector.] **Por ejemplo, se puede deducir que** la 'rabanada' es una comida y no hace falta saber el significado más preciso para comprender el texto. **O podemos inferir que** los niños tienen que dejar sus zapatos para que le dejen los regalos. **Aunque no** hacemos acá lo mismo, podemos entenderlo porque tenemos esa costumbre en el día de Reyes. **Seguramente** para lectores de otros orígenes el texto **resultaría** mucho más difícil. [Post-reading written reflection 2: **Si** pensamos que hay una historia común entre las culturas latinoamericanas y muchas tradiciones católicas comunes, lo cual nos acerca al texto y **probablemente no sería así** para otros pueblos.]
>
> **I think** the difficulties I had to understand the text were caused **mainly** by the content of the story and **not by** cultural issues. **I believe that**, with the elements that the text provides and by comparison with our own culture, **we can infer** what is **not** said **or** reconstruct the Christmas celebration that is described. [See post-reading written reflection 1 below, inserted at this point by Tess four months after data collection.] **For example, we can deduce that** 'rabanada' is a meal and there is no need to know its precise meaning to understand the text. **Or we can infer that** the children have to leave their shoes around to get gifts. **Although** we **don't do** the same here, we can understand this because we have that very custom on the Twelfth Night. **Surely** for readers from other origins the text **would** turn out to be much more difficult. [See post-reading written reflection 2 below, inserted at this point by Tess four months after data collection.]
>
> Tess, immediate reflection log

Post-reading written reflection 1: What is not said would be the 'background' of information that the author can take for granted, considering it part of the knowledge that is shared with the reader.

Post-reading written reflection 2: **If** we consider that there is a shared story among Latin American cultures and very many Catholic traditions in common, which brings us closer to the text and **would probably not be the case** for other peoples.

Discussion

Several comments seem necessary at this point. The first one is related to methodology. Some parts of my analyses of Tess's tasks may be seen as what Widdowson (2000: 22) calls 'linguistics applied', whereby texts are analysed taking into account grammatical and lexical categories in isolation and specific claims regarding their significance are made. However, this chapter should be read with the understanding that one 'cannot read discourse significance directly from a mode of signifying. The use of a [passive] construction might indeed be intended and interpreted in different ways, depending on how it figures in relation to other factors' (Widdowson, 2004: 95). In the process of scrutinizing Tess's texts, it was not possible (or desirable) to examine every feature of her texts for their significance concerning a certain aspect of her social identifications and groupings in reading. Furthermore, the significance of Tess's texts as evidence of her social identifications and groupings in this respect, as I myself saw that significance and as I report it here, needs to be seen with the awareness that 'how the language is used to construct social identity and social relationships is [not] directly inferable from linguistic forms' (Widdowson, 2004: 94). What is shown in this chapter is that these forms, grammatical and lexical, interrelate cotextually (with each other and among themselves) and contextually (with the circumstances in which Tess used them), within the contextual specificity of this study.

Second, as noted earlier, 'identity is not an essence but a positioning' (Genetsch, 2007: 15). This chapter shows Tess's constant foregrounding and/or downgrading of different aspects of her social identifications and groupings such as gender, age, race, ethnic origin or affiliation, religion, and so on. In other words, different identifications emerged at different moments in her process of understanding. These identifications were personalized, in the sense that they were 'situated, contested, dynamic and fluid and heavily dependent on context'

(Byram et al., 2009: 8–9). This means that the idiosyncrasies and nuances of interpretation described in this chapter are unique to Tess.

Third, by showing that other social and group identities – beyond the local Argentinean – can be the basis for other interpretations or readings, this chapter shows that other researchers (Lipson, 1983; Reynolds et al., 1982; Rice, 1980; Steffensen et al., 1979) have been too narrow in their interpretations of what cultural understanding involves. Their exclusive focus on the notions of schema, cultural background and culturally familiar/unfamiliar prior knowledge (by which they refer to the 'cultures' of other language groups and countries) has rendered a useful and necessary, but nonetheless narrow and static perspective on the issue. In this sense, this is an exploratory chapter which raises new perspectives for future research based on the idea that multiple social identifications mingle and interact with the local (and therefore Argentinean) in reading in this setting.

Finally, drawing from Butler (1997, 1988, 2004) and illustrated with Tess's religious identification of atheism, she clearly at times foregrounded the religious (for instance, in the association of the trainers with the 'Three Wise Men') while other times she distanced herself from it (in her identification of herself as an atheist, for example). This fluctuation can be interpreted as the realization of different 'acts' of religious identifications which helped build Tess's own sense of herself as a religious and atheist individual simultaneously, depending on the occasion. Furthermore, Butler (1997, 1988, 2004) explores issues of power in the processes of identity construction and affirmation, which may be worth investigating further. How are the (temporary) affiliations that individuals *perform*, using Butler's term, related to the distribution of legal, economic and other entitlements in society, or in other words, dominant discourses and practices? Are individuals aware of these dimensions, or are these dimensions unconscious? This chapter suggests the possibility, and need, of exploring conscious and unconscious identifications in reading in greater depth.

Conclusion

This chapter has focused on some of the multiple and simultaneous social identifications and groupings that played a role in Tess's reading of the text *Mi planta de naranja-lima* (*My Sweet Orange Tree*) (Vasconcelos, 1971), namely the social groupings of the home, the community and the country; and the identifications of age, atheism, gender, race and ethnicity. More specifically, the chapter has shown the strong influence of social groupings in Tess's interpretations, ranging from the home (i.e. Christmas as celebrated in her own home), the community and the country as a whole (Christmas as a festive celebration). Her identity as a Latin American person, beyond her national identity as an Argentinean, also surfaced at several points. Simultaneously, Tess's interpretations enacted at times an identification based on age, namely as a young adult who visits friends or goes dancing after 12 p.m. at Christmas. She also foregrounded the religious in the comparison between the placing of the trainers on the other side of the door and the religious festivity of the 'Three Wise Men' in Argentina. Furthermore, Tess's written tasks revealed several language features which have been traditionally associated with female writings.

Finally, this chapter has shown the permanent fluctuation in the social identifications that came to the surface in the different tasks based on this fragment from *Mi planta de naranja-lima* (*My Sweet Orange Tree*) (Vasconcelos, 1971). This finding points to the need to consider the subtle and varied ways in which comprehension can take place, away from standardized and generalizable interpretations.

6

Reimagining Sociolinguistic Identification in Foreign Language Classroom Communities of Practice

Deborah Cole and Bryan Meadows

Introduction

In this chapter, we build on existing examinations of the 'nationalist paradigm' (Risager, 2007), which presents a major obstacle to foreign language education by preventing it from realizing its core mission of leading students to navigate across borders of culture and language. We demonstrate how this paradigm contradicts current sociolinguistic scholarship on language use and identity. We propose an alternative: replace 'the nation' as a central model of imagined identity with 'the community of practice'. We argue that foreign language classrooms that take up the communities of practice model release classroom practice from the confines of the nationalist paradigm and provide students with learning experiences that (1) enable the exploration and cultivation of multiple identities, (2) facilitate definitions of competence that more equitably and accurately address human sociolinguistic behaviour and (3) provide students with an education that is commiserate with the realities of our complex globally connected world. We provide a model for reimagining identities in foreign language classrooms and suggestions for practical applications to foreign language programmes.

There is an ongoing critique of foreign language education. Put briefly, foreign language education operates largely detached from the social realities of multilingualism and multiculturalism in the modern global world (Dixon et al., 2012; Holliday, 2011; Pomerantz and Schwartz, 2011). Critics argue that foreign language education runs the risk of reinforcing perceived and existing borders for students rather than leading them to transcend such limitations (Swaffar, 2006), an uncomfortable predicament for a strand of education that is charged with the cultivation of cultural and linguistic border-crossers (see Kramsch, 2006). This dissatisfaction extends across geographic contexts and is apparently symptomatic of broad ideological underpinnings giving shape to foreign language education globally (see, for example, Kubota, 2002, McVeigh, 2002, Rivers, 2010a on foreign language education in Japan, and Meadows, 2010, Pomerantz and Schwartz, 2011 in the United States). This ongoing critique should be troubling for stakeholders in foreign language education because it raises a stark irony: foreign language classrooms in their present arrangement may be functioning to reinforce borders of language and culture while their core mission is to transcend them.

In this chapter, we are concerned with what we see as a formidable obstacle impeding foreign language education from realizing its mission of transcending linguistic and cultural boundaries: the imagining of national communities as the most relevant social organizations for the description and construction of sociolinguistic identity. The traditional paradigm of language teaching presupposes a sociolinguistic world neatly compartmentalized into discrete national languages corresponding to discrete cultural practices taking place within fixed geopolitical borders (Risager, 2007). Implicitly and explicitly, foreign language classrooms continue to promise students systematic encounters with others, conventionally conceptualized in nationalist terms (Holliday, 2011; Joseph, 2004), even though it has become increasingly clear across the social sciences that essentialized, nation-based representations of languages and societies no longer adequately or accurately represent the lived experiences of humans (Blommaert, 2010; Dervin, 2011; Holliday, 2011). We propose that in order to provide classroom participants with a more accurate model of lived identity as well as a more useful target for imagined belonging, foreign language classrooms replace 'nations' with 'communities of practice' (Wenger, 1998) as the central unit of social organization in the delivery of language curricula.

In what follows, we argue that such a replacement can enable foreign language instructors themselves to come to terms with the core questions raised by this volume, including how Otherness and interculturality are represented in foreign language-learning environments, how best to implement current understandings of identities as multiple and dynamic, and which mechanisms and settings best facilitate identity changes. We begin with a quick review of recent scholarship on identity within the field of sociolinguistics. We contrast this research with the traditional nation-centric concept of identity within foreign language education. This is followed by our proposal that language educators resolve the tensions between these differing conceptualizations of identity by using key elements of the communities of practice model to reimagine sociolinguistic identity in foreign language classrooms. We offer a visual illustration of 'multimembership' (Wenger, 2000) to assist with this reimagination process as well as practical suggestions for how to cultivate awareness of the multimemberships students bring into the classroom and those they may want to acquire and perform. Our goal is to help language teachers to bridge the gap between sociolinguistic research on language and identity and foreign language classroom practice.

The sociolinguistic reality of multiple and shifting identities

Sociolinguistic identities are complicated, complex, confounding and contradictory (Riley, 2007), and the practices that project and recognize them are always localized, multiple, shifting and fragmented (Bucholtz and Hall, 2004). Adding to this complexity is the rising recognition that the behavioural patterns we call identities are cut across (and are cut through by) multiple scales of time and space (Blommaert, 2010; Lemke, 2008). In addition, contemporary scholars of language-in-use are observing a steady rise in the numbers of individuals connected to each other in global communication and transportation networks (Lin, 2008) who are increasingly enacting multiple identities in the deterritorialized (Hornberger, 2007) and mediatized (Agha, 2011) economies of the current global age.

As sociolinguists come to terms with the reality of identity in the twenty-first century, they are proposing conceptual shifts in scholarly approaches to sociolinguistic study. Perhaps, the most difficult shift to accomplish, but also the shift that may be most needed, is to begin embracing the reality that all language competence is partial: No one individual, no matter how well-spoken or well-read, commands the entirety of a language, and all individuals command multiple registers and varieties of one or more languages. Blommaert (2010) has referred to these universal facts of language ability as 'truncated repertoires'. Of course these facts about language are not new, and there is important scholarship in linguistic anthropology that reaches back to the work of Mikhail Bakhtin that argued throughout the late twentieth century that all language use was definitionally heteroglossic (see, for example, Hill, 1995). Related to this shift in thinking about individual competence is a needed shift in the way we think about languages themselves. Globalization has highlighted the realization that the boundaries between what we have traditionally and synchronically defined as separate languages are historically and temporally constructed in context by those who benefit from defining and maintaining such boundaries (Hill, 2006). What on-the-ground research into actual language use illuminates instead are deterritorialized patterns in the uses of particular concrete, mobile linguistic resources occurring in localized speech events (Blommaert, 2010).

These shifts in thinking about language and language competence are inextricably linked to thinking about identity because speakers are constantly making agentive use of concrete resources (like variable pronunciations, lexical selection, pitch, etc.) to perform (and perceive) multiple personae that index affiliations with or distance from communities of Others (Agha, 2005; Bucholtz and Hall, 2004; Cole and Pellicer, 2012). These shifts are in turn supremely relevant for language education, foreign or otherwise, as they have implications for how we think about measuring competence and how classroom learning will transfer into non-classroom language use: '[e]xplicit criteria of competence are rarely the whole story in real-life communities because lived practice is not merely instrumental; it includes the production of identities' (Eckert and Wenger, 2005: 583).

Linguistic features (like accent), therefore, which may have been viewed as a marker of origin within a traditional concept of identity (i.e. as an inherent characteristic of a particular group of people living in circumscribed locale) must instead be read as an index of stance or affiliation in light of current understandings (Agha, 2005; Goebel, 2008; Mendoza-Denton, 2008). These facts also require a constant foregrounding of the realization that students will use their foreign language skills not just to make and exchange meaning, but to perform memberships in multiple communities.

Any shift in understanding or defining linguistic competence requires a focus on legitimacy, and foreign language education is inextricably tied into ongoing socio-political struggles over whose language and what language counts (Kubota, 2003; Lin, 2008; Osborn, 2006). Foreign language educators, knowingly or not, position themselves on the front line of this continued struggle, endowed as they are with the responsibility of their received authority to select what to represent to students, how to represent it, what to highlight and what to suppress. It follows that language classrooms are sites for the reproduction or transformation of existing regimes of legitimacy, and that foreign language education is directly implicated in issues of social equity (Benesch, 1993; Park, 2010).

In the following section, we build on previous critically positioned research in language education that identifies nationalism and standard language ideologies as foundational to the ongoing maintenance of inequality in language education.

As notions linking nationalism to monoglossia continue to be authorized, despite widespread evidence of the deteritorrialization of language forms and intranational speaker diversity (Heller, 2008; Meadows, 2010; Risager, 2007), foreign language education that takes national cultures and languages at face value sits in contradistinction to the current sociolinguistic scholarship outlined above. Important to our discussion of identity will be the way that nationalism dramatically reduces the variety of linguistic repertoires, and by extension the variety of identities and communities, that are legitimized and made available to foreign language students.

Traditionally imagined identities – nationalist paradigms in the foreign language classroom

Foreign language classrooms are unique within education in that their stated purpose is to draw students into meaningful engagement with Others (Holliday, 2011; Joseph, 2004), conventionally understood as a nationalized Other. The national paradigm within foreign language education rests 'on the fundamental and normally implicit conception of the national constituting the natural frame of reference for language teaching' (Risager, 2007: 191). One studies, for example, *the* Japanese language in order to engage in *the* Japanese culture. Within this well-established nation = standard language = culture equation (Sayer and Meadows, 2012; Woolard and Schieffelin, 1994), classroom practices aim to orchestrate for students encounters with native speakers of the national language in imagined locations embedded within a national culture.

We should note that in using the terms 'nationalism' and 'nationalist' here we are not referring to the conventional usage as a pejorative reference to an extreme position (e.g. nationalist right-wing groups). Rather, we use these terms to refer to an ideology (Billig, 1995; Silverstein, 2001) that circulates in discourse (Calhoun, 1998) to organize human communities into purportedly discrete and individually unique national units which are best governed by a political state that reflects the national essence – hence the term 'nation-state' (see Gellner, 2006; Kedourie, 1993). Nationalism is an endemic condition (Billig, 1995), and the fact it is difficult to imagine a world without nation-states is testament to its success in shaping commonsense. In this chapter, we use the term 'nationalist' to refer to any organizational practice that takes the nation-state unit as the fundamental unit of imagined belonging in a conscious effort on our part to recognize nationalism not as *the* unavoidable reality but as one form of constructed reality for which alternative organizational realities are imaginable, available and for the purposes of foreign language education, more relevant.

The advantages that the nationalist paradigm offers education stakeholders are easy to recognize. First and foremost, nationalism helps clarify the content to be covered in a foreign language course. National units of analysis appear to offer a relatively stable basis for the evaluation of student competence, but not because the linguistic forms that count as standard are always easy to identify or constantly stable. Rather, the processes that standardize national varieties and maintain the privileged status of their speakers also actively delineate the boundaries between what counts and what does not (Benesch, 1993). These well-guarded boundaries dramatically reduce the need for educators, curriculum designers and students to openly debate or question which forms will be taught and learned in the foreign language classroom (Chatsis et al., 2013).

Likewise, the form of community valorized by nationalism is an imagined national culture, exemplified in the practices of the idealized native-speaker subject. This idealization further reduces the complexity of course content, as those forms of human organization lying outside nationalist legitimacy can be downgraded to subcultures and dialects. For example, residents of the Osaka metropolitan region in Japan may appear in foreign language curricula, but only as speakers of Kansai dialect (not language) who practice a unique culture subordinate to an overarching culture of Japan. In short, the presuppositions of internal coherence and external distinction afforded by nationalism draw instructors and students into simplified visions of social worlds that greatly reduce the complexity of information for which classroom participants need be responsible.

Nationalist treatments of language and culture, still de rigueur in foreign language classrooms, are now understood in anthropology and sociology as essentialist (Bucholtz and Hall, 2004; Hannerz, 1999; Holliday, 2011) because they ascribe attributes to individuals that ignore the dependency of any such attributes on interactions in context. Termed 'boundary fetishism' (Pieterse, 2004: 224 as cited in Dervin and Liddicoat, forthcoming), students and teachers alike seek out cultural and linguistic differences and explain them in terms of nationalist cultural attributes that are presupposed as static, timeless, and both deterministic and explanatory of an individual's values and practices (Guest, 2002). Such reductionist, monolithic portrayals of national cultures rule out legitimate discussion of the pervasive linguistic and cultural diversity present within any so-called national culture. Traditional foreign language textbooks and curricula lead students down predetermined identity paths, exposing them to a limited range of Othered communities, sanitized to fit within prevailing nationalist imaginings (Heinrich, 2005; Matsumoto and Okamoto, 2003; Shardakova and Pavlenko, 2004). All the while, what counts as appropriate tokens of a national standard language or features of a national culture remains a moving target, as the specifics of what counts are always negotiated in local contexts according to prevailing socio-political relations and variables of time, location and interlocutor.

Seen from this perspective, the weaknesses of the nation as the most salient unit of participation and imagined belonging becomes plain for all involved in the enterprise of foreign language education (Guest, 2002; Heinrich, 2005). Our best efforts to create and deliver standardized language curricula leave students unprepared for inevitable encounters with French speakers who do not fit the mould provided in French language textbooks. Students will undoubtedly encounter an individual who speaks Mandarin but not the particular variety used in the language classroom. They will unavoidably find that classroom resources are of little help in making sense of current linguistic usages in popular culture in Bahasa Indonesia. Such incongruencies raise deep questions concerning the appropriate endpoint for foreign language programmes, leading voices in applied linguistics to question the value of judging student success according to a native-speaker norm (Cole and Meadows, 2013; Cook, 2002; Davies, 2004; Firth and Wagner, 1997; Houghton and Rivers, 2013; Leung et al., 1997; Rampton, 1990), a social category that by definition will always lie beyond the foreign language learner's reach. These incongruencies thus highlight important issues of social equity that implicate foreign language education in the ongoing marginalization of stigmatized communities (see Holiday, 2011; Lippi-Green, 2011).

Extending from this critique, we propose that foreign language educators turn away from the nation as the basic unit of analysis. What foreign language students need instead is a foreign language programme that brings to the fore sociolinguistic diversity rather than burying it within standard/non-standard, authentic/inauthentic, pure/impure dichotomies. When foreign language educators place sociolinguistic diversity at the centre of attention, space is thus created for students and teachers to pursue multimembership in a wide range of communities as an instructional goal (Kachru, 1994; Kramsch, 2006). With this chapter, we propose that the communities of practice model holds potential as an alternative means for restructuring language classrooms to be highly relevant sites for training interculturally competent individuals to interact with Others in the complex, globalized world that sociolinguistic research and theory reveal. We turn now to the communities of practice model and how we envision its utility in the kind of restructuring we promote.

Communities of practice – a model for imagining multimembership

The term communities of practice is closely associated with situated learning theory (Lave and Wenger, 1991; Wenger, 1998) which defines learning primarily as a social endeavour that emerges in specific contexts of participation in a social world (Block, 2007b; Meyerhoff, 2011). A community of practice is a particular kind of social organization that exhibits three defining characteristics (Barton and Tusting, 2005; Meyerhoff, 2011; Wenger, 1998): A community of practice involves sustained direct interaction among members, or *mutual engagement*. Such regular engagement gives life to a shared set of meaning-making resources, or *shared repertoire*. Finally, members of the community of practice must recognize themselves as sharing a definable purpose to their practice, a *joint enterprise*. It is easy to see how such a definition can be easily applied to a foreign language classroom: students and instructors are mutually engaged in the joint enterprise of acquiring a new, shared repertoire (i.e. the target foreign language).

In accordance with poststructuralist theories of identity (Lin, 2008; Riley, 2007), and research and theory in the social sciences (Brubaker and Cooper, 2000; Bucholtz and Hall, 2004), community of practice models view identity not as a personal quality but as a negotiation that lies between the social and the individual: Identity is constituted in identification practices. This is a crucial shift away from traditional conceptualizations of identity – not as something we *have* but as something we *practice*. It is through *identification*, or 'the process through which modes of belonging become constitutive of our identities by creating bonds or distinctions in which we become invested' (Wenger, 1998: 191) that identity, as an aggregate of social practices, emerges within the community of practice model. In other words, it is in the negotiation by multiple individuals in multiple social configurations that people construct multimembership (Wenger, 2000) in many communities of practice.

To demonstrate how the community of practice model enables a more accurate, flexible and inclusive concept of identity for use in the foreign language classroom than the idealized one offered by traditional, nation-based approaches, we present two contrasting figures. In the traditional foreign language classroom

(Figure 6.1), the identities of classroom participants are idealized and conceived of as 'singulars' (Rampton, 2007). Curriculum and instruction generally assume that student identities are relatively uniform (represented in the figure as 'S') and that the only relevant identity for the instructor is a teacher identity ('T'). The typical foreign language classroom relies on another kind of idealization as well (i.e. the imagined, native speakers who will be their future interlocutors ('Y')). If students are presented with the possibility of taking on a new identity in the target language at all, this identity too is the singular, idealized, native-speaking national subject (also 'Y').

As current research in second language acquisition (SLA) has rendered these idealizations problematic, for example, by demonstrating how individuals' sociolinguistic trajectories and personal biographies are inseparable from their success or failure as language students (Harklau, 2000; Wortham, 2004), foreign language educators need a better model of identity. Foreign language classroom participants must engage with a concept of identity that more accurately reflects the complex reality of identity processes, that engages with the facts of the classroom participants' identities outside the classroom, and that prepares students for the complexities of sociolinguistic identities they will inevitably encounter should they have occasion to use their acquired language outside the classroom.

In Figure 6.2, we show how a concept of identity informed by community of practice represents the relevant complexity. In this revised model, the students' and teacher's identities are represented as complex (S^n and T^n, where the superscripted variables are to be read as $S^1 + S^2 + S^3 + \ldots S^n$), because students and teachers can perform multiple and shifting personae in the classroom. For example, sometimes students act as teachers, sometimes teachers act as counsellors, sometimes students act as peer mentors, and so on. The classroom environment is represented as permeable (using dotted lines) with arrows

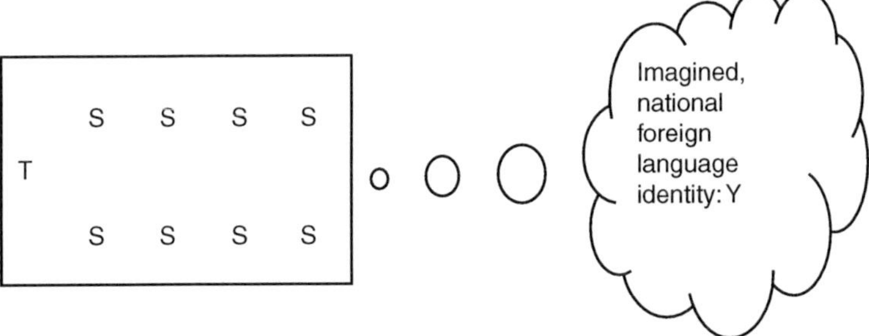

Figure 6.1 Idealized identity in traditional foreign language classroom

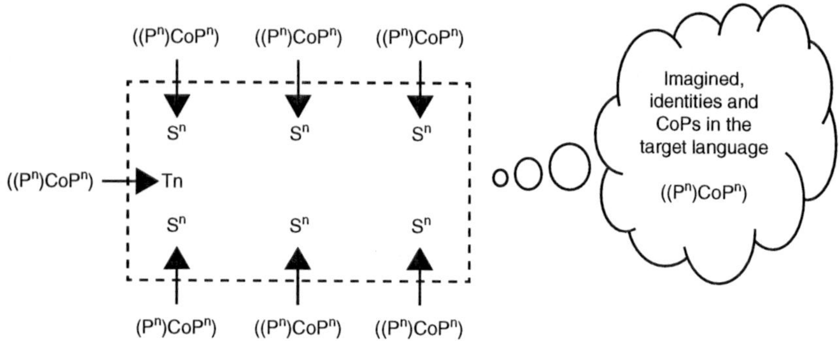

Figure 6.2 Multimemberships in foreign language classrooms informed by CoP

connecting the participants' classroom identities to their multiple identities outside of the classroom. The notation $((P^n)CoP^n)$ represents the multiple personae (P^n) that participants perform outside of the classroom within and across the multiple communities of practice (CoP^n) in which they participate. Notice that the imagined identities that become the students' targets in the language they are learning are also represented as $((P^n)CoP^n)$. This is because the shifting, complex nature of sociolinguistic identity, whether in a person's L1, L2 or Ln, is fundamentally the same.

We hope that this model will be useful to foreign language educators for two reasons. First, the community of practice model provides a metalinguistic lexicon for talking about both the identity repertoires that students bring to the classroom as well as the identity repertoires they will be expected to perform when engaging with Others in the target language. Second, the community of practice model provides the vocabulary and concepts for organizing and viewing the language classroom itself as its own community of practice, no different from the Other communities of practice to which the students already belong, thus tying together for students the classroom community and the Othered communities under study in that they both follow similar patterns of communal practice. This second point has two very important implications: First, if we can teach students to demonstrate metasemiotic awareness of the characteristics of their classroom community of practice, then we have provided them with the tools for being proactive agents in their performances (and their perceptions) of new identity repertoires in the target language. Second, such metasemiotic awareness has the potential to circumvent the limitations on the acquisition of identity repertoires that nationalist paradigms (inadvertently) promote.

We suggest that the concept of nation itself can be understood through a community of practice lens. When seen through this lens, nations become constellations of localized communities of practice, whose members align their local values and behaviours with those that are already valorized as representative of the nation by members of Other communities. Interestingly, Anderson (2006) places this at the centre of his theory of nationalism: It is the ability for individuals to visualize themselves as part of broad imagined communities that make it possible to reify nations. Viewing nations in this way means reinterpreting the endpoint of foreign language teaching. Students need no longer be restricted to imagining themselves into nationalist singulars but can be initiated into a diverse range of ways in which different communities come to identify with a nation. There are many ways of performing Americanness, Japaneseness, Germanness, and so on just as there are multiple ways of performing gender, for example. Currently, foreign language classrooms handle this reality by constructing a hierarchy that legitimizes some voices and ways of being while silencing others. But when national identities are understood as one type of identity resource available to specific communities of practice to act upon in specific contexts, classrooms are in position to recognize multiple legitimate repertoires of nationalist practice, legitimate in that each community necessarily realizes the nation in locally specific ways. From this perspective, instructors are in a position to explicitly recognize for and with students that what counts as national or standard in any particular context results from a socio-political struggle for authority and that such struggles are common to human communities.

Implications for practice in foreign language classrooms

In the previous section, we have argued that the community of practice model provides the analytical framework for students to understand how social communities work and thus how to engage successfully with diverse, unfamiliar situations. By way of constructed scenario, we develop in this section a vision for the direct application of the model we propose in the interest of equipping foreign language students for navigating an interconnected global landscape with increasing potential for identity positioning of Self and Other.

The community of practice model as an organizing framework

Welcome to Anytown High School, located in Anytown in the state of New Jersey, USA, where the foreign language Japanese programme has recently been reconstructed according to the communities of practice model. Visitors to the school now observe a series of changes that distinguish this programme from others in the district. Immediately noticeable is the fact that the name of the programme has shifted from *Japanese language* to *Japanese languages*. Instructors have been trained to present students with a variety of Japanese repertoires and to encourage students to explore specific Japanese communities, akin to Holliday's (1999) 'small cultures'. They alert students in the programme from the beginning that this focus on plurality will in turn create opportunities for them to explore multiple identity options indexed by different varieties of 'Japanese'.

During the first class meetings, instructors employ the three-part description of the community of practice model (i.e. mutual engagement, shared repertoire, joint enterprise) in describing their own classrooms as well as the sociolinguistic groups they will be studying. Rather than presenting lists of national attributes, prescribed values, practices and products, student training involves learning to look for the specific discursive practices that constitute how individual community members engage with one another, how they recognize a shared repertoire for meaning making, and demonstrate a shared alignment to a particular enterprise. Teachers and students identify and reflect on how this is done in their own classroom and then use the communities of practice model to describe the range of communities that they are engaged with outside the classroom.

The components of identity as introduced by the model (i.e. engagement, alignment and imagination (Wenger, 2000)), function as a metalanguage for students and teachers in their discussions. For example, teachers talk about alignment processes and encourage students to first reflect on when and how they align their voices with others'. Then, they identify alignment processes in the written/audiovisual texts that they have thus far been introduced to in the class. This training is simultaneous with explicit instruction in particular Japanese linguistic forms, so these discussions proceed in a combination of repertoires in the shared L1 (English) and the target L2 (Japanese).

In Figure 6.3, we show how the model we presented in Figure 6.2 can be used to visualize identification processes in the foreign language classroom. Using the scenario we have given about the Japanese Languages programme at Anytown High School (AHS), we use the model to represent identification in a particular classroom at a particular moment in time. Here, four students, Cindy, Rolando, Effy and Oscar, are engaged in the classroom community of practice with the teacher, Mr Malone. Participants are performing unique personae (notated in superscript next to their names) and drawing on other personae they perform

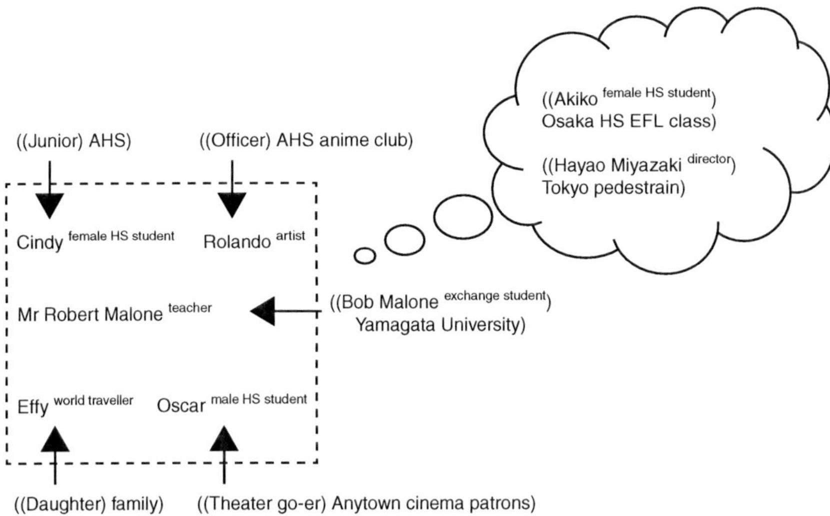

Figure 6.3 Reimagining identification in Anytown High School's Japanese languages classroom

in a community of practice outside the classroom (linked with arrows). In the immediate discourse context is a discussion about linguistic choices given varied interlocutors in imagined future encounters with speakers of Japanese. Previous course sessions have alerted students to some of the structural and functional differences between formal and informal communication, male and female speech, and Osaka and Tokyo dialects. The class has imagined two potential Japanese interlocutors: Akiko, a female high school student of the students' same age and status learning English as a foreign language, and the world-renowned director of anime films, Hayao Miyzaki.

The imagined interlocutors, speakers of different repertoires of Japanese, are also envisioned as members of a particular community of practice at the moment of imagined interaction: Akiko as a foreign language classroom participant and Miyazaki as pedestrian on the streets of Tokyo. In the discussion, each participant draws on the personae and communities of practice they think are relevant to successfully communicating with one of these imagined Japanese speakers. For example, Rolando draws on his membership in the high school anime club and his own artistic endeavours to select the forms of Japanese he would employ in a chance meeting with Miyazaki in Tokyo, and Mr Malone draws on his prior experiences as an exchange student at Yamagata University where the standard Japanese forms he had acquired in a foreign language classroom in the United States did not always suffice for making friends with other young people who spoke other than standard dialects in casual speech.

Two things about Figure 6.3 are important to note. First, this figure represents identification at one moment in time. In the very next stretch of discourse, one or more of the participants may select and perform a different persona acquired from membership in another community of practice. This constant availability of such personae was notated in Figure 6.2 as $((P^n)COP^n)$. Second, the performance and perception of these varied personae are indexed by the linguistic forms being used (Agha, 1993; Eckert and Wenger, 2005; Hill, 2002; Ochs, 1999). In other words, identification processes are inextricably linked to the availability and recognizability of multiple linguistic repertoires. Foreign language classrooms that embrace this fact inevitably, we argue, provide students with the ability to interact with a wider range of interlocutors than one where one 'standard' variety alone is presented. In doing so, such a foreign language environment has the potential to more adequately prepare students to interact with and adapt to others in target language varieties.

Teacher-directed practice

Because the *Japanese Languages* programme at Anytown does not take nationalist claims to authority at face value, instructors can construct the classroom as legitimate space to explore any language varieties actually being used by real people in real situations. Teachers introduce into the classroom a rich diversity of Japanese-speaking communities. Some might include Japanese spoken by conventionally legitimated communities: middle-class professionals, pop music celebrities, professional academics, college-bound youth. They may also include communities that struggle for legitimacy in the nationalist paradigm: Japanese spoken by people living in the Aomori region of Japan, Japanese spoken by Japanese-Americans living in Los Angeles, Japanese spoken by Japanese-Brazilians, Japanese spoken by fellow students of Japanese in Thailand, and so on.

The teacher encourages students to use and try a variety of voices tied to notions of Japanese either through role-play or through comparative analysis (see Cole, 2007). Students and teachers engage with linguistic and cultural diversity through the collaborative analysis of written/audiovisual texts. They also make generous use of online technologies to establish dialogue with Japanese-speaking communities at a geographic distance from them. Finally, teachers do not neglect the linguistic and cultural diversity that can be found in their own community directly outside the classroom (see Ruiz, 1984). They invite guest speakers from the community who speak varieties of Japanese; they arrange class excursions to areas of the local community where Japanese varieties can be heard.

This programme of course does not abandon the current Japanese standard variety, but it requires teachers to frame it as one variety of Japanese with particular significance in particular situations. In an academic classroom, it may serve a student as an alignment device to the teacher and to the wider institution of formal schooling. Conversely, standard variety could serve as a distancing device in rural regions of Tochigi if used by one local resident to another. This is to say that teachers in this programme begin with the facts of linguistic variability rather than an idealized notion of language. They make explicit that standard is one of many varieties acceptable in the foreign language classroom space. In our experience, if teachers do not openly state this, students will tend to assume the status quo, that standard is spoken here and everything else is out. Furthermore, teachers at Anytown High School regularly reflect on their own linguistic choices in the classroom and are transparent with their students about them when they can.

In facilitating the acquisition of accurate and useful models of identity for foreign language students, instructors and programme designers can be transparent about how they locate the cultural capital and the linguistic capital they associate with the linguistic forms they present to students. When they do so, teachers and programme designers take a radically inclusive approach to the notion of target language/culture that they promote for their classroom to create discursive spaces for critically analysing familiar arguments that mark communities as (in) authentic, (il)legitimate and (un)worthy. Such a self-consciously inclusive stance models for students a view of social landscapes that accords with contemporary sociolinguistic research, and it entails highlighting descriptiveness over prescriptiveness. Teachers are explicit about when they are being descriptive and when they are being prescriptive, and help students to recognize the difference.

For example, when comparing varieties of Japanese, the teacher does not characterize one variety as missing something that another has (thus implying deficiency and hierarchy). Instead, they state that the two varieties differ in identifiable ways. Students are encouraged to ask the naïve questions about languages and cultural categories and to build up from observation the discursive explanations that come to function as common sense understandings and analytical stereotypes so they can be discussed critically (e.g. 'How might someone from the Kanto region of Japan say this?, How would a speaker from the Kansai region pronounce it? How do media sources typically characterize and evaluate these differences? What evidence do we have of how speakers of these varieties evaluate their own language variety?'). The central idea behind the instructors' approach is that exposing students to a range of Japanese repertoires enables students to formulate complex perspectives that make broad generalizations, characteristic of the nationalist paradigm, difficult to accept at face value (Houghton, 2008; Liddicoat, 2006).

Student-directed practice

Not unlike theme-based instructional models, teachers in this programme build into the curriculum segments of unplanned space, which allows classroom participants to negotiate specific content as the course moves forward. Each course in the programme allows space for students to conduct exploratory projects of student-selected communities. After some teacher-led preparation, students launch into their own individual explorations of unfamiliar communities that they are interested in learning more about. Teachers provide necessary scaffolding instruction where needed as well as orchestrate valuable whole-class discussions where perspectives are compared and contrasted at specific points during the course.

Across the programme of study, students are encouraged to carry out exploratory projects in a range of communities, thus allowing them to complete the programme with direct experience in the diversity of Japanese language varieties and identities. They call upon the familiar tools of ethnography (e.g. participant observation, interview, surveys, etc.) but within the time and logistical constraints of their class semester. Students collect data on their selected communities inside and outside of class time. Specifically, they glean what information they can on how a community realizes mutual engagement, joint enterprise and shared repertoire. In many cases, they need to use online resources to collect data on their selected community. Some students will capitalize on Japanese-speaking communities in their immediate geographic area.

The value of investigating a range of communities is that it enriches the class content with empirically based diversity. With all of this diversity at hand, students and teachers can then compare and contrast the conditions for each of the communities. Students may work in groups to critically reflect on how different versions of Japanese language differ grammatically and socially. Students may then report back to the class, not unlike sociolinguists do following data collection and analysis. This empirical engagement with cultural and linguistic diversity is integrated at all levels of the foreign language programme beginning with the introductory courses of the programme. Rather than engaging with a sanitized, limited version of the foreign language, students' work in the language classroom builds on abilities they already use in navigating cultural and linguistic complexities in their everyday lives.

Summary

We hope that this constructed scenario illustrates the potential for practical application of the community of practice model to foreign language programmes and that we have, in the process, successfully argued for its potential to give shape to foreign language programmes that reinstate the linguistic and cultural diversity that conventional classrooms under the nationalist paradigm trivialize. With the community of practice as the basic unit of belonging, the language classroom is open to engaging with multiple kinds of identity work that speakers do with language because the focus is no longer on grand nationalist communities. Throughout the programme, essentialized identities are rejected and cultural homogeneity and linguistic stasis are not assumed. Students are encouraged to investigate when the target community speaks X language variety and practices X national identity. Doing so prepares students for seeing nations not as a given, but as a specific way to belong in specific contexts. Compared to the nationalist paradigm, which sharply bisects identities as authentic/inauthentic and languages as correct/incorrect, the approach we promote is self-consciously inclusive.

Conclusion

Our aim in this chapter has been to build on prior research within SLA studies that have problematized the nationalist paradigm for foreign language teaching by promoting the community of practice model as an alternative framework for imagining identity or group membership. As described here, our vision of foreign language classrooms under the community of practice model holds promise for cultivating in students a sophisticated understanding of the relationship between language/culture/identity, one that is consistent with current sociolinguistic theory. This sophisticated understanding entails a heightened awareness of Self/Other identity processes. Using the community of practice framework as an analytical guide we believe students can emerge from their foreign language programme with an established intercultural competence (Dervin, 2011; Liddicoat, 2006; Risager, 2007), or an ability to read any unfamiliar situation – regardless of the particulars – in order to gain entry into Other communities. Ultimately, we speculate that the analytical tools offered by the community of practice model will enable students not only to gain knowledge about particular communities, but to acquire the skills needed to perform legitimate identities that can participate in the negotiation of what counts as legitimate knowledge for community membership (Eckert and Wenger, 2005). We have argued that when foreign language learning is framed as increasing participation in unfamiliar communities of practice (as opposed to national cultures) and when students are given the analytical tools included in the community of practice model that foreign language education becomes exceedingly relevant in our complex, globalized world.

Without the kind of reimagining we have proposed here, we question the relevance of foreign language classrooms to the education of today's global citizens. The reality of contemporary communication and transportation technologies generates a proliferation of various kinds of potential for identity positioning as discourses travel ever more quickly across temporal and geographic space in an interconnected global network where boundaries are elusive and the Other is in close proximity (Risager, 2007). From this perspective, the clear boundaries of nationalism appear quaint and naively utopian in their simplicity. This is not to say that nationalism as an ideology is going away, because it is not. Nationalism remains a functional component of social reality today providing important organizational resources. However, the relevance of the nationalist paradigm is shifting with the new realities and practices of social communities in a global world. Language classrooms must catch up to this new reality. Without a legitimate way to conceptualize identity in complex ways, foreign language classrooms remain a hall of mirrors where student lifeworlds are uncritically reflected back to them (Swaffar, 2006) as are their preconceived views of the lifeworlds of Others who speak different languages. The corrective alternative, we have argued, is to construct language classrooms as laboratories for cultivating ways of seeing the world in diverse terms.

7

The Foreign Language Imagined Learning Community: Developing Identity and Increasing Foreign Language Investment

John W. Schwieter

Introduction

In a world of growing class size and the considerable use of electronic devices, teachers may find it increasingly challenging to actively engage their students. Indeed, for many educators, the days where adequate time could be manageably devoted to a learning which revolved around interaction have nearly evaporated. This is particularly dangerous for foreign language classes where interaction and output in the target language is critical for language acquisition (Swain, 2005). This chapter will discuss the importance of learning communities – groups of language learners who share common goals and are actively engaged in learning together from each other – in the foreign language classroom, how they underpin a genuine investment in learning, and how they foster the exploration of learners' identities in a foreign language (throughout this chapter, the terms 'learning community' and 'imagined community' are used interchangeably).

Although exceptions certainly exist, the majority of studies in sociocultural theory have been primarily rooted in the Vygotskian framework (Lantolf, 2000; Lantolf and Aljaafreh, 1995; Vygotsky, 1978). The steadfast dedication to this well-developed theoretical framework, however, may have also led to the neglect of the true interdisciplinary nature of the field (Norton, 2006). In fact, recent studies have shown fruitful results when exploring imagined learning communities in the foreign language classroom (Anderson, 2006; Kanno and Norton, 2003; Norton, 2000, 2001; Pavlenko and Norton, 2007). Not only do these learning communities foster heightened classroom dynamics through an interactive working environment, they also involve teamwork and the conceptualization of foreign language identity (Llamas and Watt, 2010; Pavlenko and Norton, 2007; Riley, 2007; and see Norton and Toohey, 2011 for a review), intercultural competence (Byram, 2008) and sensitivity to intercultural dynamics in work environments (Guilherme, 2002; Guilherme et al., 2010). Furthermore, they maximize a learner's 'investment' in foreign language learning – a notion that goes well beyond the construct of motivation (Norton, 1997, 2000; Norton Peirce, 1995).

One way these theoretical notions have been applied to the foreign language classroom is through a magazine project (Schwieter, 2010). As such, this chapter reports on a semester-long (i.e. 12 week), workshop-style foreign language writing project in which learners formed small imagined learning communities (i.e. editorial advisory boards) to create professional and marketable magazines. This methodology promoted active learning and interactive engagement among students (MacGregor et al., 2000; Yazedjian and Boyle Kolkhorst, 2007) and provided opportunity for learners to play a crucial and a distinctive role in the success of the project, their own learning and the learning development of their peers. During the project, learners submitted essays to their editorial advisory board. Essays passed through four revise and resubmit stages during which learners received feedback and debriefing sessions on how to improve their writing. Quantitative analyses from this teaching practice previously have shown both short-term and long-term development in foreign language writing (Schwieter, 2010).

At the conclusion of the project, open-ended questions were posed to the learners to gather their reactions on working in the learning communities, their investment in their language development and the success of the project, and their role as a team member. The results were analysed using a content analysis approach (Marshall and Rossman, 2010; Schwieter, 2011) and are discussed through social psychological perspectives, emphasizing how imagined learning communities in foreign language classrooms help increase investment in learning and foster creative expression of identity. Implications for how foreign language teaching and learning can be informed by work done on imagined communities are highlighted.

Background

In the field of second language acquisition (SLA), the construct *identity* has been defined as 'how a person understands [one's] relationship to the world, how that relationship is constructed across time and space, and how the person understands possibilities for the future' (Norton, 2000: 5), and speakers often do this in more than one language in everyday life. Within this definition, communication can be seen as a negotiation and renegotiation of a sense of Self as it relates to the larger speech community, leading to a reorganization and development of identity. In addition, definitions of identity may also assign importance to the ways in which relationships are socially constructed within specific relationships of power (see, for example, work on gender and sexuality by Davis and Skilton-Sylvester, 2004; King, 2008; Nelson, 2009). Current research addressing identity in SLA (see recent volumes including Blackledge and Creese, 2010; Block, 2003, 2007b; Clarke, 2008; Day, 2002; Heller, 2007; Higgins, 2009; Kanno, 2003, 2008; Kubota and Lin, 2009; Lin, 2007; Miller, 2003; Nelson, 2009; Niño-Murcia and Rothman, 2008; Norton, 2000; Norton and Toohey, 2004; Pavlenko and Blackledge, 2004; Potowski, 2007; Schwieter and Kunert, 2012; Toohey, 2000; Tsui and Tollefson, 2007) has identified several key intersections including two that will be described in more detail below: investment (Norton, 2000; Norton Peirce, 1995; Norton and Gao, 2008; Norton, 2010; Norton and McKinney, 2011; Norton and Toohey, 2011) and imagined communities (Anderson, 2006; Kanno and Norton, 2003; Norton, 2001, 2010; Norton and McKinney, 2011; Norton and Toohey, 2011; Pavlenko and Norton, 2007; Shoaib and Dörnyei, 2005).

Identity and investment

One area of SLA that has received much attention is the role that motivation plays in language learning. Pioneering work of Gardner and Lambert (1959, 1972) first introduced the distinction between instrumental motivation and integrative motivation where the former refers to the desire to learn a foreign language for utilitarian purposes and the latter relates to the desire to learn a language to successfully integrate with the target speech community. Gardner and Lambert's work on motivation in SLA has sparked a wealth of valuable research (Black, 2013; Crookes and Schmidt, 1991; Dörnyei, 2001; Dörnyei and Schmidt, 2001; Oxford and Shearin, 1994; and see MacIntyre et al., 2010 for a recent review) from psychological (Dörnyei, 2001; Reeve, 2009), social (Block, 2003) and sociopsychological (Pavlenko, 2002) perspectives (see Dewaele, 2009 for a review of approaches). Indeed, although the construct of motivation continues to be refined after more than half a century (Gardner, 2009), some researchers criticize its failure to recognize the intricate role that power and identity play in SLA (Norton and McKinney, 2011). Additional criticisms suggest that the construct of motivation has been erroneously interpreted as simply an individual character trait so that learners who have more difficulty with SLA are viewed to just not be that committed to it (Norton, 2010).

Bourdieu's (1977, 1991) work on *cultural capital* has had a significant impact on constructing an alternative to studying motivation. According to Bourdieu, cultural capital refers to the knowledge that characterizes different groups and classes of people with relation to specific sets of social forms, each having differential social values. Building on the idea of cultural capital, Norton Peirce (1995) introduced the idea of *investment* which 'signals the socially and historically constructed relationship of learners to the target language, and their often ambivalent desire to learn and practice it' (Norton, 2010: 75). One's investment in learning a foreign language goes far beyond the boundaries of motivation to imply that when foreign language learners invest in their language learning, they do so with the realization that they will gain cultural capital along with a range of symbolic and material resources (Norton and McKinney, 2011). For many foreign language learners, being a bilingual implies adding value to their cultural capital credentials.

One outcome of investment in SLA is that as learners engage in meaningful discourse in the foreign language, they not only communicate information, but they are constantly reorganizing their identity and how they see themselves fitting in a bilingual world. As cultural capital increases during this social revisioning process, foreign language learners are able to 'reassess themselves and their desires for the future' (Norton and Toohey, 2011: 420). Empirical support for the construct of investment has been demonstrated in many studies (Cummins, 2006; Duff, 2002; Haneda, 2005; Kinginger, 2004; McKay and Wong, 1996; Norton and Gao, 2008; Pittaway, 2004; Potowski, 2007; Rivers, 2012a; Skilton-Sylvester, 2002) including in a special issue of the *Journal of Asian Pacific Communication* (Arkoudis and Davison, 2008). In all, investment – as opposed to motivation – within a sociological framework makes meaningful relationships between foreign language learners' desires to acquire the target language and their dynamically changing identities.

Identity and imagined communities

How does investment ultimately transcend to the foreign language classroom and how do foreign language learners meet the needs of their changing identity? Many researchers argue that an extension of interest in identity and investment involves imagined communities. Imagined communities (Anderson, 2006; Kanno and Norton, 2003; Norton, 2001, 2010; Norton and McKinney, 2011; Norton and Toohey, 2011; Pavlenko and Norton, 2007; Shoaib and Dörnyei, 2005) refer to groups of people in the target language community who are not necessarily accessible to foreign language learners physically but through the power of the imagination. Such a community provides the possibility for a greater range of identity options for foreign language learners in the future. Furthermore, because imagined communities provide a situation in which foreign language learners may take on imagined identities, their investment to foreign language learning should be interpreted within this imagined community (Norton, 2010). As such, when foreign language learners invest in their language learning, they do so with the realization that they will gain cultural capital along with a range of symbolic and material resources.

The imagined community in the foreign language classroom allows learners to focus on the future and in particular, on whom they will become with regard to where the foreign language will take them. It is no doubt easier for teachers to envision these communities by encouraging learners to participate in imagined foreign language-learning communities that emulate their expectations in the target language community. Consequently, when learners participate in these imagined communities, language educators are provided with the opportunity to explore how foreign language learners' representations of those communities affect learning experiences and language development. Numerous studies have demonstrated positive results for language learning with imagined communities and SLA (Carroll et al., 2008; Dagenais et al., 2009; Kanno, 2008; Kanno and Norton, 2003; Kendrick and Jones, 2008; Murphey et al., 2005; Silberstein, 2003) and their impact on pedagogical practices has also gained interest among researchers.

Implications for the foreign language classroom

In the classroom setting, the notion of imagined communities and how they can effectively put into practice the theories discussed above has also been of recent research interest (Cummins and Early, 2011; Norton, 2010; Norton and Toohey, 2011; Pavlenko and Norton, 2007). In order for teaching practices to best align with these theories, foreign language educators should make every attempt to enhance the range of possibilities available to learners and to contemplate an imaginative assessment of what is possible, as well as a critical assessment of what is desirable by teachers and learners (McKinney and Norton, 2008).

Semester-length projects in which foreign language learners can reflect on their own development over an extended period of time, and explore an identity which they may aspire to have in their foreign language are especially useful pedagogical tools, especially when coupled with scaffolding techniques. Content-based foreign language courses that are geared towards certain professions such as health care or business may particularly benefit from imagined communities in which learners, for instance, create and launch a new health-related or business venture. This approach not only fosters a real-life element to foreign language learning, but also opens the door for learners to fully explore their changing identities and increase their investment in foreign language learning.

Some researchers have identified that foreign language writing classes may hold a special place for imagined communities to flourish. According to Pavlenko (2001), engaging in the process of writing appears to set up uniquely safe spaces in which new identities can be imagined and options in the foreign language can be explored by students as they write. Cummins (2006) has classified identity as a powerful construct in SLA, and illustrative examples are outlined in Cummins and Early's (2011) report of the Multiliteracies Project (www.multiliteracies.ca). This project reaches out to teachers, school boards, unions and non-government literacy organizations to explore innovative classroom writing practices that widen the identity options for learners in multilingual schools in Vancouver, Toronto and Montreal. Learner-created case studies which Cummins calls 'identity texts' in Cummins and Early (2011), and on the website, provide strong evidence for the effectiveness of the project and teaching approaches. However, even with the best intentions, the way in which foreign language educators envisioned the teaching practice often does not reflect what actually unfolds in the classroom (Lee, 2008; Ramanathan, 2005) or what actually takes shape in the school at large (Kanno, 2003). While these researchers show the challenges of imagined communities, many other studies have shown fruitful results around the world (Clemente and Higgins, 2008; Cummins, 2006; Kendrick and Jones, 2008; Kendrick et al., 2006; Stein, 2008; Wallace, 2003; and see Norton and Toohey, 2004 for a review).

Present study

The present study builds on Schwieter (2010) by fostering the creation of and participation in imagined communities of practice in a foreign language classroom. Using Vygotsky's (1978, 1986) sociocultural framework of the zone of proximal development (ZPD) and scaffolding writing (Bodrova and Leong,

1995, 1996), Schwieter reported on a foreign language writing project in which advanced language learners created professional magazines for an authentic audience. In the project, learners authored four essays which went through four peer- and instructor-edited stages of scaffolding. After each stage, ratings were given by the editors who also facilitated feedback debriefing sessions (Lidz, 1991). Significant writing development was revealed both within and across the four essays, and the results supported the notion that the use of scaffolding writing techniques and feedback debriefing sessions within learners' ZPDs can effectively develop writing skills in foreign language learning when contextualized through a writing workshop involving the creation of a professional magazine. The sections that follow report on this pedagogical approach, which has been designed in the context of the theories discussed above regarding identity, investment and imagined communities.

Participants

Twenty-four English first language learners of Spanish (as a foreign language) participated in a project in which they created a magazine at a large public university in an English-speaking region of Ontario, Canada. All participants were currently enrolled in an advanced Spanish composition course titled *Spanish Stylistics and Professional Writing* and were either specializing in Spanish as their undergraduate major or minor. The average age of these language learners was 21. For the sake of anonymity, each participant is referred to as P1, P2, P3, and so on.

Participants were asked to rate their own specific language abilities (reading, writing, speaking, listening comprehensive and overall rating) in their first language and foreign language to estimate the degree of proficiency differences and dominance levels. Table 7.1 reports the self-ratings of several language abilities and the results of pair-wised t-tests (t scores and p values). As can be seen, significant differences were reported between each first language and foreign language ability.

The magazine project

In this semester-length workshop-style project (Barnard, 2002; Schwieter, 2010), participants formed and simulated three imagined *editorial advisory boards* consisting of eight foreign language learners. Within each community, learners nominated and elected one another to take on the following identities:

Table 7.1 Self-ratings of language abilities

	First language (English)	**Foreign language (Spanish)**	*T*	*p*
Reading	7.8	6.7	4.12	< 0.001
Writing	7.3	5.9	2.71	< 0.01
Speaking	7.5	6.0	3.69	< 0.001
Listening	7.7	6.6	3.56	< 0.001
Overall rating	7.6	6.3	3.60	< 0.001

Note: Self-ratings were given on an eight-point Likert scale ranging from 1 (not fluent) to 8 (very fluent).

three textual editors, three stylistic editors, one associate editor in charge of visual design and formatting of the magazine, one associate editor in charge of administrative operations and one editor-in-chief. Once the roles were established by the learners, the instructor individually met with each of the students to ensure that they understood the critical role they would play in the project. These meetings also served as a training session on peer-editing (Lidz, 1991). All interaction was in the foreign language. A visualization of the structure for three editorial boards can be seen in Figure 7.1.

The task at hand for each editorial board was to create a professional and marketable magazine, completely authored and edited by the members of its board. During the entire project, each student authored and submitted four essays, and served as an editor for their colleagues' essays to employ a repeated scaffolding effect (Schwieter, 2010). Figure 7.2 shows the editorial cycle in which each essay was first peer-edited by a textual editor whose main purpose was to improve the grammar and clarity of the text. Following this, the textual editors reviewed the corrected essay with the author at a feedback and debriefing session during the next class meeting. The authors then made the recommended changes and resubmitted the revised version to a stylistic editor in their editorial board. The same procedure as the textual stage was repeated, and essays were debriefed and revised a second time. One final revise and resubmit stage was conducted with the associate editors and editor-in-chief before submitting the essays to the course instructor, who also participated as the final editor of the essay and publisher. The instructor also took on a facilitative role throughout the project.

The four-stage editorial process and magazine project in general has been shown to significantly improve foreign language learners' writing abilities 'in a procedural, linear manner in which editorial scaffolding techniques seek to improve the: 1) language/grammar; 2) style; and 3) fine-tuning of

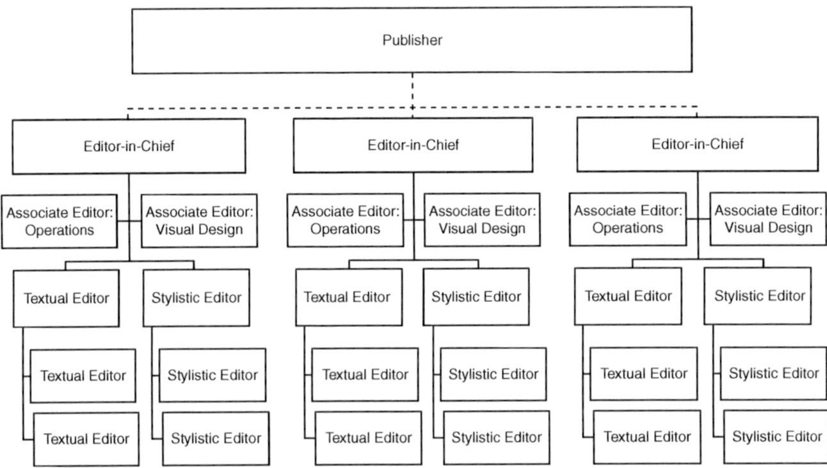

Figure 7.1 Editorial board structure for the magazine project

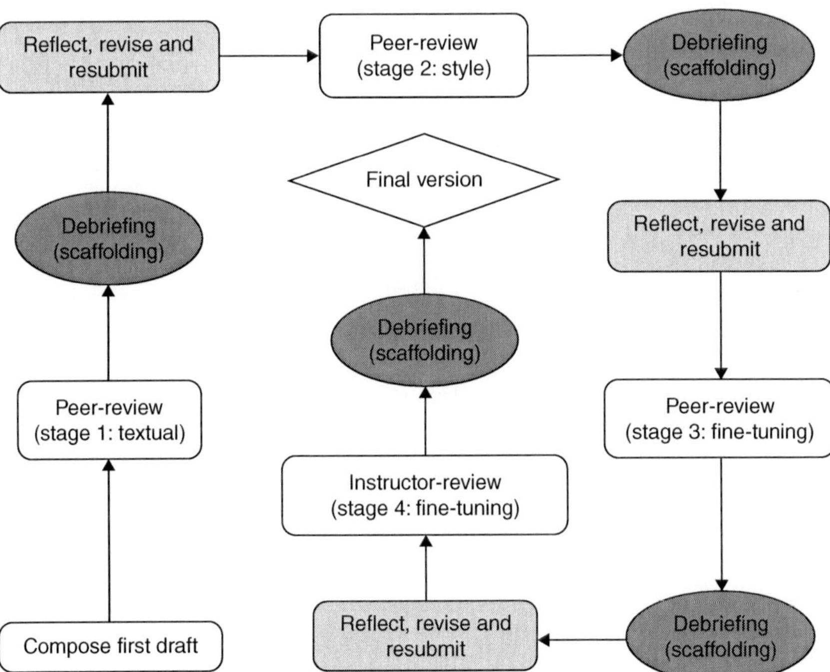

Figure 7.2 Editorial stages of scaffolding writing for each essay
Adapted from Schwieter, 2010

each essay' (Schwieter, 2010: 36). Indeed, writing development emerged not only with subsequent revisions of a single essay (see Figure 7.3), but also between the four essays (see Figure 7.4) revealing a linear, continuous writing development throughout the semester as measured by a 30-point rubric (Schwieter, 2010).

At the conclusion of the project, the editorial boards presented the magazines in their finalized and print-ready form to the university community. Electronic versions of the magazines are also uploaded on the course website (www.wlu.ca/arts/jschwieter/sp451). Although Schwieter's (2010) study investigated the extent of writing development, the magazine project allows for several research questions to be probed that look at its effectiveness through a sociological lens focusing on identity and investment. From a broad perspective, the project documented in this chapter seeks to understand the extent to which learners invest in their foreign language writing development and explore foreign language identities by participating in an imagined learning community.

Method

A case study approach consisting of open-ended interviews was employed in this study. By using this method, the researcher was able to clear up or

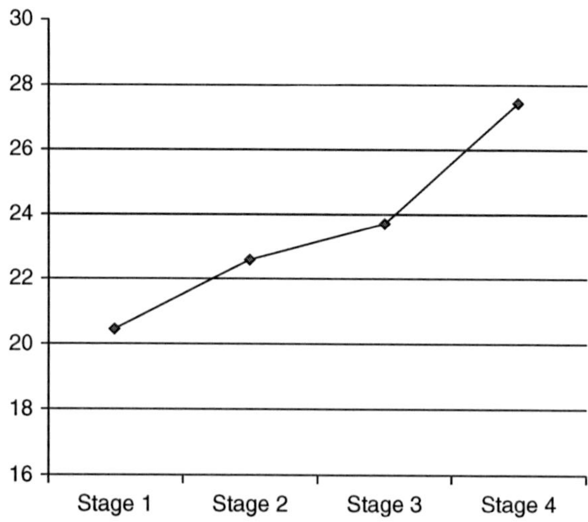

Figure 7.3 Writing development within essays
Adapted from Schwieter, 2010
Note: Each editorial stage was evaluated on a 30-point scale.

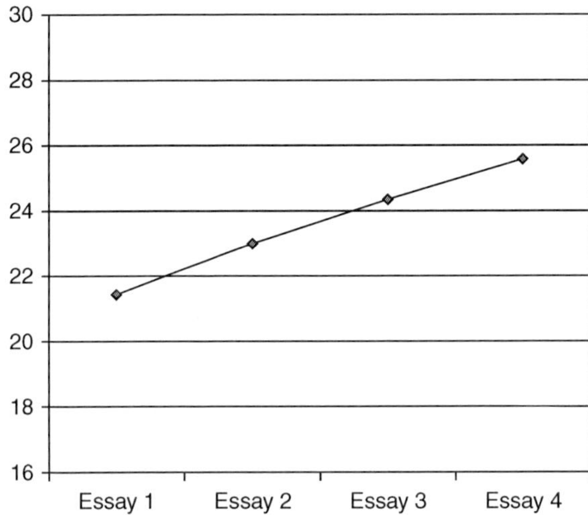

Figure 7.4 Writing development between essays
Adapted from Schwieter, 2010
Note: Each editorial stage was evaluated on a 30-point scale.

elaborate on any issues brought up in the interview, place less of a burden on the participants and promote rapport with them (Fraenkel et al., 2012). The researcher interviewed participants individually and they were given the choice to conduct the interviews in English or Spanish. The researcher transcribed all interviews and employed a content analysis approach, a holistic and systematic method of examining forms of communication to document patterns objectively (Marshall and Rossman, 2010). A content analysis approach also is effectively used in analysing narrative texts, such as transcribed interviews, as a means to clarify how respondents view and understand certain issues (Schwieter, 2011). As such, all interviews were transcribed, and then analysed thematically and coded according to the themes of the research questions in this study (see Schwieter for more information on data coding and analysis using this methodology).

Discussion of results

The open-ended questions were intended to explore learners' feelings on working in the magazine project as an imagined community and on the extent to which they were invested in learning. Several factors supporting the effectiveness of the project emerged from the responses that directly speak to issues of identity, investment and imagined communities. Shown below are the six open-ended interview questions/prompts.

- Discuss your crucial role as a team member in the project. How did this affect the success of your project?
- Discuss your reactions to working in a small learning community and the team effort that you went through to foster this environment.
- Discuss how this project affected your investment in your own language development.
- Discuss how this projected affected your investment in the language development of your peers.
- How does this project (and social environment of working on this project) help you creatively display and/or explore yourself?
- Discuss other comments and thoughts that you may have about the project that have not been addressed in the previous questions.

Base upon the responses gathered, a summary of the main findings is shown below followed by a synthesized account reporting on the three main themes that emerged from the data analysis.

- Learners clearly defined their role and responsibilities in their imagined communities and how that impacted the entire learning experience.
- Learners valued their duties in the project, making language purposeful.
- Learners deemed the magazine project as a rich collaborative experience.
- Learners effectively worked with others in constructive and creative ways that fostered common learning objectives through teamwork.
- Learners were compelled to fully succeed in their own learning because they realized that one's learning depended on another's learning.
- Learners viewed the imagined learning community as an emulation of a real-life project in which they could very well participate in the workforce in the near future.
- Learners appreciated the opportunity for freedom of creative expression where they were truly encouraged to explore foreign language identity.
- Learners reported that their self-exploration flourished because they were required to compose creative advertisements that interested them most.

Identity as team members with common learning objectives

It was clear from the interviews that learners were very much able to clearly define their role and responsibilities in their imagined communities and how that impacted the entire learning experience. P4, an editor-in-chief of one magazine, defined her professional role in the project:

> I was editor-in-chief for my group. I was responsible for organizing deadlines, delegating tasks to other members, and assuring that everyone was on the same page and understood their responsibilities. I also made decisions regarding the general direction of the magazine and reviewed article themes and ideas for my peers.

This precise definition was mirrored by P16:

> My position was Associate Editor: Operations. I kept record of the editorial board's decisions and took minutes and attendance at each meeting and then I send these out to the group to make sure that anyone who missed the meeting was informed. I also set up a special e-mail account that everyone in the group would have access to and where we could store and edit all of our magazine pages and administration files. There were a lot of details to keep track of which is why I think my position was important in our magazine's success.

The fact that learners valued the importance of their duties in the project made language purposeful which consequently led to its ultimate success. For instance, because of the value that P1 had assigned her role in the project, she remarked, 'my role is crucial for the magazine as a whole, allowing the content and quality to be as professional as possible' while P9 reflected:

> My critical role as a team member in the project was to make sure all of our essays adhered to the correct style of writing and I feel that my role affected the success of the project because we all realized that if all of us as a team does our role well, in the end the magazine would be a total success and with hardly any errors.

Perhaps P17 summarized the collaborative richness of the learning experience best when she stated, 'everyone had an essential role which made us very connected and dependent on one another. None of us wanted to let each other down, let alone let ourselves done.'

In their imagined identities, learners were challenged to meet the needs of working with others in constructive and creative ways as they worked to achieve the same learning objectives. Learners were very much aware of the importance of teamwork as revealed in P14's comment:

> I actually really enjoyed working as a team in this project because I think that is what made this experience more fun. Every one of the group members contributed something different to the project. I was happy to work with other classmates and it is interesting to see how you have to trust and rely on other people.

Other participants felt similarly: P1 stated, 'I believe that all the work done in the group was very productive and everyone had a clear understanding of what the ultimate goal was' and P7 commented, 'being a small group was certainly a great advantage, it was easier to share our opinions, frustrations, ideas, and points of view.' Finally, P18 remarked, 'I think it was great working in teams and creating something as practical as a magazine because you can picture yourself actually taking about these topics and doing these things in real life.' From the interviews, it was apparent that working as team members of imagined communities was viewed as an asset.

Investment in foreign language learning of self and others

The magazine project required constant interaction between, and reliance upon, team members in the imagined community. The fact that learners needed to rely on team members' completion of one editorial stage in order to proceed to the next editorial stage (as seen in the cyclic visualization in Figure 7.2) seemed to be a leading factor in increasing investment in foreign language learning. P5 commented that:

> The magazine project has affected my investment in my own language development because it has enabled me to write creatively, which is something that I had not done before. At first it was a bit difficult to get accustomed to, but with practice and revision by my peers, I grew more comfortable.

While P8 stated:

> It made me want to improve my language so that the other editors didn't have as much work to do. All of a sudden people other than the teacher and I were seeing what I was writing and this mattered to me.

For other learners, the magazine project increased their investment in foreign language learning simply because they saw it as an emulation of a real-life project in which they could very much participate in the workforce in the near future. P18 verified this by stating, 'in this project, I could actually see myself talking about these topics in real life and practicing what tenses to use.' Later in her interview, P18 added, 'I think that this [the magazine project] is exactly how it is in the working world where even though you are working with others, you are still given a certain amount of freedom.' P22 echoed these comments by saying, 'I think that the project is great preparation for the work force: in our group, many times our opinions differed and we would end up having to vote on many editorial referendums to come to a decision.'

Imagined communities and creative expression

In general, learners' reactions to working in imagined communities were overwhelmingly positive. P4 said that:

> This learning environment has helped me work better with others. I tend to prefer to work alone and avoid group work, especially after coming to university, but this project helps student understand what working in a group dynamic is really like, for an extended period of time. It is much more realistic (in terms of being similar to a work setting) than any other group project I have done in university.

P21 also stated that, 'working with individuals that we chose helped us to develop an honest environment in a professional yet comfortable manner to create an incredible production of a magazine.'

Perhaps one of the biggest benefits to working in the imagined communities in the magazine project, according to the participants, was the opportunity for freedom of creative expression where they were truly encouraged to explore their foreign language identity. Instead of the instructor prescribing the topics of the essays (or even the general theme of the magazine), it was left up to each editorial board to design the entire magazine's contents including the topics explored. These effects can be seen in P6's comment, 'being able to choose four essays on topics that personally interest me have really helped in developing my creative side and being able to explore my interests in a more academic way' and in P10's reaction, 'it was good to have the chance to write articles on subjects I was interested in researching'. Another participant, P17, echoed these comments:

> Instead of having to write essays about texts that I sometimes don't find particularly interesting, I was able to express myself creatively through writing about anything that interested me and this somehow fit together and complimented the work done by my peers; all of our work melding nicely together.

In addition to the actual essays that appeared in the magazines, creative expression – and for the sake of this chapter, exploration of identity – also flourished in the advertisements that learners authored and strategically placed throughout the magazines (i.e. many times in places that visually reflected and complemented surrounding essays). As with all professional magazines, learners were required to design original ads with creative slogans that display a marketable play on words. P1 reported that:

> Advertising in a different language is difficult, because many things do not translate properly. It was one of the greatest struggles that I had, but I believe that it let me explore the possibilities of being creative with a language. In my opinion, if one can master the creativity with words, and form different puns or 'play on words' in a different language, this is a huge step forward towards mastery of the language. I believe this let me explore the creativity I have with the language, and learning new ways to express myself.

P19 added:

> This project definitely helped me explore my creativity because I had the opportunity to create advertisements and work with language constructions that I had never used before for any class. I was able to make up my own ideas and incorporate them into my work.

Conclusion

This chapter has reported on a magazine project that provided the pedagogical foundation to foster a learning community in an advanced foreign language composition class, which effectively increased investment in learning and the opportunity to shape and explore foreign language identities. Overall, the responses from the interviews suggest general support for a magazine project that – when contextualized in the form of an imagined community – can allow learners to explore identities, while increasing their investment in their language learning. As Norton and Toohey (2011) note, future studies should consider implementing teaching approaches such as the one discussed in this chapter that allow learners to have a larger range of identity positions that foster the greatest opportunity for social engagement and interaction (imagined and/or real). An essential balance should be found regarding the diversity of identity positions available for learners to adopt, while additionally pinpointing those positions that do not lend themselves to this exploration and instead appear to silence or marginalize learners. This chapter and its discussion of identity, investment and imagined communities in SLA suggest that by putting into practice teaching approaches such as the magazine project, foreign language educators can reimagine their classrooms as places of possibilities for learners that are adaptable to a variety of backgrounds, investments and aspirations for the future.

8

Foreign Language Motivation and Social Identity Development

Lou Harvey

Introduction

This chapter reports on a qualitative study investigating the identity development of three foreign language learners of English in the United Kingdom, as manifested through the factors influencing their English-language learning motivation. Taking as an entry point Dörnyei's (1994: 275) claim that foreign language motivation is always contingent upon '*who* learns *what* languages *where*', the investigation expands on previous social psychological work in the field of foreign language motivation to foreground social identities through the individual voice, experience, perception and agency which have been insufficiently explored in previous motivation studies. The primary research question addressed is – How can the factors influencing foreign language learners' motivation be characterized, and how do they contribute to the development of their social identities?

To address this question, a critical review of recent language-learning motivation theory is undertaken, arguing that although the importance of identity has been acknowledged, conceptualizations of motivation have not yet sufficiently explored the various identities learners may be negotiating in their sociocultural contexts, and the ways in which these identities and contexts may engender or inhibit motivation. I then report on the semi-structured interviews conducted with three English foreign language learners in order to gain insight into how previous language-learning experiences and attitudes contribute to their motivation for learning English. The findings offer insights into the complexity of factors, choices and experiences which combine to motivate an individual, underscoring the intriguing complexity of the influence of social identity on learner motivation, and highlighting the ongoing development of these learners' social identities.

Identity in foreign language learning motivation research

Integrativeness and the L2 motivational self system

My own research into foreign language-learning motivation has taken as a starting point Gardner's (Gardner and Lambert, 1959) enduring and influential integrative/instrumental model of motivation. *Instrumentality* describes utilitarian goals and potential pragmatic gains of learning a foreign language, such as career advancement or a higher salary; *integrativeness* implies a form of psychological and/or emotional identification with the target language community (Gardner, 2001). Thus, the model recognizes social identity as playing a role in motivation and language learning. However, recent criticisms of integrativeness have centred around the role of English in globalization processes, its growing dominance as an international language and its consequent association with many more cultures than those of its 'native' speakers (Canagarajah, 2006). This carries implications for identity in that for learners of English, there is no specific 'owner' of the language with which they may identify (Dörnyei, 2009). As Ryan (2009) describes it, Gardner's model is a static characterization of language communities; but an undefined, vague and geographically disparate foreign language community may be more motivating than a fixed and readily identifiable community, as learners may more readily perceive the possibility of full, legitimate membership of that community. Therefore, access to a wider variety of social identities may become possible for learners of English. This is reflected in Dörnyei's (2009) L2 motivational self system developed as a result of these problematizations of integrativeness and increasing interest in the concept of possible selves in the field of psychology (Markus, 2006). Various studies have indicated that English learners across the world may identify not with native speakers of the language, but with an imagined future English-speaking self able to access, participate in and thereby co-create a global sociocultural context offering diverse and wide-ranging opportunities (Lamb, 2007, 2009). In Dörnyei's L2 motivational self system, it is these perceptions of their future selves which structure learners' motivation. As English potentially offers such a variety of opportunities for so many, a future English-speaking self becomes increasingly possible, moving ever-closer to reality from imagination. The L2 motivational self system, therefore, begins more clearly to connect motivation with imagination, identity and possibilities for participation in different sociocultural contexts.

However, in its uncritical foregrounding of the self, and along with cognitive approaches to motivation such as self-efficacy and self-determination theory

(Bandura, 1999; Ryan and Deci, 2000), the L2 motivational self system is limited by what Martin (2004) cites as the commonly individualistic, oversimplified and unproblematic conceptions of self cited in psychology, education and other Western cultural fields. Possible selves theory, and by extension, the L2 motivational self system, fail to consider the broader historical and sociocultural context through which the person as thinking agent is formed. This politically detached self is of little educational value, if education is understood to include the forming of persons able to critically negotiate their identities within a complex world and, importantly, capable of influencing that world (Martin, 2004). Learners are constantly negotiating an individual and collective identity, and in order to understand this process and its intersection with motivation, it is necessary to recognize learners as critically engaged and situated individuals. I would argue that a move away from an unproblematic, apolitical conception of selfhood is necessary in order to gain any meaningful insight into not only what motivates learners and why, but also into how the sociocultural context engenders or inhibits motivation. While recognizing that this is far from culturally unproblematic and grounded in a Western individualist viewpoint, there is unfortunately not enough space in this chapter to engage in a more culturally decentred debate; for the time being, this can only be considered an avenue for further research, albeit an important one.

Motivation as imagination, identity, participation

These fundamentally individualistic approaches also fail to account for how motivation may be socially negotiated and constructed. The aim of much foreign language-learning motivation research has been to uncover generalizable rules and laws to explain how context affects motivation, rather than to explore the person as a multifaceted, self-reflective, intentional agent, socially situated, constituting and constituted by their own context in a dynamic and complex relationship (Lantolf and Pavlenko, 2001). Individual agency is shaped, and facilitated or constrained, by context – but context is multifaceted and dynamic, meaning individual agency is always unpredictable and has the potential to overcome social disadvantage (Lamb, 2009; Reay, 2004).

Kormos and Csizér (2007) draw attention to the impact of intercultural contact on language-learning motivation, pointing out that one of the main aims of learning languages is to communicate with members of other cultures, that these interactions provide occasions for developing foreign language competence, and that intercultural encounters can have an important influence on attitudes to the foreign language, its speakers and its culture. Culhane (2003) points out that learners' attitudes towards the target language, based on previous learning experience and knowledge of the associated culture, will influence not only their motivation for learning English per se but also their motivation for contact with English speakers, directly influencing their use of the first language and the foreign language in the target culture. Culhane suggests that the greater the positive social and psychological contact with the foreign language community, the greater the likelihood of successful foreign language acquisition. Although still based in the social psychological paradigm, this acknowledges that motivation is constructed in interaction, shaped by and shaping the identities that emerge in intersubjective relations (Bucholtz and Hall, 2010). The 'Otherness' encountered in intercultural contact leads to the construction of an intersubjective reality, in which identities 'acquire social meaning in relation to other available identity positions and other social actors . . . [i]dentities emerge only in relation to other identities within the contingent framework of interaction' (Bucholtz and Hall, 2010: 23–5). This has been developed further by the (as yet few) qualitative studies of motivation, which draw on concepts of *imagination* and *participation* to characterize the social construction of motivation.

Yashima (2009) points out that learners' visions of using English are often visions of participation in an imagined English-speaking international community. Such an imagined community could be best understood within the context of learners' investment (Norton, 2000), where motivation is the investment learners make with the potential of increasing their cultural capital, self-concept and identity. Furthermore, as language is used to socially construct an image or identity (Benwell and Stokoe, 2006; Block, 2007b; Joseph, 2004, 2010), identity cannot be separated from the context of the social interaction in which it originates, and if 'to the extent that we have individual voices, we fashion them out of the social voices already available to us' (Lemke, 1995: 24–5), foreign language learners may potentially be lacking the opportunity to fashion the voices of the communities in which they wish to participate. Thus, they cannot move from legitimate peripheral participation to full participation (Lave and Wenger, 1991), and are thereby constrained in the transformation of their identities (Ushioda, 2009); the identity to which a learner aspires may not be recognized by other community members, or may create tension with their aspirations towards membership of other communities. As a result, individual learners may not be granted 'legitimate' speaker status, and may have unequal access to social and cultural resources (Lamb, 2009; see also Norton, 2000). In this way, agency is constrained externally 'by the framework of opportunities and constraints the person finds [oneself] in', and internally by 'an internalised framework that makes some possibilities inconceivable, others improbable, and a limited range acceptable' (Reay, 2004: 435). This sociocultural, constructivist understanding of motivation provides insight into the community, relational dimensions of motivation not facilitated by social psychological and cognitive approaches.

Participants

Participant 1: Alima

Alima (pseudonym) was a 28-year-old female learner from a city in North-East Iraq, on a Cambridge First Certificate in English course at the college where I was teaching at the time of the study. Alima contacted me via email telling me she would be willing to be interviewed after I had introduced myself to her class and asked for volunteer participants. Alima was a student in Iraq, and did not work in the United Kingdom. She had lived in the United Kingdom with her husband for eighteen months and was planning to stay for anything up to another five years, depending on the progress of her education – they are, however, definitely planning to return and did not wish to live in the United Kingdom permanently.

Participant 2: Mariona

Mariona (real name requested) was a 28-year-old Catalan/Spanish bilingual woman from Girona, near Barcelona, Spain. Mariona had been in the United Kingdom since January 2008, and did not know when she would return to Spain. She worked as a freelance photographer and graphic designer in Manchester, as she had in Barcelona. She took private, one-to-one English lessons with me in order to improve her general English. Mariona and I were friends, having met within a shared social circle.

Participant 3: Katka

My third participant was Katka (pseudonym), a 45-year-old woman from Bratislava, Slovakia. I met Katka through a mutual friend who had suggested she might be willing to be interviewed. Katka had been in the United Kingdom since

April 2006, and was planning to leave within a few years. She worked as a carer at a convent in Manchester; in Bratislava, she was a manager at the city transport offices. She was an ESOL Level 1 (mid-intermediate level) learner at a college of further education.

Methodology and design

Although motivation research has traditionally espoused quantitative methods, there now appears to be a move towards recognition of the value of a qualitative approach in the motivation literature. According to Ushioda (2001), qualitative methods may be particularly appropriate to explore conceptions of motivation as dynamic, multifaceted and rooted in a particular context. It was thus felt that a semi-structured interview would be most appropriate to allow participants to recount their experiences according to their own narratives and contexts, and develop and expand their answers in as much detail as they wanted to, without feeling 'penned' into a prestructured format. Based on a roughly chronological language-learning history, the following questions were asked:

- When you were growing up, did you hear much English spoken?
- How did you feel about the English language?
- What were your attitudes towards what you perceived as British culture?
- How old were you when you started learning English?
- Did you choose to learn English? Why? If not, how did you feel about that?
- Did you enjoy your English lessons?
- Can you tell me about your experiences speaking English in your country?
- When and why did you come to the UK?
- Can you tell me about your experiences speaking English in the UK?
- Have your experiences with people in the UK affected your motivation for learning English?

Interviews were transcribed and inductively analysed (following Richards, 2003). From the analysis, the following four themes were derived, representing the factors influencing these learners' motivation:

- Learner perception of choice and agency in the learning of English
- Nature of English contact experience
- Perceived benefits of learning English
- Wish to participate in UK social life

These four themes are now exemplified and explained in relation to the development of the participants' social identities, using their voices to assist in the telling of their stories.

Findings

Learner perception of choice and agency in the learning of English

Alima

Perhaps the most striking theme from Alima's interview was the lack of choice she felt she had been given, particularly in terms of the *big decisions* in her life. However, it became clear that in her home context she did not always mind this lack of choice, and was sometimes glad of the choices which had been made for her:

A: Actually my family they say to me you have to complete university master and PhD, and – I want, I thought I had to learn English, there's no choice and I didn't interest in English.

L: How did you feel about that, about not really having a choice?

A: Actually, it wouldn't matter for me. I found it interesting to know another language.

Although Alima had perhaps not begun to develop a particular English-speaking social identity due to a lack of interest in English, the beginnings of a foreign language identity are suggested by her claim that she 'found it interesting to know another language'. When she came to the United Kingdom, however, her agency was restricted by the legal–educational requirements of English-language providers, which became a significant source of distress and frustration for her, constraining her ability to participate in social life and to develop a socially recognized identity through English:

A: When I came to [this college in Manchester] they didn't accept me because they say you must live in England more than a year that we accept you . . . [I felt] embarrassed, actually. I cried very much because I don't want to stay at home and do nothing.

Mariona

Mariona's motivation for learning English and subsequent social identity development through English was closely linked to her own sense of agency and choice. Her father made the original choice for her to learn English when she was 12, a decision which was not to her liking. However, she became more motivated when she began to make her own choices:

L: So you didn't feel particularly motivated [to learn English]?

M: No, not until I was – eighteen, maybe? Seventeen, eighteen. I started to the university, and yeah, I was feeling more interested in English, because I wanted to go abroad . . . I had the option, and I chose.

Mariona's motivation increased when she started to enjoy English lessons, and when she decided she wanted to go abroad, a choice influenced only by her own desire and not by external pressures. This, coupled with her sense of agency, enhanced her motivation; an English-speaking social identity began to develop alongside her sense of agency.

Katka

Agency as a theme in Katka's interview manifests itself rather differently, in her perception of English as potentially offering freedom and opportunities which would not otherwise be available to her. Growing up under a Communist regime in Soviet Czechoslovakia (which collapsed when she was 26), she felt lucky to have had the chance to learn English, the good fortune of which she claimed to be very aware. Katka too was learning English by parental dictate, but did not appear to have chafed against this dictate as Mariona did. As Katka's parents had both been to university and mixed with the Bratislava intelligentsia, she associated English with sophistication and elitism, representing an international outlook in times of political oppression; thus, she seemed to have accepted her parents' decision for her to learn English in the knowledge that it would give her access to their world:

K: I told you my parents were the Slovak intelligence, yeah? And this society in Slovakia, it was small group. It was group people with the higher education . . . and my parents had many many friends . . .

Thus, Katka was able to begin to develop a social identity through a perception of English as offering participation in an elite community within her world, and an imagined international community outside her world, seeing English as an investment with the potential of increasing her cultural capital and developing an 'international' identity (Norton, 2000).

Nature of English contact experience

Alima

Alima's contact experiences with both the English language and its speakers also appear to have had an impact on her motivation for learning English. She talked about positive contact experiences with English in Iraq:

> A: My older brother had a lot of English friends – actually not English, from Turkey, from Syria, and they don't speak our language when they visit us, they know English – we communicate in English, and it is very interesting for me.

Although she did not explicitly state that these experiences had a positive impact on her motivation, she did mention that they contributed to her interest and enjoyment; thus, insofar as interest and enjoyment lead to motivation, it could be said that her motivation was being constructed through these intercultural social interactions. She had no negative learning experiences, although being unable to attend English lessons for a year after she came to the United Kingdom led to a temporary deprivation of contact experience, which significantly affected her emotional state (as evident in the quotation above). All contact with English speakers in the United Kingdom was negative; the only positive contact experience in the United Kingdom was with her Iraqi friends. However, she looked for positive contact with British people, and hoped that improving her English would also lead to an improved social life:

> A: [In the UK] sometimes when I'm go to shopping, to hospital, anywhere there's someone – they hate us, they act as they hate foreign people – not everyone, but I feel embarrassed why they hate us.
>
> A: When I came to England – actually now I haven't got any English friends . . . [My friends are] from Iraq. I don't work, and I came to college, and nothing else.
>
> L: So the fact that you don't have any British friends, has this affected your motivation for learning English?
>
> A: Not really – maybe a little, because I watch TV very much, and listen to news, and I want to move into Huddersfield in one month, I want to find a volunteer work to help older people, maybe with their shopping, I think it's better . . . I want to improve my English and have English friends, and maybe when I go back to my country visit them in UK or visit them to Iraq.

The deprivation of contact and negative contact experiences seemed to have constrained social identity development for Alima in the United Kingdom; her identity was unrecognized, and remained so as long as she lacked opportunities to develop her own voice within the communities she wished to be part of.

Mariona

In Mariona's learning experience, there was an important social factor which appears to have simultaneously stimulated her motivation and been reinforced by it. She acknowledged that she may have enjoyed early English lessons because of the people rather than the language or the lessons per se. Her first experiences with native English speakers, during her visits to Detroit and London, were very positive; she had no negative experiences and experienced no particular cultural difficulties, although she recognized that Detroit offered a more limited opportunity because she was with her sister and speaking more Catalan than English. As her English improved, she discovered more contact opportunities, and often felt that her lower level of language was one of the limits on her opportunities for contact. Her feeling that social contact was her greatest motivation was perhaps most clearly manifested in her recognition that social immersion has highlighted, and continues to highlight to her, the limitations of her own English:

> M: I had this interest [in learning English] before going to America, I was more interested in English. But yeah, maybe if you are going a foreign – well, you know, you stay in an English-spoken country, then yeah, you feel even more motivated. Yeah, because you realise that you have to understand even more than you think you do. I feel, I always feel that during my English lessons – I mean, well, it's not useless, but – when you really start to learn English, it's when you're going to live in the foreign country, not during the lessons. The first time when I went to Detroit I realised that my English lessons was quite useless, because okay, I understand nothing, I've been studying many years.

Katka

Katka, as well as having positive associations of education, knowledge, sophistication and freedom with English, also had positive contact experiences with English as she was growing up, reinforcing her associations with the language. Her contact experiences in the United Kingdom were similarly positive; she enjoyed her English classes and classmates, and her contact experience outside her English class had also, for the most part, been positive. Furthermore, her social contact in the United Kingdom consisted almost exclusively of British people, although she seemed a little hesitant to express her attitude towards her friends and her definitions of friendship and social life, and made no mention of its influence on her motivation in the way that Mariona did:

K: [My social life is] Only British. Only, only. When I moved in the convent I changed the town, I changed society, and I spend my time with only British people.
L: Have you found it easy to make friends?
K: It is hard to say who is friend. I have many acquaintance – many many – but friends, well – I think, I want . . . and I work at night. Five nights I work, and when I want to go to school and improve my English, I am very happy that I can work at the weekend, and the night.

Perceived benefits of learning English

Alima

Alima evinced an interest in learning languages, and in other nationalities and cultures. Her interest appeared to be intrinsic, owing to her background and upbringing, and was an important aspect of her social identity in Iraq:

A: [My second language is] Arabic, and when I was a child my family sent me to a private school – in Iraq we call it college, not school, and in that school we learned Turkish, and because our city is near to Iran, we went to Iran many times, I know Persian also. I find something very interesting in country foreign.

However, the harsh practical realities of her situation in Iraq may also have been an influence, as she explicitly mentioned the attractiveness of the United Kingdom in light of the Iraq war of the 2000s. Alima's primary motivation, however, was towards her goal of education. The emphasis placed on English in her Iraqi education was clear, as was the importance she attached to education in general:

A: My family they say to me you have to complete university master and PhD . . . I want to do CAE and start my education – they ask me to have CAE certificate.
L: So your motivation, from when you started English, was always education.
A: Yeah. Education and language learning – not just English, but language.

Thus, insofar as her education is part of her social identity, learning and speaking English also appeared to be part of the construction of this identity. However, she only mentioned her educational ambitions with regard to her family, rather than to herself; her goal of attaining the Certificate in Advanced English (CAE) indicated a specific educational ambition she held for herself, but this appeared to be a stepping stone towards achieving her wider educational goals, or perhaps her family's goals for her, rather than an end in itself.

Mariona

A major opportunity English offered to Mariona was that of travel, which was clearly very important to her. She decided when she went to university that she wanted to go abroad and chose to learn English in the knowledge that it would help her achieve this, and she actively took the travel opportunities offered to her by participating in the ERASMUS scheme at both of her universities. Her travel experiences also became progressively more positive, particularly as regards her use of English; she enjoyed her first visit to Manchester even more than her previous visit to London, which was likewise a more positive language experience than Detroit, and she chose to return to Manchester in 2008 because she enjoyed her time here in 2005 so much. She described her Detroit experience thus:

> M: It was positive to – yeah, to know all about there, and yeah, to – it was my first big travel, and – yeah, it was positive. I think it's always positive to travel.

Mariona, then, developed a strong social identity through her desire for travel and the opportunities for social participation this offered her, as facilitated by learning and speaking English, and substantially enhancing her motivation towards this learning.

Katka

Katka and her family's perception of English being associated with freedom appears at least in part to be based on considerations of education and future opportunity; if English cannot offer a physical and political freedom, then it may at least offer an intellectual freedom. She acknowledged that her reasons for coming to the United Kingdom were at least partly to improve her job opportunities in Slovakia:

> K: [I came to the UK for] Two reasons: first it was my improve English, because I would like to change my job, and second to improve my stammer, because I still have little stammer, and now it is 'nevermind' good.
>
> L: So you didn't come here for economic reasons? You have a good job in Slovakia . . .

> K: It was in last place . . . Many many people have these reasons like first. And I thought we, in Slovakia, we will have next year like second country of Eastern Europe, because Slovak economy is very fast growing. And I am very proud, for sure, because we had very hard life, and I am very happy that almost twenty years after revolution more and more people are satisfied with life. It is very well, very good.

Although her reasons are economic only insofar as she wanted to change her job in Slovakia, she acknowledged (as above) that many Slovaks come to the United Kingdom for the more overtly economic purpose of earning money to send home, though this was not such an important consideration for her. She thus sets herself apart somewhat from this trend in her country; through her early development of a social identity through English based on investment in an imagined international community and the opportunities associated with it, she saw herself as being motivated and equipped to improve her own life in Slovakia through the use of English.

Wish to participate in UK social life

Alima

Alima, in contrast to Katka and Mariona, did not really mix socially with English speakers and had a very strong motivation towards the particular goal of furthering her education. She seemingly felt an absence of social interaction in general, having a very limited social circle and no British friends. She felt that improving her English would correct this, as demonstrated in the *Nature of English contact experience* section. Although Alima was not content with her situation, she was perhaps accepting of her circumstances, or likely to assume responsibility for them herself. She tended to blame not having as many friends as she would like on her level of English, rather than attributing it to any negative attitudes or cultural differences. She stated that her lack of British social life had not much affected her motivation because she did not see it as her only means of social participation; if she couldn't work or socialize, she could do volunteer work instead:

> A: When I came to England – actually now I haven't got any English friends . . . [My friends are] from Iraq. I don't work, and I came to college, and nothing else.
>
> L: So the fact that you don't have any British friends, has this affected your motivation for learning English?

A: Not really – maybe a little, because I watch TV very much, and listen to news, and I want to move into Huddersfield in one month, I want to find a volunteer work to help older people, maybe with their shopping, I think it's better . . . I want to improve my English and have English friends, and maybe when I go back to my country visit them in UK or visit them to Iraq.

In Alima's case, then, a lack of a strong social identity connected to English may have facilitated her motivation to overcome the problems she faced. Because her motivation to learn was so strongly associated with education, she didn't feel constrained by the need to participate socially in a particular way, and as a result she was perhaps able to recognize a wider array of opportunities for such participation.

Mariona

Mariona was frustrated by the difference between learning in the first language and foreign language contexts, and the awareness it brought of the disparity between her proficiency and that of native speakers:

M: [I'm having English lessons now] 'Cause I feel quite frustrated sometimes that I cannot talk as much as I'd like. I can do it but – it tooks [*sic*] ages for me, and – I don't know. I don't feel I have a good English. I'd like to be more spontaneous – I used to be more spontaneous, yeah? And a lot of times here, I want to say something, and it's just like yeah, it doesn't matter, it's all the same, like, never mind . . . And I want to understand more what all my friends are talking about, because sometimes we are here all together, talking, chatting, and – yeah, I just disconnect because I cannot follow everything and sometimes I disconnect and I'm here, maybe, but – I'm like not.

Mariona's sense of herself as a social participant, as formed through her previous travel and participation experiences, was constrained for her by her level of language as she felt that this particular social identity had not being recognized; her motivation to improve was driven by this urge to participate more fully and to be recognized as a participant.

Katka

Katka, too, was motivated by her wish to participate in UK social life. Like Mariona, Katka was very aware of the difference between using English in a classroom context in her own country and using it in an English-speaking context, and this too was a source of frustration. She compared her frustration at being unable to express herself as fully as she would like to with regressing back to childhood:

> K: I'm not satisfied with my English, because at home when I am spoke about foreign situations, I am now not able to express exact what I want to say. It is hard for me, of course, of course – you [indicating me] have very higher level of English, and if you change your life from one day you would speak like five years old child, it was hard. You have knowledge about life, about work, about many many things, and now you have few words what you can have. It is hard, it is hard. Now I have very different words I can understand and I am able to say.

Katka also had a desire to have her social identity as an adult with a variety of experience and many things to say recognized through English; she felt that her level of language was a constraint upon this recognition, and was thus motivated to improve.

Discussion

Factors influencing motivation and the development of social identities

Learner perception of choice and agency in the learning of English

Although clearly couched in very different cultural contexts, this was an important theme for both Mariona and Katka. Both participants' stories illustrate facilitations of and constraints upon their agency which have shaped their social identities, which in turn facilitate or constrain their agency. In Mariona's case, when able to make the choice to learn for herself, she was able to begin to develop a social identity as an international traveller which motivated her to learn; for Katka, her social awareness of having been offered a choice available only to a privileged few in her country was highly motivating, and spurred her on in her desire to participate in this elite community and the wider imagined English-speaking community. Overall, Mariona, Katka's parents, and Katka herself, saw English as a personal tool for social action with which they could forge a place in the world, making language use for them an act of agency (Bucholtz and Hall, 2010; Reay, 2004).

Alima, in contrast, indicated a striking lack of choice. Although she was aware of this, she did not appear to mind, sometimes even seeming glad of the choices which had been made for her. This indicates that choice and agency may also be culturally contingent, as it may be that a lack of choice in the immediate term is unlikely to foster a strong motivation in a European context; in other contexts it may have a very different effect. However, she was more painfully aware of the constraints on her agency in the United Kingdom, where even a language-learner identity was denied by her college's refusal to accept her as a student. Thus, she was unable to gain access to a form of social participation she particularly desired, depriving her of a potential community which might have offered her resources for fashioning a voice of her own (Lemke, 1995; see also Lave and Wenger, 1991), and was constrained in the development of her identity (Ushioda, 2009).

Nature of English contact experience

Mariona's contact experience facilitated the development of, and consistently reinforced, her social identity and her motivation for learning English. Mariona exemplifies Culhane's (2003) theory of contact motivation: she developed an enhanced exploration motivation, and her social experiences over the years have led to greater foreign language contact, higher foreign language use and increased foreign language friendships (Culhane, 2003). For Katka, contact appeared to be a less encouraging motivational factor than for Mariona, but it certainly contributed to her continuing social identity development, particularly through the contact she experienced in Slovakia and the real and imagined communities to which it gave her access.

As discussed in the section *Learner perception of choice and agency in the learning of English*, Alima's social identity development was constrained in the United Kingdom. In particular, social contact experience in the United Kingdom had a direct impact on her social identity. Alima, again in contrast to the other two interviewees, experienced negative attitudes to a far greater extent. Ethnic background may have played a role here – Mariona and Katka are white Europeans who dressed in common European high street fashions and are less obviously foreign in appearance, whereas Alima was a Kurdish Muslim who wore *hijab*. Thus, there was a more visually obvious 'Otherness' which may make her a more likely target for inappropriate treatment or abuse, and affected her desired level of engagement with speakers of English, or with whom she perceived as British people. As a result, Alima felt distanced from what she perceived as the English-speaking community while also wanting to be part of it at the same time. She therefore had to negotiate conflicting feelings regarding her social identity and its development. Alima saw her English lessons as a social outlet, clearly because she had almost no other opportunities to form social networks. It may be, then, that negative or very limited contact experience affects the type or amount of value ascribed to, or personal investment put into, English lessons (Norton, 2000). Furthermore, I suggest that her motivation to further her education was so strong that other issues become peripheral – she perhaps prioritized the English language over engagement with its speakers, and so although she would have liked to make friends, it seemed to be less important to her than to Katka and Mariona.

Perceived benefits of learning English

Alima was multilingual and had a lively interest in other languages and cultures, and one of her reasons for wanting to make friends in the United Kingdom is that they could visit her in Iraq when she returned, in a kind of cultural exchange. However, her education was her main goal. For Mariona, although she extended her social and employment opportunities by learning English and living in the United Kingdom, it seems that these were secondary advantages compared to what she considered to be her most important opportunity, the chance to travel. Learning English and living in the United Kingdom also offer her the opportunity to expand her social network; she realized how limited her opportunities for contact were when she had a lower level of English, and hoped that learning English again now would offer further social opportunities. Katka's opportunities likewise arose from her background and circumstances, in spite of as well as because of them. Katka's chief motivation for learning English was that she could change her job in Bratislava; this was the main opportunity English could offer her now. I would argue that Katka, in her desire to return to and remain in Slovakia with a better level of English and improved job prospects, was displaying a form of identification with her own country and the global English-speaking community. She was learning English in order to ultimately partake in the growth of her country, and may have wished to be perceived as a member of her own community who is competent in a language of wider communicative reach.

In sum, I suggest that all three women were motivated throughout their learning histories by the prospect of access to social, professional and academic opportunities they would not otherwise have been able to enjoy. As a result, these three learners were perhaps moving towards an enhanced level of participation in the communities of which they aspire to be part, be these in the United Kingdom, their home countries or globally.

Wish to participate in UK social life

Both Mariona and Katka felt frustrated with their level of English since they came to the United Kingdom, a frustration which sprang from their desire for increased social participation. Mariona's frustration derived, on the whole, from social situations, from feeling that she couldn't participate fully in a social group because she was limited by her level of English. Katka expressed her frustration much more generally, in terms of living in the United Kingdom as compared to living in Slovakia with her level of English. Alima did not really mix socially with English speakers and felt an absence of social interactions in general, having a very limited social circle and few non-Iraqi friends; as a result of this lack of participation, she was constrained in her agency and the construction or transformation of her identity (Ushioda, 2009). Although she felt that improving her English would facilitate increased social friendships, she never explicitly stated that she desired this, perhaps feeling that the constraints on her agency would render it improbable (Reay, 2004). However, she was able to perceive other opportunities for participation which were perhaps less dependent on others' recognition of her desired social identity, such as volunteer work. The emerging pattern, then, appears to be that positive contact experience may engender an enhanced wish to participate; if positive contact leads to increased foreign language friendships (Culhane, 2003), or a desire for increased foreign language friendships, a learner's enthusiasm to be part of a group and for intimacy within that group may enhance their wish to participate. Alima, not having had the same degree of positive contact experience, did not feel this desire.

An interesting point arising from this is the women's sense of *absence* concerning their lack of language and/or social interactions opportunities. This feeling of linguistic and communicative inadequacy and their frustration at being unable to express themselves resulted in a metaphorical loss of voice; although they could speak the language, they found it difficult to speak their minds because they had not yet mastered the language to the point where they could use it for their own purposes and make it real for them (Lemke, 1995). However, they are independent, educated women who *want* to be able to use English for their own ends and to forge a place in the world, positioning themselves as members of a global community and partaking of the opportunities this offers. Clearly they felt that English offered them a voice in the world, and they wished to participate in the global sociocultural context as well as in the immediate society in which they lived. This may be indicative of the reverence in which the 'native speaker' is still held; none of them felt that they had good English, although they had a high level of communicative competence. This raises important considerations regarding the position of the native speaker in the twenty-first century (Canagarajah, 2006).

Conclusion

Gardner (1985: 169) has claimed that 'the source of the motivating impetus is relatively unimportant, provided that motivation is aroused.' However, I have attempted in this chapter to show that understanding 'the source of the motivating impetus' is fundamental if learners' motivation is to be understood as the complex, contextually grounded and relational construction that it is. In the four factors influencing motivation that I have constructed – *Learner perception of choice and agency in the learning of English*, *Nature of English contact experience*, *Perceived benefits of learning English* and *Wish to participate in UK social life* – a central concept is that of identity, manifested in the extent to which participants' choice and agency was facilitated or constrained by their home contexts and the global status of English; their social experiences in English and the ways in which they may have felt positioned by others; the extent to which English could offer them opportunities for personal and professional development; and the extent to which they wished to participate locally and globally through the use of English. Identity, which Bucholtz and Hall (2010: 18) characterize as 'the social positioning of self and other', is thus central to motivation.

While much past and present foreign language motivation research points to some of the social aspects of identity, it retains what Benwell and Stokoe (2006: 8) call an 'internalised understanding of a pre-discursive self', rather than a constructed, individually articulated and dynamic range of forms of participation in various communities. As English speakers and learners, these individuals are constantly negotiating a range of social identities, while aspiring to participate in a variety of communities at local and global levels with differing degrees of agency and power to accept or resist these identities and the wider pressures and influences they face. These learners, and many other English and foreign language learners, are in the interstices between the various communities in which they wish to participate, negotiating those margins where, as Joseph (2010: 17) points out, 'identities matter most'. By bringing learners' individual voices, experiences, perceptions and agency to the fore, we can illuminate ways in which different identities may be negotiated, perpetuated and resisted.

9

Emotive Accounts of the Self during an ERASMUS Sojourn Abroad

Sonia Gallucci

Introduction

Research on overseas study sojourns (referred to in this chapter as the 'year abroad') has been proliferating over the past three decades, with a growing focus on the sociocultural and pedagogic dimensions of the experience abroad. A number of recent studies have also investigated the development of the 'new linguistic identities' of year abroad students (e.g. Block, 2007b; Crawshaw et al., 2001; Jackson, 2008; Kinginger, 2009). However, the expression of emotions during the year abroad is still an underexamined field of research which requires greater attention (see Pavlenko, 2005, 2006).

The study documented in this chapter brings together perspectives on emotions and identities from the fields of social psychology, pragmatics, applied linguistics and sociolinguistics. The fields of pragmatics and sociolinguistics, in particular, have experienced a shift within the past decade towards the use of new, unified conceptual frameworks in researching emotions. For many years, as Pavlenko (2005: 113) points out, 'emotions in language have been examined only through the lens of vocal communication, concepts, or metaphors. It is only in the past decades that we have begun seeing theoretical proposals for a unified pragmatics of emotive communication.' Within these pragmatic discursive frameworks, emotions are considered as part of socially constructed, dynamic and fundamentally interactive processes expressed through specific emotive linguistic devices, such as prosodic or lexical cues. According to Arndt and Janney (1991: 529), 'emotional communication' needs to be clearly distinguished from 'emotive communication'. They define 'emotional communication' as spontaneous and often unintentional responses to internal states, whereas 'emotive communication' is described as the conscious 'strategic modification of socially learned, cognitively mediated and intentionally performed affective signals'. Research on emotive and emotional communication can be found in the hitherto embryonic, interdisciplinary research tradition that combines linguistics, sociology and psychology (see Arndt and Janney, 1991; Bloch, 1996; Caffi and Janney, 1994; Holden and Hogan, 1993; Retzinger, 1991; Scheff, 1990; Scheff and Retzinger, 1991; Selting, 1994)

I link this cross-disciplinary approach of emotions to a poststructuralist stance on identities, which consider them as dynamic, multiple and contradictory sites of struggle, where practices of societies are 'heterogeneous arenas characterized by conflicting claims to truth and power' (Norton, 2000: 14; see also Bourdieu, 1977, 1991; Bourdieu and Passeron, 1977, 1990; Heller, 1982; Weedon, 1987, 1997). Relations of power are at the heart of poststructuralist thought about discourse. They are considered as key elements for the understanding of the shaping of individuals' identities. In this view, discourses about identity are continually being imposed, negotiated or contested. Individuals' understanding of their relationship to the world is central to this standpoint, since they are seen as active agents of their own life, capable of taking up different subject positions and to resist others' positioning with a particular social discourse (Norton Peirce, 1995).

This chapter aims to explore the significance of emotions in the shaping of foreign language identities in particular intercultural encounters through a case-study analysis of a female British citizen who lived in Italy for an academic year as an ERASMUS student. As in Pavlenko and Lantolf's (2000) study, which provides revealing insights into the life stories of people who have struggled through cultural border crossing before (re)constructing their identities, I analyse the concept of foreign language identity through the first-person narratives of my case-study participant. As will be demonstrated, her lived experiences, including her struggles for acceptance in the new Italian contexts, are central to her sense of Self, hence to the negotiation of her social identity. I will focus on the ways in which she consciously expressed her emotions, namely through the 'emotive dimension' of her speech. More specifically, I will consider the emotion lexicon that the participant used in her narratives to describe and represent her experience of emotion. I will analyse this aspect of the data in relation to the following research question:

- In what ways did the participant in this study make use of affective lexicon in her emotive discourse of Self and to what extent was her affective lexicon influential in the construction of her foreign language identity during the year abroad in Italy?

Researching affective lexicon

I approached the lexical analysis of my participant's emotions from a social psychological perspective, namely through the identification of affective lexicon based on Clore et al.'s (1987) taxonomy of psychological conditions, specifically on the emotion terms that refer to the internal–mental–affect focal condition. The authors proposed eight different categories which when combined can be divided into four broader classes. Mental conditions give rise to a fifth category, depending on which of the three major meaning components, behaviour, affect or cognitive, are mainly focused upon (see Figure 9.1, derived from Clore et al., 1987: 753). The four primary categories and classes were: (1) Subjective Evaluations and Objective Descriptions (External Conditions); (2) Cognitive Conditions and Cognitive-Behavioural Conditions (Cognitive Conditions); (3) Physical and Bodily States (Non-Mental Conditions); (4) Affective States, Affective-Cognitive Conditions and Affective-Behavioural Conditions (Affective Conditions).

On the basis of the above, the authors hypothesized that the best examples of emotion words would be those that refer to internal (as opposed to external) conditions, those that refer to mental (as opposed to non-mental) conditions and those that have a significant focus on affect. The taxonomy shown in Figure 9.1 emerged from an analysis of a sample of almost 600 English words in which the authors considered what kind of condition each term referred to. More than 400 undergraduate psychology students participated in the original study conducted at the University of Illinois. The participants were divided into groups of 20 to 30 with each person being required to rate a sample of affective terms. The study was designed in a way which allowed the average rating for each item to be based on approximately 20 individual observations. The empirical results confirmed that the lexical items related to 'Affect–Focal Mental Conditions' that had shown little difference between feeling and being could be confidently rated as emotions (e.g. feeling/being happy).

In their study, Clore et al. (1987: 754) provided a summative list of 282 terms for emotion (see Clore et al., 1987 for the full list of affective terms). The 24 terms presented in Table 9.1 refer to the lexical items used by my case-study participant either in English or in Italian. These advances offer a valid contribution to the study of emotions, nevertheless, as the authors clearly state, their study is not a theory of emotions, but 'rather it is one possible heuristic approach to the identification of the psychological states that need to be considered in theories of emotions.'

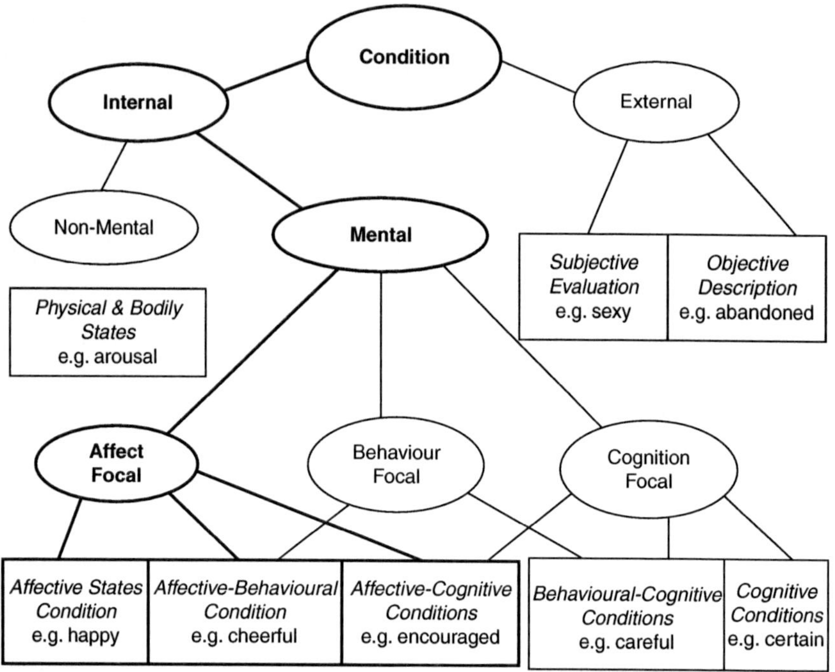

Figure 9.1 Taxonomy of psychological conditions: Affective lexicon

Methodology

Participant and research settings

The case-study participant was a female English native speaker and a British citizen spending a year abroad in Italy as ERASMUS student as a part of her undergraduate studies. More specifically, Daphne (pseudonym) lived in Ferrara (a city in Northern Italy) for ten months between September 2006 and June 2007.

Data collection

The research was primarily undertaken by means of semi-structured and in-depth interviews. Some of these interviews were based on photographs, with accompanying captions (written by the participant) (see Knight, 2002; Martin-Jones et al., 2009; Nikula and Huhta, 2008). Data was also obtained through diary entries written by Daphne during her year aboard (see Alaszewski, 2006; Jones et al., 2000). All interviews were audio recorded.

Table 9.1 Affective lexicon used by the case-study participant

1. angry	2. irritated
3. annoyed	4. isolated
5. ashamed	6. moved
7. bored	8. nervous
9. comfortable (psychologically)	10. pleased
11. contented	12. pleasure
13. embarrassed	14. proud
15. emotional	16. relaxed
17. excited	18. sad
19. frustrated	20. satisfied
21. happy	22. surprised
23. homesick	24. upset

Adapted from Clore et al., 1987

Data analysis procedures

In the study, the emotive dimension of Daphne's speech was evaluated, namely the terms for emotion, which she used consciously and strategically in her written and oral narratives. In order to understand the expression of her emotions in her accounts of intercultural encounters, a lexical analysis of her discourse, using Clore et al.'s (1987) taxonomy of psychological conditions, was conducted allowing the participant's affective lexicon to be characterized. In this chapter, I have focused exclusively on Daphne's direct verbal cues in naturally occurring situations. These 'cues to emotions' have previously been described in detail (see Planalp et al., 1996).

Throughout my analysis of her affective lexicon, I first identified the statements Daphne made orally (in audio- and video-recorded interviews) and in writing (in diary entries and photo-descriptions). Since my research methods were ethnographically informed, I did not ask Daphne to carry out any particular task. Instead, I encouraged her to talk about her lived experiences in Italy on her own terms. During the analysis of the interview transcripts and diary entries, I identified those terms for emotions which Daphne used in her narratives. These included lexical items with a significant focus on affect, and, in line with Clore et al.'s (1987) theoretical approach, I rated them as 'emotions' in all instances where there was little difference in meaning between the terms for emotion preceded by the verbs 'to feel' and 'to be' (e.g. I feel/am happy). The analysis of Daphne's emotive lexicon facilitated my characterization of her sense of Self while negotiating her social identities as foreign language learners during her year aboard in Italy.

Emotive accounts of self

Throughout Daphne's emotive communication, I have adopted a pragmatic standpoint. In other words, I have approached emotions as part of a 'process of interaction' rather than as a 'product of interaction'. As previously mentioned, in this study, I focus on the 24 terms used orally or in writing by Daphne to describe her emotions (see Table 9.1). In the following sections, I detail the specific ways in which emotions were indicative in the negotiation of Daphne's social identities.

Daphne's affective lexicon and the construction of her foreign language identity

From the analysis of Daphne's use of affective lexis in accounts of her experiences abroad, it emerged that she expressed emotions in a variety of interactional contexts. She made use of the following terms for emotion: angry, annoyed, **ashamed**, bored, comfortable (psychologically), **contented**, **embarrassed**, **emotional**, **excited**, frustrated, irritated, **isolated**, **proud**, happy, homesick, **moved**, **nervous**, nervous, pleased, **pleasure**, relaxed (psychologically), sad, **surprised**, satisfied, upset. The emotion words in bold font were expressed in Italian. I now turn my attention to the term for emotion which had the highest frequency in Daphne's accounts of her year abroad, 'nervous'. My main aim in the following sections is to describe the ways in which Daphne made use of this and other related terms for emotion through her narratives, and to consider how this term was related to the construction of her foreign language identity.

Transcription conventions can be found at the end of this chapter. In the interview transcripts, the following abbreviations have also been used: G: Gallucci (me), I: Ilaria (participant), L: Lucy (participant), D: Daphne (participant).

Nervous

Daphne used the adjective 'nervous' several times throughout her narratives, alternatively in English and in Italian. The first time she expressed this emotion during the year abroad was in her diary on 25 October 2006, where she used the Italian term 'nervosa' to indicate her particular state in regard to the Italian oral examination. Daphne wrote, 'I am very happy that in England all exams are written, I would be too nervous to speak.' Daphne was happy (and presumably relieved) that she did not have to take many oral examinations in the United Kingdom. This point was also revisited during our second interview in November 2006:

Excerpt 9.1

[. . .] when I do, like, the oral exam, in England, for the languages, I get so[:] nervous before, I can feel my hands are shaking: . . . I think if I don't know what to say . . . you can't leave a big **s**ilence or something . . . whereas in the written exam if I don't understand the question, I can go to the next question and **c**ome back, but with speaking you have to say something [laugh].

Daphne's main linguistic concern at the beginning of her experience was to speak the target language in instructed environments. However, despite this nervousness, she decided to overcome this emotion by taking part in formal conversations during the lectures and by sitting the oral examination at the end of the academic year in Italy. This aspect is shown in the two Excerpts 9.2 and 9.3 which were taken from a diary-based interview conducted in November 2006.

Excerpt 9.2

G: I see, I see, ok, then you had a terrible experience [both laugh], because you said "The Professor asked me to stand and talk about English history in front of the Italian class! It was terrible" [. . .] I can read here, that you had this experience on Tuesday, and then on Wednesday again you said "I had to talk again in front of the whole class", so you had to talk.

D: Yeah, I knew he was going to ask me.

G: Ah, so you were prepared?

D: Yeah, I wasn't quite as nervous, because I was expecting it.

Excerpt 9.3

G: And what about the[:] your opinion about the university, the Italian university system? And . . have you taken any exam? Or . . did you like them or not?

D: Erm . . yeah . . I did an exam, last week, which was an oral exam, because almost all the exams are oral, which erm . . . was quite a change because in England all the exams are written. I was quite' no, I was **very nervous** in the beginning, I was shaking and I was so nervous [. . .]

G: [[How]] did it go, your exam?

D: It was all right, eh eh, even the teacher was **so nice**, I think he liked the foreign students, because he gave me and my friend the top marks. Even though, eh eh, . . yeah

Daphne admitted feeling very nervous when she had to speak in front of others, even in her first language, because she defined herself as being a shy person and therefore, she said that she would get embarrassed and would feel awkward if she had to speak. Indeed, when I asked her why she felt nervous about speaking in front of other people in the class, this was her reply:

Excerpt 9.4

{. . .} I don't . . I don't like speaking in front of a group, even in English, because I just know I get red and that makes me even more nervous, but I didn't actually know the answer to the question he asked, which was a bit . . erm . . awkward, and also . . I got so nervous I couldn't think in Italian, I couldn't think at [:]all, and I couldn't think enough to say "I don't know the answer, or just to say "oh I can't speak" but the fact that I could **feel** myself going red and it was horrible, I think . .I don't know I just felt a bit silly in front of the other students, because I want to be **p**art of the class, and I don't want or be THE foreign student. When I have to speak in front of them, when I can't say anything, this makes it **obv**ious that I am **E**nglish and . . I feel . . I don't feel as much of the class if I look[:] like I can't speak Italian.

Daphne's feeling of nervousness (as well as embarrassment and frustration) can be understood in her refusal to be positioned in a marginal role by Italian native speakers. Excerpt 9.5 shows quite clearly Daphne experiencing negatively a power asymmetry in foreign language interactions.

Excerpt 9.5

G: Ok, ok on Friday the 27th you went to a party, again, and you said 'it was very nice' . . . but 'I felt a bit er . . . excluded' 'sometimes I feel a bit excluded because I'm a foreigner' . . . so what do you mean by that? You felt a bit . . . isolated.

D: Mmm. I think it was because I was in another party for graduation, and it was quite, there's a lot of traditions[:] a n d . . . I just don't know, and 'cause (. . .) well it's hard to explain, but I didn't know the traditions, so[:] I didn't know what was going on some of the time, so I felt really awful, I don't know . . . and a lot of times, not a lot of time, WHEN I **feel** excluded, it's quite often because there's a . . . it with jokes a lot of times. And I think because erm . . . they're quite subtle sometimes, I think it's a quite hard thing, they usually play on words or . . . like swear words or . . . they're quite particular and also if somebody else is talking, you don't understand, it's a kind of **ann**oying but it's all right, it's kind of **wait** until they change their subject to something I understand. If everyone starts **LAUGHING** and I don't get it, it's a, I don't know it's a . . . quite, maybe it's just a more obvious s i g n than a conversation, I don't know if it does make sense.

In Excerpt 9.6, taken from an interview conducted in April 2007, we can see Daphne taking control of foreign language interaction when ordering foods in an Italian restaurant, since her Italian friends were too drunk to speak. In this particular situation, she became the primary interlocutor in the foreign language conversations and she manages to deal successfully with this situation. This shows that public discourses, which position foreign language users as disadvantaged, can be challenged and, despite the truth of the events, also shows the vulnerability and basic state of disempowerment of Daphne as being someone who can only speak when her oppressors are drunk.

Excerpt 9.6

G: Then you had a very amusing evening, with your friends, a friend wasn't very happy, she was a bit down, because something had happened to her, however, you say, that 'it is strange because it was me who was the most able to speak Italian'. Why?

D: [[yes]] because the other two . . were a bit drunk (eh), so they hadn't spoken a lot, because usually in a restaurant I[:] don't order, because for an Italian it's easier, but this time the other two were not able to speak, so I did it.

Daphne felt nervous also when she experienced power asymmetries within the academic environment (see Excerpt 9.2). Despite this nervousness, however, she decided not to remain silent in the face of such inequalities, but her way to challenge them, was indeed to speak out loud in front of Italian native speakers (students and professors) and make them hear her voice as a potentially knowledgeable and confident foreign language learner. This aspect is shown in Excerpt 9.7.

Excerpt 9.7

D: [[mh mh, yeah]] and I think it's probably because it's just make . . . mmm . . . he [the Professor] always **points** out that I'm a foreign student' although there are others, there are quite a few Americans in the class, and we're always . . . we all sit together and if somebody doesn't understand the question, we can help each other to work out how to say it. But . . . yeah it just **makes** . . . points out the difference between me and the Italian students, I think.

G: And you stand up in front of the class now?

D: No, I don't stand up, but I do speak if he asks, sometimes.

Daphne's choice to speak when facing power asymmetries in the academic environment and thus, her refusal to be silenced by others' positioning, is also shown by her decision to take the end of the course oral exams (see Excerpt 9.3). Daphne constantly challenged being marginalized by Italian native speakers in relative positions of power. Indeed, when confronted with unequal relations of power, especially in the Italian academic environments, Daphne decided to speak up by making them hear her voice as worth listening to. Daphne's proactive attitude and her perseverance in trying to achieve her goals seemed to help her to re-establish more balanced relations of power, and her struggles for acceptance in society were appeared to be compensated through gaining apparent access to 'formal' and 'informal' interactions with native speakers of the target language.

Over the course of the year abroad, Daphne felt less nervous and shy when facing new situations in the face of Otherness. This aspect can be understood in her awareness of her identity changing over time in the new Italian contexts. Indeed, as shown in Excerpt 9.8, taken from an interview conducted in November 2006, she felt progressively more confident and more relaxed about deadlines and being prompt for meetings. She also started to use Italian forms of verbal communication, such as using her hand, raising her voice and engaged in cultural practices such as not queuing or arriving late. These changes made Daphne feel very different as a person. She felt changed in her personality, emotions and thoughts. Thus, her sphere of subjectivity, namely her sense of being and her ways of understanding her relations with the world made her feel a different person (see Weedon, 1997).

Excerpt 9.8

D: I think [. . .] I'm more confident, than I was, even just er . . I haven't got my ticket to go home, or just things like that, I'm not like I was . . like rigid 'I have to do this now; I have to be at the lesson at ten o'clock exactly' Now I'm just going like ten past ten and it doesn't matter. [. . .] I've noticed when I speak I use my hands, all the time, which I never used to do, but now I'm . . . so which is really not an English thing to do, I think, so[:] . . .

G: When you come back in England, do you think you will be like you are now? Like a different person? Or would you go back to the old Daphne?

D: Er . . I think I will be a bit different, I think so, yeah[:]

Interestingly, this feature of Daphne's personality changed significantly after her experience abroad, as shown in our last interview undertaken in the United Kingdom during November 2007, where she stated that she did not feel as shy as before the year abroad, and she did not care about what other people may think of her. Excerpt 9.9 reveals Daphne's awareness of the ways in which her identity had changed during the year aboard, and how these changes made her feel the person she wanted to be.

Excerpt 9.9

G: Do you feel changed?

D: yes a lot, I'm not as shy as before and . . (. . .) now I'm don't mind what other people think, whereas before, maybe because in England (. . .) erm . . the environment is different and . . in Italy is freer. So now I'm more . . myself.

G: Do you feel more European now?

D: Yes, because er . . erm . . there are stereotypes about other countries, but when one lives in another country s/he understands why Italians are like that . . and it's not . . it's understandable, because you understand another culture and.

G: So do think you have understood Italian culture, or at least now can you accept it better?

D: Yes, I hope so.

G: Do you feel a bit Italian now?

D: A little bit yes, eh eh.

G: For example what do you do which is Italian? Which is not typically English?

D: Erm[:] I'm noisier than before and . . I don't want to wait

G: Do you queue?

D: mm . . I don't want to [laugh]

Daphne was also aware of the struggles that individuals may experience when learning another language, therefore, she seemed neither surprised nor discouraged by her first few unsuccessful attempts. Excerpt 9.10 shows Daphne's awareness of such struggles in language learning, when commenting on an Italian native speaker struggling to speak English with her, and on the reasons why she did not want to laugh at him.

Excerpt 9.10

G: . . . then you went to this party and you found it really really funny, because there was somebody trying to speak English. [both laugh]

D: Yeah.

G: What happened? [laugh]

D: erm, quite often the Italian people like to kind of try out their English because even . . there was this girl's dad, and I think he hadn't actually spoken English for like twenty **years[:]** or something . .

G: *[laugh]* [[oh]]

D: He was really nice, and it was really strange because all of a sudden he thought of an English word and he kind of shouted across the room to me, just like, I don't know like interrupting, trying to speak English, and usually I could see . . . like if I'd heard the conversation so I knew when he said something, but this one time he started shouting 'ankle' at me, ankle I don't understand what's going on, I thought "I missed something", and then I realised he was having a conversation about his family and was trying to say 'uncle', so, so I didn't want to laugh at him because I thought "I know how it feels when you say something to somebody in another language." But it was so[:] funny.

The emotion of being/feeling 'nervous', also emerged in relation to informal conversations in Italian, such as the one Daphne undertook with her flatmate when trying to comfort her (see Excerpt 9.11) or when trying to deal with day-to-day things in informal encounters (see Excerpt 9.13). As shown in Excerpts 9.11 and 9.12, this aspect emerged very clearly in a diary-based interview undertaken in November 2006, where Daphne used the term 'nervous' as many as 11 times. It made her feel really nervous as well as frustrated, annoyed, angry and psychologically stressed when she couldn't express herself as she wanted to, for instance, when talking about complex things (see Excerpt 9.12).

Excerpt 9.11

G: Ok, on Saturday the 21st again you start . . your diary by saying 'it is too frustrating' and then something happened, you went out with Sara [your flatmate], you went to a restaurant and then she told you something about her life, yeah?

D: Oh yeah.

G: And you wanted to give her some advice?

D: Yeah she was having like a . . a problem with a colleague or a boyfriend or something like that, and I think she was quite . . not upset, but she was quite . . it was like a proper problem, and I was really pleased that we could talk about something like quite . . personal, like a proper friend, and I wanted to help her, like saying 'maybe you could do this or do that, maybe it's because of this or something'

G: Yeah.

D: And I couldn't (. . .) it was like vocabulary I didn't know and I couldn't, I couldn't find a way to say it, and I wanted to help her and it was quite annoying because I wanted, I wanted to help, but I couldn't even think what or say so . . mm . . it was quite hard because I felt like I wasn't being helpful, but it wasn't because I didn't want or be helpful, but it was because I couldn't work out how to say what I wanted to say . .

Excerpt 9.12

G: Do you enjoy speaking Italian?

D: Yeah, I do when I can express myself, but I do, I do get quite frustrated sometimes, if I can't, because it's just . . . it's quite hard if there's something I really want to say and I can't say it. [. . .] I think, because I'm getting better, I'm more confident about speaking, so I speak more, which means I find more . . . thingsss I can't say, because I'm trying more [laugh] so I think I'm getting maybe a bit more frustrated but I don't think it's because I'm getting 'worse, I think it's because probably I'm getting better, I don't know, maybe not.

G: Yeah, maybe you want to say more complex things.

D: [[yeah that's why I think]], yeah maybe I can actually say more and I'm finding the things . . . like really complicated thoughts I have and I can't say them . . .

Overall, Daphne felt nervous when she had to cope with things in Italian. This included a sense of frustration about not being able to either understand or reply to Italian native speakers. However, at the same time, it also made her feel very proud and pleased when she was eventually able to understand what was being said in the target language, and when she was able to take part in conversations. Excerpt 9.13 illustrates these contrasting emotions quite clearly.

Excerpt 9.13

G: Ok, and are you proud about your progress in Italian?

D: I think so, because in the beginning I was quite nervous, and I did find it really hard when I first came here, just err . . . just to cope with **eve**rything. But I **think** I'm quite, I'm especially pleased to understand[:] not everything, but I do understand almost everything that people say to me, and I think although my speaking got better, I really, it really frustrates me when I can't reply, because I understand what somebody says and I know what I want to say, but if I can't say it, I think they think I haven't understood . . . but I think I'm quite pleased.

As time passed by, Daphne felt generally less nervous, which is shown by the fact that, in later interviews, she made lesser use of this and other associated terms, such as 'frustrated' or 'embarrassed', to signal her emotions. Indeed, as shown in Excerpt 9.14, taken from an interview conducted in April 2007, Daphne claimed to be less nervous about making mistakes when speaking Italian.

Excerpt 9.14

G: And then do you feel . . changed? I mean, do you see yourself as being the same Daphne as before Christmas? Or do you feel different?

D: I am **v e r y** different, and yes I'm less shy and . . yes if I make mistakes . . . it's not important, yes I am less nervous about speaking Italian, if I make mistakes, because it happens . . it doesn't mean that **I can't** speak Italian, it' only because . . . I'm an **English** [person] who speaks, I'm not Italian.

Daphne was conscious about her nervousness when she arrived in Italy and about the ways in which she changed over time. In an interview carried out in June 2007, she used this term for emotion as many as four times, but only to recall some episodes related to her past fear of making mistakes and to take oral examinations, which she was able to successfully overcome. This is shown in the Excerpt 9.15.

Excerpt 9.15

[. . .] I was really nervous when I arrived and I found it hard to speak to people, and I found it quite hard . . to get to know at beginning, 'cause I was nervous of making **mistakes**, as soon I spoke Italian and . . but now er . . (. . .) I don't mind if I make mistakes because . . people

> `still understand what I'm trying to say, and everyone is really friendly and (. . .) [sigh] I think I'm a lot more` **`confident,`** `about speaking Italian, and I just get out and meet people in general . . yeah . . .`

It seems that the more she managed to position herself as a confident and capable second language learner, by establishing more equal relations of power in the new linguistic and cultural environments, the less use of negative terms for emotions she made, such as the affective lexicon: nervous, frustrated, embarrassed, annoyed, and so on. This shows that emotions are indeed linked to individuals' perceptions of Self and Otherness, and ought to be considered in our analysis of factors which can contribute to one's construction of 'new linguistic identities'.

Discussion

The main aim of this chapter was to explore the significance of emotions in the shaping of 'new language identities' in a study abroad context. I have looked at this from a case-study perspective. Daphne, as the sole participant in this study, expressed her emotions in various ways both verbally and non-verbally. In this chapter, only the direct verbal dimension of her emotive communication has been taken into consideration. This was approached by means of qualitative analysis of the affective lexicon used by the participant to articulate her emotions during her sojourn abroad. From the analysis of the data, it emerged that Daphne made use of a wide range of affective lexical items to express her emotions during my fieldwork with her over her the course of the year.

The verbal expression of emotions was influenced by the particular intercultural contexts in which Daphne found herself during the year abroad, and by the ways in which she perceived and dealt with them. Daphne made extensive use of affective lexical items, switching from English to Italian, depending on the context she was referring to, and on the particular inner state she wanted to describe (e.g. being/feeling nervous, being/feeling happy). Daphne used affective terms to describe a variety of formal and informal environments in which she found herself, with self-reflection and willingness to understand them. In this context, particular attention has been paid to the affective lexical item 'nervous'. This term was chosen for emotion because it had the highest frequency in Daphne's emotive accounts of her lived experiences during her year abroad in Italy. I have described the ways in which Daphne made use of this and other related terms for emotion in her narratives, and I have evaluated the extent to which this specific affective lexicon was influential in the construction of her foreign language identity.

As mentioned earlier, Daphne made a large use of the term 'nervous' and other related affective terms (such as embarrassed, frustrated, annoyed) during her sojourn in Italy, especially when she experienced (often unequal) power relations with people from the local communities of practice. Despite her initial struggles to take part in public discourse, she managed to gain access to informal interaction with Italian native speakers and she also managed to successfully gain access to formal interactions within the academic environment, with both students and professors. When confronted with power asymmetries, Daphne refused to be silenced by other's positioning and decided to speak instead. Hence, she was able to reverse unequal relations of power by making others hear her voice as worth listening to.

Daphne's construction of her foreign language identity during her year abroad confirms the poststructuralist perspectives introduced earlier in this chapter. In her case, we see that foreign language identities are dynamic, multiple and sites of struggle. Indeed, through her struggles, she managed not only to recover from an initial phase of loss and to become a competent foreign language speaker, but also to grow as a person and to overcome her emotions when pursuing her linguistic goals. These were mostly driven by a personal desire to change some aspects of her personality. In fact, during and also after her experience abroad, she admitted feeling and being a different person. She became less shy and less nervous than before her year abroad, which made her feel glad and satisfied, since she could express herself more freely as she became the person she wanted to be.

Daphne seemed to have gone through a process of continuous self-reflection, which involved making a compromise between her personal and social identity, namely, a balance between her internal thoughts and emotions, and the happenings around her. Through reflexivity, Daphne managed to give voice to her 'emotional commentaries' as defined by Archer (2000: 195), gaining access to interaction not only with the social world but also with her inner-self. Emotions helped her to become more aware of the situations and to select a set of new social roles during her year abroad. Daphne seemed to have used reflexivity and introspection intensely, and for an extended period of time. This is shown for instance in the diary entries, which she continued to provide after the diary-based interview had been carried out and in our last interview, which shows the continuous and dynamic negotiation of her social identity, her commitment to adjust pre-existing social roles according to the context and to the creative ways her identity was negotiated. Hence, it seems that the ways in which an individual uses specific lexicon to express emotions, can be highly influenced by the ways in which they perceive themselves and others in new sociocultural and linguistic environments.

Daphne's use of specific affective lexis shows quite clearly that 'words' indexing emotions are strictly linked to the sociocultural contexts in which they are used, and in which an individual continuously negotiates identity as a foreign language learner capable of constructing legitimate emotive discourse (see Norton Peirce, 1995, 2000). Hence, the need for ethnography by year abroad students, and also by teachers, educationalists and researchers involved in the experience abroad, along with close analysis of language in use. This can shed light on identity development and the expression of emotions, and eventually help students to have a successful year abroad experience.

As researchers and as language teachers, we need to consider year abroad students as individuals embarking on a journey of personal growth, who constantly negotiate and reconstruct their cultural identities as an ongoing process of becoming (see Byram, 1997; Meinhof and Galasiński, 2005). We also need to put more emphasis on the emotional processes involved in the experience abroad, in order to raise awareness of the ways in which emotions are bound up with the year abroad experience of language learning, and to build an understanding of the ways in which students have access to social networks in the target language communities.

Transcription conventions

word	stressed syllable/word/sentence
w o r d	slowing down
w o r d	stressed syllable/word/sentence and slowing down
WORD	louder tone of voice
WORD	louder tone of voice and stressed syllable/word/sentence
W O R D	louder tone of voice and stressed syllable/word/sentence, slowing down
. .	micro pause (less than 2 seconds)
. . .	short pause (less than 3 seconds)
(. . .)	pause (between 3 and 6 seconds)
{. . .}	long pause (more than 6 seconds)
{. . .} {. . .}	very long pause (more than 12 seconds)
[[word]]	overlapping speech
word	misspelling/mispronunciation
[word]	my insertion (comment/lexical item or paralinguistic feature)

{ }	inaudible speech
[:]	prolonging the pronunciation of the final vowel/syllable
word'	truncation
'word	truncation
"words"	Italian or English lexical items (reported speech or diary entries)
words	relevant turns at talk
[. . .]	stretches of talk between turns that have been omitted
words	relevant turns at talk

10

Setting Standards for Intercultural Communication: Universalism and Identity Change

Stephanie Ann Houghton

Introduction

The purpose of this chapter is to explore and showcase different kinds of identity development in students in relation to standard setting for intercultural communication, and particularly in relation to the valuing of universalism. An action research case study was conducted at a university in Japan by applying the Intercultural Dialogue (ID) Model (Houghton, 2012; Houghton and Yamada, 2012) over a 13-week semester in an English as a Foreign Language (EFL) course designed to develop students' Intercultural Communicative Competence (ICC) (Byram, 1997) and identity development within it. As we shall see, the identity development located in the final stage of the ID Model involves reasoned reflection on the part of students, who have progressed through earlier stages of the model, upon whether or not to change in response to their interlocutor(s), which provides them with the opportunity to consciously change if they wish. This chapter starts by providing an overview of the ID Model, and the study, before tracking the development of three students through the ID Model, all of which ultimately lead to students' decisions to change in some way in response to interviewee(s). Decision making about identity development is evident in students' statements that they have either already changed, or that they do (or do not) intend to change, in response to intercultural dialogue, and it may refer back to earlier stages of the model.

The Intercultural Dialogue Model

The purpose of the ID Model is to help teachers systematically develop students' ICC, and identity development within it, by building sequenced and staged learning objectives into materials design. While it accords theoretically with Byram's (1997) ICC Model, some of Byram's *savoirs* were split and recombined, and/or sequenced, and an additional *savoir* was added to take account of identity development. The course of learning is sequenced through five stages, which involve student attention to task, student change and the development of student meta-awareness.

- **Stage 1** (Analysis of Self) involves student reflection upon their own values with reference to a given conceptual framework. This relates to Byram's concepts of *savoir* and *savoir être* (the generation of new knowledge about the Self, and the partial description of one's own values and associated concepts).
- **Stage 2** (Analysis of Other) involves student exploration of their interlocutor's values by using non-judgemental, empathy-oriented communication strategies. This relates to Byram's concepts of *savoir* and *savoir apprendre/faire* (the generation of new knowledge, and the elicitation of information about an interlocutor's perspective in real time to clarify points and develop detail).
- **Stage 3** (Critical Analysis) involves student identification of value similarities and differences between Self and Other. This relates to Byram's concepts of *savoir s'engager* and *savoir comprendre* (comparing and contrasting one's own values with one's interlocutor's, interpreting and bringing both into relation in the process).
- **Stage 4** (Critical Evaluation) involves student evaluation of the values of Self and Other with reference to a clear standard. This relates to Byram's concepts of *savoir s'engager* and *savoir être* (evaluating one's own values and one's interlocutor's with reference to an explicitly stated standard).
- **Stage 5** (Identity Development) involves student reasoned reflection, having progressed through Stages 1–4, upon whether or not to change in response to the interlocutor which provides the opportunity to change consciously. None of the main concepts characterizing Byram's model relate directly to this component, so the term *savoir se transformer* was coined. Decision making is evident in students' statements that they have either already changed, or that they do (or do not) intend to change, in response to intercultural dialogue, and it may refer back to earlier stages of the model.

Within the ID Model, a value system is conceptualized as a complex, hierarchically organized and unstable system that forms part of a person's broader identity, which contains various interconnected values that include stated values, real, ideal and target values, all of which may be evidenced in, yet sometimes contradict, behaviour and feelings. The complex and dynamic functioning of the value system was termed 'within-self diversity' (Houghton, 2011), a view that broadly accords with Rogers' (1951) description of self-structure and Dörnyei's (2005, 2009) description of the L2 motivational self system which was in turn rooted in Higgins' (1987) Self-Discrepancy Theory and related influential research into cognitive dissonance (Festinger, 1957), imbalance (Heider, 1958) and multiple selves (Markus and Nurius, 1986). Notably, the resolution of self-discrepancy is considered to be a key mechanism in identity development in both Houghton ID Model and Dörnyei's description of the L2 motivational self system, but key distinctions between them have been explored elsewhere (Houghton, in press).

For the purposes of this chapter, it is worth highlighting the point that the key cognitive processes underpinning identity development are considered to include the selection, rejection and reprioritization of values within the existing value hierarchy that forms part of the broader structures of the Self. As students identify and resolve discrepancies arising among their own competing values in response to dialogue, they can make conscious decisions about what (not) to value, and what (not) to become. Confusion and identity change can be triggered by any discrepancy arising among any of a student's values at any stage of the ID Model, and the ability to do this reflectively, analytically and evaluatively is considered to be a skill within the concept of *savoir se transformer*.

The study

The purpose of this chapter is to explore and showcase different kinds of identity development in students in relation to standard setting for intercultural communication, and particularly in relation to the valuing of universalism, as evidenced in students' written work in statement patterns that indicated identity change had already happened, was underway, or was being planned by the students concerned. In this study, triangulated qualitative data were gathered in English over one 13-week semester at a university in Japan from 17 consenting student participants in an EFL course designed to develop students' ICC and from the author (as teacher-researcher). The data included audio recordings of lessons and documentary evidence (including student work, and student and teacher diaries). Ethical issues related to informed consent, participant anonymity and the safe storage of data, for example, were duly considered (Cohen et al., 2000; Creswell, 2003; McDonough and McDonough, 1997). An overview of the double-looped syllabus design is presented in Table 10.1.

Table 10.1 An overview of syllabus design

Weeks 1–5	**Stage 1** (Analysis of Self)	• Reflection upon values referring to a taxonomy of 10 universal values
LOOP 1		
Week 6	**Stage 2** (Analysis of Other)	• Exploration of another student's values using non-judgemental, empathy-oriented communication strategies
Week 7	**Stage 3** (Critical Analysis)	• Identification of value similarities and differences between Self and the Other student
Week 8	**Stage 4** (Critical Evaluation)	• Apply own, explicit standard to evaluate one's own values and those of the other student
	Stage 5 (Identity Development)	• Reflect upon whether or not to change in response to the other student
LOOP 2		
Weeks 1–5 (homework)	**Stage 2** (Analysis of Other)	• Write a (30-question) questionnaire with which to interview a foreigner about their values (3 questions for each of the 10 values studied in Weeks 2–5) • Exploration of a foreigner's values using non-judgemental, empathy-oriented communication strategies
Weeks 9–10	**Stage 3** (Critical Analysis)	• Identification of value similarities and differences between Self and the foreigner
	Stage 4 (Critical Evaluation)	• Apply own, explicit standard to evaluate one's own values and those of the foreigner
	Stage 5 (Identity Development)	• Reflect upon whether or not to change in response to the foreigner
Weeks 11–13	Presentations	• Make a presentation to the class about the interview with a foreigner

Student self-reflection was structured around the taxonomy of ten universal values, adapted from Schwartz and Sagiv (1995) and Schwartz et al. (1997), which included power, achievement, universalism, benevolence, tradition, conformity, security, self-direction, stimulation and hedonism. Definitions of the values presented to students in teaching materials relevant to this chapter are presented in Table 10.2.

Data analysis

Qualitative data were categorized and coded using Atlas.ti software. For the purposes of this chapter, student homework was prioritized over other data

Table 10.2 Definitions of the terms presented to students in Weeks 2 and 4

Week 2	• **Universalism:** People who value universalism care about the welfare of all people and nature as a whole (even people they do not know). They recognize and value the fact that people of all countries and cultures, along with nature, inhabit the same universe. They value wisdom, have a strong sense of social justice and aspire towards a world at peace. They tend to be broad-minded and value equality between people. They see beauty in the world, value unity with nature and seek to protect the environment. • **Benevolence:** People who value benevolence care about the welfare of people around them; people they know and see often. They are very active in helping those around them, are loyal and honest, tend to be forgiving and value true friendship.
Week 4	• **Tradition**: People who value tradition accept, respect and are committed to their culture, its religion, customs and ideas. They accept their role in life and are humble. • **Conformity**: People who value conformity care about respecting social expectations and norms. They do not wish to upset or harm others and value restraint. They are obedient, value self-discipline, politeness and honour their parents and elders. • **Security**: People who value security care about safety, harmony and the stability of society, relationships and the Self. They value family security, national security and social order. They believe that if someone does you a favour, you should do them a favour back. They also tend to value cleanliness.

types to identify patterns or types of statement indicative of student identity development primarily framed in terms of change rooted in the past, present and/or future. To carefully delimit this kind of data within the data stock, unclear examples and examples of no change were included in the initial analysis. It can be seen in Table 10.3 that four main types of student change emerged through data analysis, that six examples were unclear and that there were four examples of no change. Student change fell into four main types as listed below.

- In Change/Type 1, Student 7 reflected upon past behavioural tendencies (in terms of what she didn't used to do) before making a statement about what she thought she should do followed by a statement expressing the intention to change in the future.
- In Change/Type 2, Student 10 claimed she had changed the evaluative standard she had selected to support intercultural communication.
- In Change/Types 3 and 4, Students 2, 3, 5, 13, 14, 15, 16, 17 and 18 all claimed that their ideas had already changed in response to their foreign interviewees, but Students 2, 3, 18, 13, 14 and 16 also claimed that they wanted to change in some way in the future.

Table 10.3 Statement patterns indicative of student identity development

<table>
<tr><td colspan="5">CHANGE</td></tr>
<tr><td>Type</td><td colspan="2">Past</td><td>Present</td><td>Future</td></tr>
<tr><td>1</td><td colspan="2">I didn't used to . . .
(Student 7)</td><td colspan="2">I should . . . and I want to change
(Student 7)</td></tr>
<tr><td>2</td><td rowspan="3">I changed . . .</td><td>. . . my standard
(Student 10)</td><td></td><td></td></tr>
<tr><td>3</td><td rowspan="2">. . . my ideas
(Students 2, 3, 5, 13, 14, 15, 16, 17, 18)</td><td colspan="2" rowspan="2">I want to change
(Students 2, 3, 18, 13, 14, 16)</td></tr>
<tr><td>4</td></tr>
<tr><td colspan="5">No Change
(Students 2, 12, 13, 15)</td></tr>
<tr><td colspan="5">Unclear
(Students 1, 4, 6, 8, 9, 11)</td></tr>
</table>

Illustrative data for each type of change is presented in Table 10.4, where it can be seen that by chance, Students 7, 10 and 15 all focused on the value of universalism. For this reason, the personal journey of these three students was tracked through the course to showcase different kinds of student identity development in relation to standard setting for intercultural communication, and particularly in relation to the valuing of universalism, as evidenced in students' written work in statement patterns that indicated identity change had already happened, was underway or was being planned by the students concerned. More detailed data illustrating each of these three cases will be presented in the next section.

Data presentation

Change/Type 1

In Data 1, Student 7 wrote:

> After interview, I have thought I should actively do something for universalism. There are so many suffering people all over the world. Until now, I have never done for them. So, I want to do voluntary work if I have a chance.

Table 10.4 Data illustrating the statement patterns indicative of student identity development

Change/Type 1	**Data 1:** After interview, I have thought I should actively do something for universalism. There are so many suffering people all over the world. Until now, I have never done for them. So, I want to do voluntary work if I have a chance. (Student 7)
Change/Type 2	**Data 2:** During interview, I find that she used the words 'family'. So I think she values conformity and security best, and I felt that she loved her family and her country. After I finished interview, I changed my standard (from universalism to conformity and security). (Student 10)
Change/Type 3	**Data 3:** My idea about universalism and benevolence changed in response to my interviewee. (Student 15)
Change/Type 4	**Data 4:** After this interview, I thought that if I avoided trying new things, I might lose chances which made me grown. I want to try new things, while I respect the tradition. (Student 3)
No change	**Data 5:** Also, my interviewee thinks that it is important to ask people whatever when he wants to know what should he does. But I think it is not good to ask people whatever. (Student 15)
Unclear	**Data 6:** My idea changed after I understood her idea. For example, I regard achievement as very important things in my life, because achievement develops me more. So, I will continue to value achievement in my life. (Student 6)

In other words, he intended to change. How had this dynamic unfolded over time? In Stage 1 (Analysis of Self), Student 7 did not submit a paragraph reflecting upon his values related to universalism, but he did write about it in the Week 5 Essay on Values. A discrepancy between Student 7's valuing of universalism and his actual behaviour is evident in Data 7.

> **Data 7:** People who value universalism think about welfare of all people and nature as whole. I think I'm not Universalism because I never do something for people who I don't know. So If I have a chance to do for welfare of people and nature, I want to challenge.

In week 7 of Stage 3 (Critical Analysis/Loop 1), Student 7 critically analysed Self and Other by identifying value similarities and differences between himself and his partner. In Data 8, similarities are underlined and differences are italicized for emphasis. A notable difference between Student 7 and his interviewee is that while Student 7 did not seem to take act upon the universalism, the interviewee did seem to take action by raising money for earthquake victims. Notably, and in contrast to himself, Student 7 encounters a lack of discrepancy between his interviewee's valuing of universalism and that person's apparent actual behaviour.

Data 8: I think I'm not universalism because I never do something for people who I don't know. And my partner think that he tend to raise money for the Great Eastern Japan Earthquake. Also, earthquakes and floods have happened all over the world, and many people round the world have suffered from such problems, so he intends to do what he can. We both think about universalism. I think that it can't say I'm universalism person. However, my partner thinks if he has a chance something, he can really help people.

In his critical evaluation essay, which was written in Stage 4 (Critical Evaluation/Loop 1) of the course, Student 7 did not write about the need for universalism in intercultural communication, which suggests that universalism was not a priority for him as suggested above. Having interacted with students in his own class in Loop 1 of the course, Student 7 then interviewed a foreigner in Loop 2. He chose not to describe his foreign interviewee's values related to universalism, but in Stage 3 (Critical Analysis/Loop 2), he did. The value differences identified by Student 7 between his own values and those of his foreign interviewee on universalism are presented in Data 9. One apparent difference between Student 7 and his foreign interviewee is that while Student 7 did not seem to take act upon the universalism, the foreign interviewee did by raising money for earthquake victims, making this the second person Student 7 had interviewed who not only claimed to value, but who also took action through fund-raising. Notably, and again in contrast to himself, Student 7 encounters a lack of discrepancy between his foreign interviewee's valuing of universalism and that person's apparent actual behaviour.

Data 9: I think I'm not universalism because I have never done something for people who I don't know. And my partner thinks she tend to raise money for the Great Eastern Japan Earthquake. Also, various disasters happened all over the world and many people round the world have suffered from such problems, so she intends to do what she can.

In Stage 4 (Critical Evaluation/Loop 2), Student 7 evaluated himself and his foreign interviewee by applying the standard set in Part 1 in Parts 4 and 5 of the final essay. The standard related to universalism is presented in Data 10.

Data 10: I think universalism is important to support intercultural communication, too. People who value universalism think about welfare of all people and nature as whole.

It can be seen in Data 16 and 17 that Student 7 evaluated his partner positively in relation to universalism partly because this involves taking action (i.e. there is no apparent discrepancy between value and behaviour) and evaluated himself negatively partly because he tends not to take action (i.e. there is an apparent discrepancy between value and behaviour). Notably, this was followed by an expression of the desire to take action (i.e. this seems to be an attempt to remove or at least reduce the discrepancy between value and behaviour), and a clear and final reiteration of the valuing of universalism.

> **Data 16:** For universalism, my partner thinks she should try to do something for people who has troubles. For example, voluntary work, donation and so on. When Great Eastern Japan Earthquake happened, my partner donated some money. Also, she tends to visit foreign Country for voluntary work. So I think she values universalism and it correspond with my own value.

> **Data 17:** Next, I evaluate my own values by applying the standards I set. For universalism, I think I'm not universalism because I don't tend to do something for people who I don't know. But I think universalism is important in intercultural communication. So if I have a chance something. I can really help people and I want to donate as much as possible for them. I value universalism.

The reader is now asked to refer back to Data 1, which completes the data analysis loop by showcasing the decisions made by Student 7 related to identity development in relation to universalism in Stage 5 (Identity development/Loop 2) of the course.

Change/Type 2

In Data 2, Student 10 wrote 'During interview, I find that she used the words "family". So I think she values conformity and security best, and I felt that she loved her family and her country. After I finished interview, I changed my standard.' In other words, she intended to change. How had this dynamic unfolded over time?

There was no content change between Student 10's Week 3 homework paragraph on universalism and benevolence, her Week 4 paragraph on tradition, conformity and security, or the corresponding paragraphs in the third version of her Week 5 Essay on Values. Her (Week 5) reflections upon universalism and benevolence in Stage 1 (Analysis of Self) are presented in Data 18, and her reflections on tradition, conformity and security are presented in Data 19. In Data 18, it can be seen that she seems to be drawing a conceptual line between universalism and benevolence along the national boundary between people in Japan and people overseas, and that she also seems to be drawing a conceptual line within the given definition of universalism between caring about the welfare of all people (i.e. not just people in Japan) and caring about nature, the former of which she claims not to care about and the latter of which she does. And further, she partly attributes her lack of care about the welfare of all people to the fact that her school teachers tended not to emphasize it as they emphasized the protection of nature instead.

Regarding conformity, it can be seen in Data 19 that there appears to be some discrepancy between Student 10's present Self and future Self insofar as she claims that while she does not tend to oppose parents and elders in the present, she wants to become independent of them when she grows up.

> **Data 18:** I think that I value benevolence because I find it difficult to care about the welfare of all people, who are distant from me. To be honest, I don't feel that they are close to me. For example, I am more interested in the Tohoku Earthquake disaster in Japan rather than people overseas. And to give another example, I would like to teach children as voluntary work because I am interested in teaching. There is another reason, I think. In Japan, teachers tell us to protect nature, and to save electricity, but they only seem to emphasize only nature. Other problems, such as the welfare of people overseas, are not emphasized so much. Therefore, Japanese people, including me, seem to be more interested in nature than the welfare of people overseas. I am interested in nature because nature is as familiar as people by education.

> **Data 19:** [A]s to conformity, I don't want to harm others, and because I like to live in harmony, I do not oppose my parents and elders. Last, as to security, I care about the stability of society since I would like to live a stable life. In the future, I want to become a person who values tradition and security. I don't want to obey my parents even when I grow up. When I grow up, I think that I will need the 'give and take' spirit in work relations.

In week 7 of Stage 3 (Critical Analysis/Loop 1), Student 10 critically analysed Self and Other by identifying value similarities and differences between herself and her partner. Her critical analysis of values related to universalism and benevolence, and tradition, conformity and security are presented in Data 20 and 21 respectively. Similarities are underlined and differences are italicized for emphasis.

> **Data 20:** When I read my partner's essay, I found some similarities. First, she values benevolence more than universalism, and I don't value universalism. She

thinks that she should appreciate food and not waste it. However, she tends to waste food because she doesn't know people directly who don't have enough food to eat in the world. She tends to help people around her because she knows them directly. This is the same as my opinion. *However, I am interested in nature problems only, which is related to universalism.*

Data 21: Second, she values tradition, conformity and security severally as like my opinions. *However, I don't want to value conformity very much in the future because I don't want to obey my parents even when I grow up.*

In Data 20, regarding universalism, Student 10 reiterates the distinction made in Data 18 within the given definition of universalism between caring about the welfare of all people (which she does not value), and caring about nature (which she does), identifying a similarity between her and her partner insofar as her partner claims to value benevolence more than universalism. In Data 21, regarding conformity, the discrepancy evident between Student 10's present Self and future Self in Data 19 is reiterated in Data 21 as Student 10 notes that while both she and her partner value conformity in the present (i.e. a similarity), she wants to become independent of her parents when she grows up (i.e. a difference).

Having twice claimed that she did not value universalism (caring about the welfare of all people), Data 22 shows that in her critical evaluation essay, which was written in Stage 4 (Critical Evaluation/Loop 1) of the course, Student 10 freely chose to set universalism as the evaluative standard needed to support intercultural communication for the reasons stated, which resulted in a negative self-evaluation that opened up a discrepancy between her own values and the values she thought were needed to support intercultural communication.

Data 22: As I evaluate my own value, I find some negative points. I don't value universalism. When I judge by my international standards, I should value universalism. These days international cooperation is important and I know people who need to help all over the world.

Having interacted with students in her own class in Loop 1 of the course, Student 10 then went on to interview a foreigner in Loop 2. In Stage 3 (Critical Analysis/ Loop 2), the value similarities and differences identified by Student 10 between her own values and those of her foreign interviewee related to universalism and power, and then to conformity and security, are presented in Data 23 and 24 respectively. Similarities are underlined and differences are italicized for emphasis. It can be seen in Data 23 that Student 10's foreign interviewee not only values universalism (caring about the welfare of all people) but also acts upon it by donating money to help people regardless of geographical location. This is a difference between Student 10 and her partner, and notably, her partner's value on this point approximates the value she set for supporting intercultural communication more than her own, highlighting the discrepancy between the two in the process. Regarding conformity, the discrepancy evident between Student 10's present Self and future Self in Data 19 and 21 is reiterated for a third time in Data 24 as Student 10 notes that she wants to become independent of her parents when she grows up, which differentiates her from her partner.

> **Data 23:** First, she doesn't value power because she thinks that power is unsuitable for her, she is weak character. I don't value power, too. The purpose of it is only to get wealth and authority. I neither like those ideas nor need power for me. *Then, if she has power, she wants to help people regardless of around and all over the world. So she values universalism. She has donated money to charity, but she has not restricted to around people in particular. Although she values universalism, she is not interested in global warming. This is a big point that is different from my opinion. I value universalism because I am interested in nature problem, not people in trouble all over the world, and nature problem is as familiar as people in trouble by education. On the other hand, she doesn't think that nature problem, such as global warming is serious.*

> **Data 24:** She loves her family very much. So, she values security. And she values conformity because she is obedient to her parents who she respects. She doesn't want to make them sad by breaking social expectations which she think it good for her. Then if she were against someone's opinion, she keeps her opinion because she likes harmony, but she will try to explain her idea in debate. I value security, too because I like to live in harmony. I care about the stability of society since I would like to live a stable life. *However, there is a different point. I don't value conformity very much because I don't want to obey my parents in the future. When I grow up, I want to decide by myself.*

In Stage 4 (Critical Evaluation/Loop 2), in her final essay, Student 10 was supposed to evaluate herself and her foreign interviewee by applying the standards she set for supporting intercultural communication, which included universalism (caring about the welfare of all people), but instead, she reports on how her standards had changed as a result of the interview. Although it is a little difficult to interpret the content and implications of Data 25 accurately, Student 10 seems to have been influenced by her foreign interviewee's feelings towards family, which Student 10 understood in terms of valuing conformity and security. This seems to have highlighted possible and more complex connections between multiple values in Student 10's mind, triggering a reprioritization of values in the process, which resulted in her replacement of universalism (caring about the welfare of all people) as the value needed to support intercultural communication with the two values of conformity and security, both of which she claimed were connected to the values of universalism and tradition. Regarding conformity, it remains unclear what is happening to the discrepancy evident between her present Self and future Self in Data 19, 21 and 24 as Student 10 seems to have shifted consideration of wanting to become independent for her parents in the future to prizing family more in Data 25.

> **Data 25:** During interview, I find that she used the words 'family'. So I think she values conformity and security best, and I felt that she loved her family and her country. After I finished interview, I changed my standard. At first, I thought that I should set the standard for universalism in terms of supporting intercultural communication because it is necessary in the future to do worldwide. I think that we have to help each other in the future, not only own country but also other countries by globalization which makes the border crossed. However, I set the standard for conformity and security after interview. This is connected with universalism and tradition. As to universalism, to help people around me relates to help people all over the world. I don't think I can help other people if I can't help my family and friends. Tradition influenced my parents and me, and I love my family. Therefore, I love tradition, too because I think that to like people equals to like the environment where people has been brought up. I have never considered about my family deeply before which is always around me. If I didn't interview a foreign student who left her family and lives alone in foreign country, I wouldn't do so. After interview, I could find that this narrow unit connects wide supporting intercultural communication in terms of conformity and security. I want to communicate with foreign people because I am interested in many Other cultures and ideas. As to my standard, I have already put value on conformity and security for intercultural communication. Therefore, I want to prize my family much more.

The reader is now asked to refer back to Data 2, which completes the data analysis loop by showcasing the decisions made by Student 10 related to identity development in Stage 5 (Identity development/Loop 2) of the course.

Change/Type 3

In Data 3, Student 15 wrote 'My idea about universalism and benevolence changed in response to my interviewee.' In other words, her ideas had changed in response to her interviewee. How had this dynamic unfolded over time?

There was no content change between Student 15's Week 3 homework paragraph on universalism and benevolence, or the corresponding paragraphs in the third version of her Week 5 Essay on Values. Her (Week 5) reflections upon universalism and benevolence in Stage 1 (Analysis of Self) are presented in Data 26, where it can be seen that she claims to value both universalism and benevolence. Notably, the conceptual line drawn by Student 10 between universalism and benevolence along the national boundary between people in Japan and people overseas in Data 18 does not seem to have been drawn by Student 15 in Data 26 as she claims to have tried to help both people suffering from the earthquake in Japan and people suffering from poverty around the world.

> **Data 26:** Next, I say about universalism and benevolence. I donated money to help people who suffered in the great earthquake in Eastern Japan. When I first found out about the news, I was greatly shocked by it. Then, I thought I should do what I can do help the earthquake victims because I simply couldn't treat it as having nothing to do with me, so I tend to save water and electricity, and I don't tend to hoard up things like a toilet roll and bottle of water and so on. And I tend to donate a few money to people that live in need. I wanted to give some kind of assistance to them. I bought fair trade goods that from poverty area in the world. Actually, fair trade goods are more expensive than other goods, but I think I should contribute toward people living in poverty, so when I find fair trade goods, I buy it as many as I can.

In week 7 of Stage 3 (Critical Analysis/Loop 1), Student 15 critically analysed Self and Other by identifying value similarities and differences between herself and her partner. In Data 27, similarities are underlined and differences are italicized for emphasis. It can be seen in Data 27 that Student 15 has noticed that while both she and her partner claimed to value universalism (caring about the welfare of all people), their points of view actually differed.

> **Data 27:** We both wrote about universalism and we both wrote about welfare of all people. *However, our point of view are different. She wrote that she thinks that people getting universalism are hypocrite. But when she watched news about great earthquake in Eastern Japan, she noticed all people who have universalism aren't hypocrite. Because if all people have benevolence, suffering people are not saved. Therefore, she thinks mind of welfare is very important. On the other hands, I wrote that I wanted to give some kind of assistance to people that live in need. So I wrote universalism very important in my life too.*

Data 28 shows that in her critical evaluation essay, which was written in Stage 4 (Critical Evaluation/Loop 1) of the course, Student 15 set universalism (caring about the welfare of all people) as the standard to support intercultural communication. Although she had twice claimed to value universalism (caring about the welfare of all people) in both Data 26 and 27, this actually results in a negative self-evaluation, which seems to indicate emergent instability within the value.

> **Data 28:** As I evaluate my own value, I find some negative points. I don't value universalism. When I judge by my international standards, I should value universalism. These days international cooperation is important and I know people who need to help all over the world.

Having interacted with students in her own class in Loop 1, Student 15 interviewed a foreigner in Loop 2 of the course. Her description of her foreign interviewee's values related to universalism and benevolence in Stage 2 (Analysis of Other/Loop 2) is presented in Data 29, where the instability within her valuing of universalism (caring about the welfare of all people) starts to become more apparent as she reports on her foreign interviewee's support for governmental acceptance of foreign refugees into Australia.

> **Data 29:** First, he doesn't value about benevolence. In other words, he values about universalism. He thinks that receiving refugees is good things because he want to help worried people. Also, Australian government have accepted refugees legally yet every year. He thinks it is not good to receive refugees illegally, but follow certain steps to promote a project is good.

In Stage 3 (Critical Analysis/Loop 2), the value differences identified by Student 15 between her own values and those of her foreign interviewee on universalism and benevolence are presented in Data 30, where the limitations of Student 15's valuing of universalism (caring about the welfare of all people) start to become clear as she expresses her opposition to governmental acceptance of foreign refugees into Japan for the reasons stated.

> **Data 30:** First, I have value about benevolence. My idea is difference from my interviewee's idea. I'm negative for receiving refugees because if a lot of refugees come to Japan, Japan might be unable to deal with their life. Also, Japanese government receive refugees more, jobs for Japanese might decrease and it is more difficult to me to find job. So I don't think it is important to receive refugees.

In Stage 4 (Critical Evaluation/Loop 2), Student 15 evaluated herself and her foreign interviewee by applying the standards set in her final essay as shown in Data 31. Having claimed to value universalism (caring about the welfare of all people) in Data 26 and 27, and having then brought this into question into Data 28, 29 and 30, Student 15 then sets universalism as the standard needed to support intercultural communication, opening up a discrepancy between this and her own valuing of universalism, in some aspects, in the process.

> **Data 31:** I think that having a value of universalism is more important than having a value of benevolence is the standard and it support intercultural communication, because I think that world has gone global, so international cooperation is more needed.

It can be seen in Data 32 and 33 respectively that Student 15 evaluated her interviewee positively and herself negatively for the reasons stated, which resulted in a negative self-evaluation that seems to have triggered opinion change on the issue of refugees as shown in Data 34, apparently closing the discrepancy between universalism as the standard needed to support intercultural communication and her own valuing of universalism in the process.

> **Data 32:** My interviewee thinks that having a value of universalism important. It corresponds with my standard and I think that his idea promote intercultural communication.

> **Data 33:** I think my idea for benevolence is difference to my standards because I only think about myself. This behavior can't promote intercultural communication and it reduces the opportunities that I can meet people who come from other countries.

> **Data 34:** My idea about universalism and benevolence changed in response to my interviewee. It is not good to think about only around me and Japanese. I think that Japanese government should accept more refugees because I think Japanese attention should not be paid only to the interior of Japan, but to worried countries as well. This behavior help a lot of worried people in foreign countries and bring me connection with foreign people.

The reader is now asked to refer back to Data 3 and 5, which completes the data analysis loop by showcasing the decision made by Student 15 related to identity development in Stage 5 (Identity development/Loop 2) of the course.

Discussion

In the description of the ID Model at the start of this chapter, it was suggested that a value system can be conceptualized as a complex, hierarchically organized and unstable system that forms part of a person's broader identity, which contains various interconnected values that include stated values, real, ideal and target values, all of which may be evidenced in, yet sometimes contradict, behaviour and feelings.

One kind of contradiction is illustrated by Student 7 who claimed to value universalism, but did not tend to act upon it in practice. This discrepancy between the valuing of universalism and actual behaviour was brought into question as Student 7, having explored the values of another student and a foreign interviewee using non-judgemental, empathy-oriented communication strategies, noticed a lack of discrepancy between the valuing of universalism and actual behaviour in both cases. Student 7 then set universalism as the standard to support intercultural communication evaluating the foreign interviewee positively for taking action and himself negatively for not following this up with an expression of the desire to change in the future by taking action in support of universalism. This can be considered an attempt to resolve self-discrepancy, which is considered to be a key mechanism in identity development in Houghton's ID Model as noted earlier.

This chapter has focused primarily upon showcasing student identity development in relation to values, and in particular, in relation to universalism, but as pointed out in the brief description of Stage 1 of the ID Model earlier in the chapter, this is integrally connected to student concepts. Possible conceptual differences between students can be illustrated by way of comparing and contrasting Students 10 and 15's conceptualizations of universalism. In Table 10.2, a particular definition of universalism was presented to students who, while using it as a common reference point, also chose to adapt it to suit them personally, perhaps by prioritizing some components and deprioritizing others differently (as in the case of student 10, who chose to value nature but not people outside Japan), or by drawing different conceptual distinctions between universalism and benevolence (as in the cases of Students 10 and 15, the former of whom drew the conceptual distinction between people inside and outside Japan, and the latter of whom initially did not although she seemed to do this later).

Universalism did not seem to be initially valued at all by Student 10 whose conceptualization of universalism and benevolence was based upon pivotal distinctions between the welfare of all people and the protection of nature (within the concept of universalism), and between people in Japan and people overseas (in the distinction between universalism and benevolence). Of these, Student 10 only claimed to care about nature. Having explored the values of another student using non-judgemental, empathy-oriented communication strategies, Student 10 reiterated the claim that she did not value universalism (caring about the welfare of all people) while somewhat contradictorily going on to set it as standard to be used to support intercultural communication. The application of this standard resulted in negative self-evaluation as a discrepancy emerged between her own values and values supportive of intercultural communication.

Having explored the values of a foreign interviewee using non-judgemental, empathy-oriented communication strategies, Student 10 noticed a difference between her own valuing of universalism and her foreign interviewee's valuing of universalism/action upon it. However, although she had set universalism as the standard to support intercultural communication, and although her foreign interviewee also valued it, she replaced it with conformity and security (in connection to universalism/tradition) in response to her foreign interviewee. She did not clearly evaluate herself or her foreign interviewee by applying the old or new standard(s). Regarding conformity, despite earlier discrepancy between present/future selves in wanting to become independent from her parents in the future, Student 10 claimed that she wanted to want to prize her family more, although the meaning and implications remain unclear. What can be said, however, is that both her personal understandings and conceptualization of the values, and the ways in which she was making connections between them, were changing in response to her foreign interviewee in ways that did not correspond to the other two students whose development was tracked in this chapter. Other than requiring students to select values supportive of intercultural communication, the teacher did not guide students' choices leaving them free to find their own person pathway through the ID Model.

Indeed, a key feature of the ID Model is that if it is applied systematically by the teacher over time (in this case, over a 13-week period), students are given plenty of time to reflect upon and develop clearer understandings and descriptions of their values, and plentiful opportunities in weekly written tasks to revise past positions freely in response to new experience and ideas. Thus, while students may claim unequivocally to value universalism (or any particular value) at the start of the course, they may come to realize the limitations of their value through encounters with Otherness. This is exemplified by Student 15, who claimed to value both universalism and benevolence at the start of the course, and although she not seem to draw a conceptual line between universalism and benevolence along the national boundary between people in Japan and people overseas like Student 10, the limitations of her conceptualization and valuing of universalism became clear later.

Having explored the values of another student using non-judgemental, empathy-oriented communication strategies, she noticed that while both she and her partner valued universalism (caring about the welfare of all people), their viewpoints differed. She set universalism (caring about the welfare of all people) as the standard to support intercultural communication, but despite twice claiming to value universalism (caring about the welfare of all people), she evaluated herself negatively when applying that standard indicating the emergence of value instability. Then, having explored the values of a foreign interviewee using non-judgemental, empathy-oriented communication strategies, she noticed her foreign interviewee's support for governmental acceptance of foreign refugees into Australia, and her own opposition to governmental acceptance of foreign refugees into her own country, Japan. She then set universalism as the standard to support intercultural communication, evaluating her foreign interviewee positively and herself negatively when applying the standard, which seems to have triggered opinion change on the issue of refugees, thus reducing the discrepancy between universalism as the standard she chose to support intercultural communication and her own limited valuing of it.

The valuing of universalism differed insofar as while all students at least initially set universalism as a value to support intercultural communication, Student 10 did not actually value (parts of it) herself, Student 7 claimed to value it but did not tend to take action in support of it, and Student 15, while initially claiming to care about people from Other countries, came to find that the scope of her care was more limited than she expected when she came to consider the particular issue of governmental acceptance of refugees into her own country, although recognition of the inconsistency of her own position in this regard appears to have triggered opinion change.

In all three cases, students' (de)valuing of universalism was brought into question by encounters with Otherness in the form of both Japanese classroom peers and foreign interviewees, but they responded to it in different ways. In the cases of Students 7 and 15, exploring the values of Others, and in particular noticing the ways in which universalism was valued, ultimately seems to have strengthened the students' valuing of universalism in the final analysis as self-discrepancies of different kinds were attended to and resolved. Student 10, however, basically did not value universalism although she seemed to think she should for the purposes of supporting intercultural communication, at least in the beginning, although she came to replace it with other values.

Conclusion

In this chapter, different kinds of identity development in students in relation to standard setting for intercultural communication, and particularly in relation to the valuing of universalism, have been explored and showcased. Statement patterns in students' written work that indicated identity change had already happened, was underway, or was being planned by the students concerned were presented and discussed in relation to the broader data set to track students' personal journeys through the course. As we have seen, identity development in Stage 5 of the ID Model seems to involve reasoned reflection on the part of students, who have progressed through Stages 1–4 of the model, upon whether or not to change in response to their interlocutor(s), which provides them with the opportunity to change consciously if they so wish. Decision making is evident in students' statements that they have either already changed, or that they do (or do not) intend to change, in response to intercultural dialogue, and it may refer back to earlier stages of the model.

References

Abrams, D. and Hogg, M. A. (1990). *Social Identity Theory: Constructive and Critical Advances*. London: Harvester-Wheatsheaf.

Agha, A. (1993). Grammatical and indexical convention in honorific discourse. *Journal of Linguistic Anthropology*, 3(2), 131–63.

— (2005). Voice, footing, enregisterment. *Journal of Linguistic Anthropology*, 15(1), 38–59.

— (2011). Meet mediatization. *Language and Communication*, 31(3), 163–70.

Aguilar Río, J. I. (2010). Pour une analyse de la « présentation de soi » de l'enseignant de L2 : Style revendiqué, aspects relationnels, décisions interactionnelles. Unpublished Ph.D. dissertation, Sorbonne Nouvelle-Paris 3 University, Paris.

— (2011). L'étude de la cognition enseignante à travers l'auto-confrontation : problématiques de recherche et précautions méthodologiques. In V. Bigot and L. Cadet (Eds), *Discours d'enseignants sur leur action en classe : Enjeux théoriques et enjeux de formation*, Actes académiques (pp. 61–73). Paris: Riveneuve éditions.

Alaszewski, A. (2006). *Using Diaries for Social Research*. London: Sage.

Anderson, B. (2006). *Imagined Communities: Reflections on the Origins and Spread of Nationalism* (Revised Edition). London: Verso.

Antaki, C. and Widdicombe, S. (Eds) (1998). *Identities in Talk*. London: Sage.

Appadurai, A. (1996). *Modernity at Large: Cultural Dimensions of Globalization*. Minneapolis, MN: University of Minnesota Press.

Appleby, R. (2012). Desire in translation: White masculinity and TESOL. *TESOL Quarterly*, 47(1), 122–47.

Archer, M. S. (2000). *Being Human: The Problem of Agency*. Cambridge: Cambridge University Press.

Arditty, J. and Vasseur, M.-T. (1999). Interaction et langue étrangère : présentation. *Langages*, 134, 3–19.

Arkoudis, S. and Davison, C. (Eds) (2008). Chinese students: Perspectives on their social, cognitive, and linguistic investment in English medium interaction. *Journal of Asian Pacific Communication*, 18(1), 1–133.

Arndt, H. and Janney, R. (1991). Verbal, prosodic, and kinesic emotive contrast in speech. *Journal of Pragmatics*, 15(6), 521–49.

Ashforth, B. E. and Mael, F. (1989). Social identity theory and the organization. *Academy of Management Review*, 14(1), 20–39.

Atlantic Provinces Education Foundation (1997). *Programme de français immersion tardive – 7e, 8e et 9e année – version provisoire.*

Auerbach, E. R. (1993). Reexamining English only in the ESL classroom. *TESOL Quarterly*, 27(1), 9–32.

Bailey, K. (2007). Akogare, ideology, and 'Charisma Man' mythology: Reflections on ethnographic research in English language schools in Japan. *Gender, Place and Culture*, 14(5), 585–608.

Ball, S. J. (2000). Performativities and fabrications in the education economy: Towards the performative society. *Australian Educational Researcher*, 17(3), 1–24.

— (2003). The teacher's soul and the terrors of performativity. *Journal of Educational Policy*, 18(2), 215–28.

Ballmer, T. T. (1981). A typology of native speakers. In F. Coulmas (Ed.), *A Festschrift for Native Speaker* (pp. 51–67). The Hague: Mouton.

Bamberg, M. (2006). Stories: Big or small? Why do we care? *Narrative Inquiry*, 16(1), 139–47.

— (2010). Who am I? Narration and its contribution to self and identity. *Theory & Psychology*, 21(1), 1–22.

Bandura, A. (1999). Social cognitive theory: An agentic perspective. *Asian Journal of Social Psychology*, 2(1), 21–41.

Barker, D. (2003). Why English teachers in Japan need to learn Japanese. *Language Teacher*, 27(2), 7–11.

Barkhuizen, G. (2011). Narrative knowledging in TESOL. *TESOL Quarterly*, 45(3), 391–414.

Barnard, I. (2002). Whole-class workshops: The transformation of students into writers. *Issues of Writing*, 12(2), 124–43.

Barton, D. and Tusting, K. (2005). Introduction. In D. Barton and K. Tusting (Eds), *Beyond Communities of Practice: Language, Power and Social Context* (pp. 1–33). New York: Cambridge University Press.

Befu, H. (1983). Internationalisation of Japan and Nihon Bunkaron. In H. Mannari and H. Befu (Eds), *The Challenges of Japan's Internationalisation: Organization and Culture* (pp. 232–66). Tokyo: Kwansei Gakuin and Kodansha International.

— (2001). *Hegemony of Homogeneity*. Melbourne: Trans Pacific Press.

Behan, L., Turnbull, M. and Spek, J. (1997). The proficiency gap in late French immersion: Language use in collaborative tasks. *Le Journal de l'Immersion*, 20(2), 41–4.

Beijaard, D., Meijer, P. C. and Verloop, N. (2004). Reconsidering research on teachers' professional identity. *Teaching and Teacher Education*, 20(2), 107–28.

Bellah, R. N. (1965). Japan's cultural identity: Some reflections on the work of Watsuji Testsurō. *Journal of Asian Studies*, 24(4), 573–94.

Benesch, S. (1993). ESL, ideology, and the politics of pragmatism. *TESOL Quarterly*, 27(4), 705–17.

Benwell, B. and Stokoe, E. (2006). *Discourse and Identity*. Edinburgh: Edinburgh University Press.

Bertin, J.-C., Gravé, P. and Narcy-Combes, J.-P. (2010). *Second Language Distance Learning and Teaching: Theoretical Perspectives and Didactic Ergonomics*. Hershey: IGI Global.

Bhabha, H. K. (1994). *The Location of Culture*. London: Routledge.

Bhatia, V. (2008). Genre analysis, ESP and professional practice. *English for Specific Purposes*, 27(2), 161–74.

Billig, M. (1995). *Banal Nationalism*. London: Sage.

Black, C. (2013). Motivation: A key factor in L2 teaching and learning. In J. Schwieter (Ed.), *Studies and Global Perspectives of Second Language Teaching and Learning*. Greenwich, CT: Information Age Publishing.

Blackledge, A. and Creese, A. (2010). *Multilingualism: A Critical Perspective*. London: Continuum.

Bloch, C. (1996). Emotions and discourse. *Text*, 16(3), 323–41.

Block, D. (2003). *The Social Turn in Second Language Acquisition*. Edinburgh: Edinburgh University Press.

— (2007a). The rise of identity in SLA research, post Firth and Wagner (1997). *Modern Language Journal*, 91(s1), 863–76.

— (2007b). *Second Language Identities*. London: Continuum.

Blommaert, J. (2010). *The Sociolinguistics of Globalization*. Cambridge: Cambridge University Press.

Bodrova, E. and Leong, D. (1995). Scaffolding the writing process: The Vygotskian approach. *Colorado Reading Council Journal*, 6, 27–9.

— (1996). *Tools of the Mind: The Vygotskian Approach to Early Childhood Education*. Englewood Cliffs, NJ: Merrill/Prentice Hall.

Boreham, N. and Gray, P. (2005). *Professional Identity of Teachers in Their Early Development*. Paper presented at the Dublin Symposium. Retrieved from www.ioe.stir.ac.uk/research/projects/epl/docs/ProfidentityNB.pdf

Borg, S. (2009). Language teacher cognition. In J. C. Richards and A. Burns (Eds), *The Cambridge Guide to Second Language Teacher Education* (pp. 163–71). Cambridge: Cambridge University Press.

— (2011). Teacher learning on the Delta. *Research Notes*, 45, 19–25.

Bourdieu, P. (1977). The economics of linguistic exchanges. *Social Science Information*, 16(6), 645–68.

— (1991). *Language and Symbolic Power*. Cambridge: Polity Press.

Bourdieu, P. and Passeron, J.-C. (1977). *Reproduction in Education, Society, and Culture*. Beverly Hills, CA: Sage.

— (1990). *Reproduction in Education, Society, and Culture* (2nd Edition). Beverly Hills, CA: Sage.

Bredella, L. (2000). Literary texts. In M. Byram (Ed.), *Routledge Encyclopedia of Language Teaching and Learning* (pp. 375–82). London: Routledge.

Brewer, M. B. and Pierce, K. P. (2005). Social identity complexity and outgroup tolerance. *Personality and Social Psychology Bulletin*, 31(3), 428–37.

Brubaker, R. and Cooper, F. (2000). Beyond 'identity'. *Theory and Society*, 29(1), 1–47.

Bucholtz, M. (2011). *White Kids: Language, Race, and Styles of Youth Identity*. Cambridge: Cambridge University Press.

Bucholtz, M. and Hall, K. (2004). Language and identity. In A. Duranti (Ed.), *A Companion to Linguistic Anthropology* (pp. 369–94). Malden, MA: Blackwell.

— (2005). Identity and interaction: A sociocultural linguistic approach. *Discourse Studies*, 7(4/5), 585–614.

— (2010). Locating identity in language. In C. Llamas and D. Watt (Eds), *Language and Identities* (pp. 18–28). Edinburgh: Edinburgh University Press.

Bueno, E. P. and Caesar, T. (2003). *I Wouldn't Want Anybody to Know: Native English Teaching in Japan*. Tokyo: JPGS Press.

Burgess, C. (2004). Maintaining identities: Discourses of homogeneity in a rapidly globalizing Japan. *Electronic Journal of Contemporary Japan*. Retrieved from www.japanesestudies.org.uk/articles/Burgess.html

Butler, J. (1988). Performative acts and gender constitution: An essay in phenomenology and feminist theory. *Theatre Journal*, 40(4), 519–31.

— (1990). *Gender Trouble: Feminism and the Subversion of Identity*. London: Routledge.

— (1997). Merely cultural. *Social Text*, 52/53, 265–77.

— (2004). *Undoing Gender*. New York: Routledge.

Butzkamm, W. and Caldwell, J. A. W. (2009). *The Bilingual Reform: A Paradigm Shift in Foreign Language Teaching*. Tübingen: Narr.

Byram, M. (1997). *Teaching and Assessing Intercultural Communicative Competence*. Clevedon: Multilingual Matters.

— (2008). *From Foreign Language Education to Education for Intercultural Citizenship: Essays and Reflections*. Bristol: Multilingual Matters.

Byram, M. and Morgan, C. (1994). *Teaching-and-Learning Language-and-Culture*. Clevedon: Multilingual Matters.

Byram, M., Barrett, M., Ipgrave, J., et al. (2009). *Autobiography of Intercultural Encounters: Context, Concepts and Theories*. Strasbourg: Language Policy Division, Council of Europe Publishing.

Cachet, O. (2009). Professionnalisme des enseignants et complexité : vers une conception dynamique de l'agir. *Lidil*, 39, 133–50.

Caffi, C. and Janney, R. (1994). Towards a pragmatics of emotive communication. *Journal of Pragmatics*, 22(3/4), 325–73.

Caldas-Coulthard, C. R. and Iedema, R. (Eds) (2008). *Identity Trouble: Critical Discourse and Contested Identities*. Houndmills: Palgrave Macmillan.

Calhoun, C. (1998). *Nationalism*. Minneapolis: MN: University of Minnesota Press.

Calvé, P. (1993). Pour enseigner le français . . . en français (To teach French . . . in French). *Canadian Modern Language Review*, 50(1), 15–29.

Cambra Giné, M. (2003). *Une approche ethnographique de la classe de langue*. Paris: Crédif-Didier.

Canagarajah, A. S. (1999). *Resisting Linguistic Imperialism in English Teaching*. Oxford: Oxford University Press.

— (2006). TESOL at forty: What are the issues? *TESOL Quarterly*, 40(1), 9–34.

Carlile, P. R. (2004). Transferring, translating and transforming: An integrative framework for managing knowledge across boundaries. *Organization Science*, 15(5), 555–68.

Carroll, S., Motha, S. and Price, J. (2008). Accessing imagined communities and reinscribing regimes of truth. *Critical Inquiry in Language Studies*, 5(3), 165–91.

Carter, R. (2010). Issues in pedagogical stylistics: A coda. *Language and Literature*, 19(1), 115–22.

Chambers, G. (1992). Teaching in the target language. *Language Learning Journal*, 6(1), 66–7.

Chang, H. (2008). *Autoethnography as Method*. Walnut Creek, CA: Left Coast.

Chatsis, A., Miyashita, M. and Cole, D. (2013). A documentary ethnography of a Blackfoot language course: Patterns of variationism and standard in the organization of diversity. In S. Bischoff, D. Cole, A. Fountain and M. Miyashita (Eds), *The Persistence of Language: Constructing and Confronting the Past and Present in the Voices of Jane H. Hill* (pp. 277–310). Amsterdam: John Benjamins.

Chen, X. M. (1995). *Occidentalism: A Theory of Counter-Discourse in Post-Mao China*. New York: Oxford University Press.

Cicurel, F. (1991). L'identité discursive d'un apprenant. In G. Russier, H. Stoffel and D. Véronique (Eds), *Interactions en langue étrangère* (pp. 259–69). Aix-In-Provence: Publications de l'Université de Provence.

— (2005). La flexibilité communicative : un atout pour la construction de l'agir enseignant. Le français dans le monde : *Recherches et applications*, 167, 145–64.

Clandinin, D. J. and Connelly, F. M. (1995). *Teachers' Professional Knowledge Landscapes*. New York: Teachers College Press.

Clarke, M. (2008). *Language Teacher Identities: Co-constructing Discourse and Community*. Bristol: Multilingual Matters.

Clemente, A. and Higgins, M. (2008). *Performing English with a Postcolonial Accent: Ethnographic Narratives from Mexico*. London: Tufnell Publishing.

Clore, G., Ortony, A. and Foss, M. (1987). The psychological foundations of the affective lexicon. *Journal of Personality and Social Psychology*, 53(4), 751–66.

Codd, J., Gordon, L. and Harker, R. (1990). Education and the role of the State: Devolution and control post-Picot. In H. Lauder and C. Wylie (Eds), *Towards Successful Schooling* (pp. 15–32). London: Routledge.

Cohen, L., Manion, L. and Morrison, K. (2000). *Research Methods in Education*. London, New York: Routledge.

Coldron, J. and Smith, R. (1999). Active location in teachers' construction of their professional identities. *Journal of Curriculum Studies*, 31(6), 711–26.

Cole, D. (2007). Online voice tools can help us teach and learn about language attitudes (and be attentive to prescriptivism in academic written English). *Anthropology News*, 48(6), 11.

Cole, D. and Meadows, B. (2013). Avoiding the essentialist trap in intercultural education: Using critical discourse analysis to read nationalist ideologies in the language classroom. In F. Dervin and A. Liddicoat (Eds), *Linguistics for Intercultural Education* (pp. 29–47). Amsterdam: John Benjamins.

Cole, D. and Pellicer, R. (2012). Uptake (un)limited: The mediatization of register shifting in U.S. public discourse. *Language in Society*, 41(4), 449–70.

Comer, D. R. and Vega, G. (2011). *Moral Courage in Organizations: Doing the Right Thing at Work*. Armonk, NY: M. E. Sharpe.

Comoroff, J. (1985). *Body of Power, Spirit of Resistance: The Culture and History of a South African People*. Chicago, IL: University of Chicago Press.

Compton, L. K. L. (2009). Preparing language teachers to teach language online: A look at skills, roles, and responsibilities. *Computer Assisted Language Learning*, 22(1), 73–99.

Conle, C. (2000). Narrative inquiry: Research tool and medium for professional development. *European Journal of Teacher Education*, 23(1), 49–63.

Connelly, F. M. and Clandinin, D. J. (2006). Narrative inquiry. In J. L. Green, G. Camilli and P. Elmore (Eds), *Handbook of Complementary Methods in Education Research* (3rd Edition) (pp. 477–87). Mahwah, NJ: Lawrence Erlbaum Associates.

Cook, V. (2002). Language teaching methodology and the L2 user perspective. In V. Cook (Ed.), *Portraits of the L2 User* (pp. 327–43). Clevedon: Multilingual Matters.

— (2005). Basing teaching on the L2 user. In E. Llurda (Ed.), *Non-Native Language Teachers: Perceptions, Challenges and Contributions to the Profession* (pp. 47–61). New York: Springer.

Council of Europe (2001). *Un Cadre Européen de Référence pour les Langues : Apprendre, Enseigner, Évaluer*. Strasbourg: Editions du Conseil de l'Europe.

Council of Local Authorities for International Relations (2010). *JET Programme FAQs*. Retrieved from www.jetprogramme.org/e/faq/faq01what.html

Crawshaw, R., Callen, B. and Tusting, K. (2001). Attesting the self: Narration and identity change during periods of residence abroad. *Language and intercultural communication*, 1(2), 101–19.

Creswell, J. W. (2003). *Research Design: Qualitative, Quantitative and Mixed Method Approaches*. Thousand Oaks, CA: Sage.

Crookes, G. and Schmidt, R. (1991). Motivation: Reopening the research agenda. *Language Learning*, 41(4), 469–512.

Culhane, S. (2003). Sojourner acculturation attitudes: Suggestions for learner motivation in second language acquisition (SLA). *Bulletin of the Faculty of Education, Kagoshima University*, 54, 59–74.

Cummins, J. (2006). Identity texts: The imaginative construction of self through multiliteracies pedagogy. In O. García, T. Skutnabb-Kangas and E. Torres-Guzmán (Eds), *Imagining Multilingual Schools. Language in Education and Globalization* (pp. 51–68). Bristol: Multilingual Matters.

Cummins, J. and Early, M. (Eds) (2011). *Identity Texts: The Collaborative Creation of Power in Multilingual Schools*. Stoke-on-Trent: Trentham.

Dale, P. N. (1986). *The Myth of Japanese Uniqueness*. London: Routledge.

Dagenais, D., Moore, D., Lamarre, S., Sabatier, C. and Armand, F. (2009). Linguistic landscape and language awareness. In E. Shohamy and D. Gorter (Eds), *Linguistic Landscape: Expanding the Scenery* (pp. 253–69). New York: Routledge.

Davies, A. (2004). The native speaker in applied linguistics. In A. Davies and C. Elder (Eds), *The Handbook of Applied Linguistics* (pp. 431–50). Malden, MA: Blackwell.

Davis, K. and Skilton-Sylvester, E. (Eds) (2004). Gender in TESOL. *TESOL Quarterly*, 38(3), 377–544.

Day, E. (2002). *Identity and the Young English Language Learner*. Clevedon: Multilingual Matters.

Dervin, F. (2011). A plea for change in research on intercultural discourses: A 'liquid' approach to the study of the acculturation of Chinese students. *Journal of Multicultural Discourses*, 6(1), 37–52.

Dervin, F. and Liddicoat, A. (forthcoming). Introduction. In F. Dervin and A. Liddicoat (Eds), *Linguistics for Intercultural Education*. Amsterdam: John Benjamins.

Dewaele, J. (2009). Perception, attitude, and motivation. In V. Cook and L. Wei (Eds), *Contemporary Applied Linguistics: Language Teaching and Learning* (pp. 163–92). London: Continuum.

Dick, K. and Kofman, A. Z. (2005). *Derrida: Screenplay and Essays on the Film*. Manchester: Manchester University Press.

Diehl, M. (1988). Social identity and minimal groups: The effects of interpersonal and intergroup attitudinal similarity on intergroup discrimination. *British Journal of Social Psychology*, 27(4), 289–300.

Dixon, L., Zhao, J., Shin, J., et al. (2012). What we know about second language acquisition: A synthesis from four perspectives. *AERA*, 82(1), 5–60.

Dörnyei, Z. (1994). Motivation and motivating in the foreign language classroom. *Modern Language Journal*, 78(3), 273–84.

— (2001). *Motivational Strategies in the Language Classroom*. Cambridge: Cambridge University Press.

— (2005). *The Psychology of the Language Learner: Individual Differences in Second Language Acquisition*. Mahwah, NJ: Lawrence Erlbaum Associates.

— (2007). Creating a motivational classroom environment. In J. Cummins and C. Davidson (Eds), *International Handbook of English Language Teaching* (pp. 719–31). New York: Springer.

— (2009). The L2 motivational self system. In Z. Dörnyei and E. Ushioda (Eds), *Motivation, Language Identity and the L2 Self* (pp. 9–24). Bristol: Multilingual Matters.

Dörnyei, Z. and Schmidt, R. (2001). *Motivation and Second Language Acquisition*. Honolulu, HI: University of Hawaii Press.

Duff, P. (2002). The discursive co-construction of knowledge, identity, and difference: An ethnography of communication in the high school mainstream. *Applied Linguistics*, 23(3), 289–322.

Duff, P. and Uchida, Y. (1997). The negotiation of sociocultural identity in post-secondary EFL classrooms. *TESOL Quarterly*, 31(3), 451–86.

Dupuis, V., Heyworth, F., Leban, K., Szesztay, M. and Tinsley, T. (2003). *Face à l'avenir : Les enseignants de langues étrangères à travers l'Europe*. Strasbourg: Editions du Conseil de l'Europe.

Eckert, P. and Wenger, E. (2005). Communities of practice in sociolinguistics: What is the role of power in sociolinguistic variation? *Journal of Sociolinguistics*, 9(4), 582–9.

Edwards, D. (1994). Script formulations: An analysis of event descriptions in conversation. *Journal of Language and Social Psychology*, 13(3), 211–47.

Edwards, J. (2009). *Language and Identity: An Introduction*. Cambridge: Cambridge University Press.

Ellis, N. C. (2008). The dynamics of second language emergence: Cycles of language use, language change, and language acquisition. *Modern Language Journal*, 92(2), 232–49.

Fairclough, N. (1989). *Language and Power*. London: Longman.

Fanon, F. (1967). *Black Skin, White Masks*. New York: Grove Press.

Farquhar, J. (2002). *Appetites: Food and Sex in Post-socialist China (Body, Commodity, Text)*. Durham, NC: Duke University Press.

Fenton-Smith, B. and Torpey, M. J. (2013). Orienting EFL teachers: Principles arising from an evaluation of an induction program in a Japanese university. *Language Teaching Research*, DOI: 10.1177/1362168813475946.

Festinger, L. (1957). *A Theory of Cognitive Dissonance*. Evanston, IL: Row Peterson.

Firth, A. and Wagner, J. (1997). On Discourse, Communication, and (Some) Fundamental Concepts in SLA Research. *Modern Language Journal*, 81(3), 285–300.

Foucault, M. (1984). *The Foucault Reader* (P. Rabinow, Ed.). New York: Pantheon Books.

— (1990 [1978]). *History of Sexuality, Vol. 1: An Introduction*. New York: Vintage Books.

Fraenkel, J., Wallen, N. and Hyun, H. (2012). *How to Design and Evaluate Research in Education* (8th Edition). New York: McGraw-Hill.

Freeman, D. (2002). The hidden side of the work: Teacher knowledge and learning to teach. A perspective from North American educational research on teacher education in English language teaching. *Language Teaching*, 35(1), 1–13.

Gardner, R. C. (1985). *Social Psychology and Second Language Learning: The Role of Attitudes and Motivation*. London, ON: Edward Arnold.

— (2001). Integrative motivation and second language acquisition. In Z. Dörnyei and R. Schmidt (Eds), *Motivation and Second Language Acquisition* (pp. 1–19). Honolulu, HI: University of Hawaii Press.

— (2009, May). *Perceptions on Motivation for Second Language Learning on the 50th Anniversary of Gardner & Lambert (1959)*. Paper presented at the annual meeting of the Canadian Association of Applied Linguistics, Ottawa, Canada.

Gardner, R. C. and Lambert, W. E. (1959). Motivational variables in second language acquisition. *Canadian Journal of Psychology*, 13(4), 266–72.

— (1972). *Attitudes and Motivation in Second Language Learning*. Rowley, MA: Newbury House.

Geertz, C. (2000 [1973]). *The Interpretation of Cultures*. New York: Basic Books.

Gellner, E. (2006). *Nations and Nationalism* (2nd Edition). Malden, MA: Blackwell.

Genetsch, M. (2007). *The Texture of Identity*. Toronto, ON: TSAR Publications.

Georgakopoulou, A. (2011). Teachers, students and ways of telling in classroom sites: A case of out-of-(work) place identities. In J. Angouri and M. Marra (Eds), *Constructing Identities at Work* (pp. 151–76). Houndmills: Palgrave Macmillan.

Gini, G. (2006). Bullying as a social process: The role of groupmembership in students' perception of inter-group aggression at school. *Journal of School Psychology*, 44(1), 51–65.

Giroux, H. A. (2003). Pedagogies of difference, race, and representation: Film as a site of translation and politics. In P. P. Trifonas (Ed.), *Pedagogies of Difference: Rethinking Education for Social Change* (pp. 83–109). New York: Routledge.

Goebel, Z. (2008). Enregistering, authorizing, and denaturalizing identity in Indonesia. *Journal of Linguistic Anthropology*, 18(1), 46–61.

Goffman, E. (1959). *The Presentation of Self in Everyday Life*. New York: Double Anchor Books.

Graham, S. and Juvonen, J. (2002). Ethnicity, peer harassment, and adjustment in middle school: An exploratory study. *Journal of Early Adolescence*, 22(2), 173–99.

Greenwood, D. (1989). Culture by the pound: An anthropological perspective on tourism as a cultural commoditization. In V. Smith (Ed.), *Hosts and Guests: The Anthropology of Tourism* (2nd Edition) (pp. 171–86). Philadelphia, PA: University of Pennsylvania Press.

Guest, M. (2002). A critical 'checkbook' for culture teaching and learning. *ELT Journal*, 56(2), 154–61.

Guilherme, M. (2002). *Critical Citizens for an Intercultural World: Foreign Language Education as Cultural Politics*. Clevedon: Multilingual Matters.

Guilherme, M., Glaser, E. and Del Carmen Méndez-García, M. (Eds) (2010). *The Intercultural Dynamics of Multicultural Working*. Bristol: Multilingual Matters.

Guiora, A. (2005). The language sciences – The challenges ahead. A farewell address. *Language Learning*, 55(2), 183–9.

Gumperz, J. J. (1982). *Discourse Strategies*. Cambridge: Cambridge University Press.

— (1997). *Language and Social Identity*. Cambridge: Cambridge University Press.

Hall, I. P. (1998). *Cartels of the Mind: Japan's Intellectual Closed Shop*. New York: W.W. Norton.

Hall, S. (1995). Fantasy, identity and politics. In E. Carter, J. Donald and J. Squires (Eds), *Cultural Remix: Theories of Politics and the Popular* (pp. 63–9). London: Lawrence & Wishart.

Handley, K., Sturdy, A., Fincham, R. and Clark, T. (2006). Within and beyond communities of practice: Making sense of learning through participation, identity and practice. *Journal of Management Studies*, 43(3), 641–53.

Haneda, M. (2005). Investing in foreign-language writing: A study of two multicultural learners. *Journal of Language, Identity, and Education*, 4(4), 269–90.

Hannerz, U. (1999). Reflections on varieties of culturespeak. *European Journal of Cultural Studies*, 2(3), 393–407.

Haraway, D. (1989). *Primate Visions: Gender, Race, and Nature in the World of Modern Science*. New York: Routledge.

Harbord, J. (1992). The use of the mother tongue in the classroom. *ELT Journal*, 46(4), 350–5.

Harklau, L. (2000). From the 'good kids' to the 'worst': Representations of English language learners across educational settings. *TESOL Quarterly*, 34(1), 35–67.

Hashimoto, K. (2009). Cultivating 'Japanese who can use English': Problems and contradictions in government policy. *Asian Studies Review*, 33(1), 21–42.

Hayes, B. E. (2013). Hiring criteria for Japanese university English-teaching faculty. In S. A. Houghton and D. J. Rivers (Eds), *Native-Speakerism in Japan: Intergroup Dynamics in Foreign Language Education* (pp. 132–46). Bristol: Multilingual Matters.

Heider, F. (1958). *The Psychology of Interpersonal Relations*. New York: Wiley.

Heimlich, E. (2013). The meaning of Japan's role of professional foreigner. In S. A. Houghton and D. J. Rivers (Eds), *Native-Speakerism in Japan: Intergroup Dynamics in Foreign Language Education* (pp. 169–82). Bristol: Multilingual Matters.

Heinrich, P. (2005). Language ideology in JFL textbooks. *International Journal of the Sociology of Language*, 175/176, 213–32.

Heller, M. (1982). Negotiation of language choice in Montreal. In J. Gumperz (Ed.), *Language and Social Identity* (pp. 108–18). Cambridge: Cambridge University Press.

— (2007). *Linguistic Minorities and Modernity: A Sociolinguistic Ethnography* (2nd Edition). London: Continuum.

— (2008). Language and the nation-state: Challenges to sociolinguistic theory and practice. *Journal of Sociolinguistics*, 12(4), 504–24.

Heyworth, F. (2003). Language educators as agents of change: New developments in language pedagogy and their influence on the status of language education. In P. Rádai (Ed.), *The Status of Language Educators* (pp. 95–100). Graz: Council of Europe Publishing.

Hicks, S. K. (2013). On the (Out)Skirts of TESOL networks of homophily: Substantive citizenship in Japan. In S. A. Houghton and D. J. Rivers (Eds), *Native-Speakerism in Japan: Intergroup Dynamics in Foreign Language Education* (pp. 147–58). Bristol: Multilingual Matters.

Higgins, C. (2009). *English as a Local Language: Post-colonial Identities and Multilingual Practices*. Bristol: Multilingual Matters.

— (Ed.) (2011). *Identity Formation in Globalizing Contexts: Language Learning in the New Millennium*. Berlin: De Gruyter Mouton.

Higgins, E. T. (1987). Self-discrepancy: A theory relating self and affect. *Psychological Review*, 94(3), 319–40.

Hill, J. (1995). The voices of Don Gabriel. In B. Mannheim and D. Tedlock (Eds), *The Dialogic Emergence of Culture* (pp. 96–147). Urbana, IL: University of Illinois Press.

— (2002). Japan and the *New York Times*: An intertextual series as evidence for retrieving indirect indexicals. In K. Kataoka and S. Ide (Eds), *Culture, Interaction, and Language* (pp. 135–54). Tokyo: Hitzuzisyobo.

— (2006). The ethnography of language and language documentation. In Jost Gippert, Nikolaus P. Himmelmann and Ulrike Mosel (Eds), *Essentials of Language Documentation* (pp. 113–28). DEU: Walter de Gruyter.

Hogg, M. A. and Abrams, D. (1988). *Social Identifications: A Social Psychology of Intergroup Relations and Group Processes*. London: Routledge.

Holden, K. and Hogan, J. (1993). The emotive impact of foreign intonation: An experiment in switching English and Russian intonation. *Language and Speech*, 36(1), 67–88.

Holliday, A. (1999). Small cultures. *Applied Linguistics*, 20(2), 237–64.

— (2011). *Intercultural Communication and Ideology*. London: Sage.

Horio, T. (1988). *Educational Thought and Ideology in Modern Japan: State Authority and Intellectual Freedom*. Tokyo: University of Tokyo Press.

Hornberger, N. (2007). Biliteracy, transnationalism, multimodality, and identity: Trajectories across time and space. *Linguistics and Education*, 8(3/4), 325–34.

Houghton, S. A. (2007). Managing the Evaluation of Difference in Foreign Language Education: A Complex Case Study in a Tertiary Level Context in Japan. Unpublished Ph.D. thesis, University of Durham, UK.

— (2008). Enhancing diversity in the mono-lingual, mono-cultural foreign language classroom: A case study in Japan. *International Journal of Diversity in Organisations, Communities and Nations*, 8(4), 93–100.

— (2011). Within-self diversity: Implications for ELT materials design. In S. M. Thang, P. Krish, F. F. Wong, L. L. Lin, Mustafa Jamilah and Maros Marlyna (Eds), *Language and Cultural Diversity: Global Realities and Challenges* (pp. 106–29). Serdang: Universiti Putra Malaysia Press.

— (2012). *Intercultural Dialogue in Practice: Managing Value Judgment in Foreign Language Education*. Bristol: Multilingual Matters.

— (2013). The overthrow of the foreign lecturer position, and its aftermath. In S.A. Houghton and D.J. Rivers (Eds), *Native-Speakerism in Japan: Intergroup Dynamics in Foreign Language Education* (pp.60–74). Bristol: Multilingual Matters.

— (in press). Making intercultural communicative competence and identity development visible for assessment purposes in foreign language. *Language Learning Journal Special Issue: Intercultural Communication*, 1.

Houghton, S. A. and Rivers, D. J. (Eds) (2013). *Native-Speakerism in Japan: Intergroup Dynamics in Foreign Language Education*. Bristol: Multilingual Matters.

Houghton, S. A. and Yamada, E. (2012). Developing Criticality in Practice through Foreign Language Education. Frankfurt Am Mein: Peter Lang.

Houghton, S. A., Furumura, Y., Lebedko, M. and Song, L. (Eds) (forthcoming). *Developing Critical Cultural Awareness: Managing Stereotypes in Intercultural (Language) Education*. Newcastle-upon-Tyne: Cambridge Scholars Publishing.

Huzzard, T. (2004). Communities of domination? Reconceptualising organisational learning and power. *Journal of Workplace Learning*, 16(6), 350–61.

Imai, Y. (2010). Emotions in SLA: New insights from collaborative learning for an EFL classroom. *Modern Language Journal*, 94(2), 278–92.

Iwabuchi, K. (2005). Multinationalizing the multicultural: The commodification of 'ordinary foreign residents' in a Japanese TV talk show. *Japanese Studies*, 25(2), 103–18.

Jackson, J. (2008). *Language, Identity and Study Abroad*. London: Equinox.

Johnson, K. E. and Golombek, P. R. (2002). Inquiry into experience: Teachers' personal and professional growth. In K. E. Johnson and P. R. Golombek (Eds), *Teachers' Narrative Inquiry as Professional Development* (pp. 1–14). Cambridge: Cambridge University Press.

Jones, K., Martin-Jones, M. and Bhatt, A. (2000). Constructing a critical, dialogic approach to research on multilingual literacies. In M. Martin-Jones and K. Jones (Eds), *Multilingual Literacies: Reading and Writing Different Worlds* (pp. 319–51). Amsterdam: John Benjamins.

Joseph, J. E. (2004). *Language and Identity: National, Ethnic, Religious*. Houndmills: Palgrave Macmillan.

— (2010). Identity. In C. Llamas and D. Watt (Eds), *Language and Identities* (pp. 9–17). Edinburgh: Edinburgh University Press.

Kachru, Y. (1994). Monolingual bias in SLA research. *TESOL Quarterly*, 28(4), 795–800.

Kanno, Y. (2003). *Negotiating Bilingual and Bicultural Identities: Japanese Returnees Betwixt Two Worlds*. Mahwah, NJ: Lawrence Erlbaum Associates.

— (2008). *Language and Education in Japan: Unequal Access to Bilingualism*. Houndmills: Palgrave Macmillan.

Kanno, Y. and Norton, B. (Eds) (2003). Imagined communities and educational possibilities. *Journal of Language, Identity, and Education*, 2(4), 241–49.

Kedourie, E. (1993). *Nationalism* (4th Edition). Oxford: Blackwell.

Kendrick, M. and Jones, S. (2008). Girls' visual representations of literacy in a rural Ugandan community. *Canadian Journal of Education*, 31(3), 372–404.

Kendrick, M., Jones, S., Mutonyi, H. and Norton, B. (2006). Multimodality and English education in Ugandan schools. *English Studies in Africa*, 49(1), 95–114.

Kiely, R. (2009). Small answers to the big question: Learning from language program evaluation. *Language Teaching Research*, 13(1), 99–116.

Kiernan, P. (2010). *Narrative Identity in English Language Teaching*. Houndmills: Palgrave Macmillan.

Kim, J. M. (2005). Stress assignment rules in Korean English. *Studies in Phonetics, Phonology and Morphology*, 11(2), 247–58.

King, B. (2008). 'Being gay guy, that is the advantage': Queer Korean language learning and identity construction. *Journal of Language, Identity, and Education*, 7(3/4), 230–52.

Kinginger, C. (2004). Alice doesn't live here anymore: Foreign language learning and identity reconstruction. In A. Pavlenko and A. Blackledge (Eds), *Negotiation of Identities in Multilingual Contexts* (pp. 219–42). Clevedon: Multilingual Matters.

— (2009). *Language Learning and Study Abroad. A Critical Reading of Research.* New York: Palgrave Macmillan.

Knight, P. T. (2002). *Small-Scale Research: Pragmatic Enquiry in Social Science and the Caring Professions.* London: Sage.

Kormos, J. and Csizér, K. (2007). An interview study of inter-cultural contact and its role in language learning in a foreign language environment. *System*, 35(2), 241–58.

Kowalski, K. (2003). The emergence of ethnic and racial attitudes in preschool-aged children. *Journal of Social Psychology*, 143(6), 677–90.

Kramsch, C. (2006). Preview article: The multilingual subject. *International Journal of Applied Linguistics*, 16(1), 97–110.

— (2009). *The Multilingual Subject.* Oxford: Oxford University Press.

Krashen, S. D. and Terrell, T. D. (1983). *The Natural Approach: Language Acquisition in the Classroom.* London: Prentice Hall Europe.

Kubota, R. (2002). The Impact of globalization on language teaching in Japan. In D. Block and D. Cameron (Eds), *Globalization and Language Teaching* (pp. 13–28). London: Routledge.

— (2003). Critical teaching of Japanese culture. *Japanese Language and Literature*, 37(1), 67–87.

Kubota, R. and Lin, A. (2006). Race and TESOL: Introduction to concepts and theories. *TESOL Quarterly*, 40(3), 471–654.

— (Eds) (2009). *Race, Culture, and Identities in Second Language Education: Exploring Critically Engaged Practice.* London: Routledge.

Labov, W. (1973). *Sociolinguistic Patterns.* Philadelphia, PA: University of Pennsylvania Press.

Lahire, B. (1998). *L'homme pluriel : Les ressorts de l'action.* Paris: Nathan.

Lamb, M. (2004). 'It depends on the students themselves': Independent language learning at an Indonesian state school. *Language, Culture and Curriculum*, 17(3), 229–45.

— (2007). The impact of school on EFL learning motivation: An Indonesian case study. *TESOL Quarterly*, 41(4), 757–80.

— (2009). Situating the L2 Self: Two Indonesian school learners of English. In Z. Dörnyei and E. Ushioda (Eds), *Motivation, Language Identity and the L2 Self* (pp. 229–47). Bristol: Multilingual Matters.

Lambert, P. (2009). (Dé)construction de clôtures identitaires dans un espace scolaire : un regard sociolinguistique impliqué. *Lidil*, 39, 43–56.

Lantolf, J. P. (Ed.). (1994). *Vygotskian Approaches to Second Language Research. Second Language Learning.* New Jersey: Ablex.

— (Ed.) (2000). *Sociocultural Theory and Second Language Learning.* Oxford: Oxford University Press.

Lantolf, J. P. and Aljaafreh, A. (1995). L2 learning in the zone of proximal development: A revolutionary experience. *International Journal of Educational Research*, 23(7), 51–64.

Lantolf, J. P. and Genung, P. (2003). 'I'd rather switch than fight': An activity theoretic study of power, success, and failure in a foreign language classroom. In C. Kramsch (Ed.), *Language Acquisition and Language Socialization* (pp. 175–96). London: Continuum.

Lantolf, J. P. and Pavlenko, A. (2001). (S)econd (L)anguage (A)ctivity theory: Understanding second language learners as people. In M. P. Breen (Ed.), *Learner Contributions to Language Learning: New Directions in Research* (pp. 141–58). Harlow: Pearson Education.

Larsen-Freeman, D. and Cameron, L. (2008). Research methodology on language development from a complex systems perspective. *Modern Language Journal*, 92(2), 200–13.

Lave, J. and Wenger, E. (1991). *Situated Learning: Legitimate Peripheral Participation.* Cambridge: Cambridge University Press.

Lee, E. (2008). The 'other(ing)' costs of ESL: A Canadian case study. *Journal of Asian Pacific Communication*, 18(1), 91–108.

Lemke, J. L. (1995). *Textual Politics: Discourse and Social Dynamics.* London: Taylor and Francis.

— (2008). Identity, development, and desire: Critical questions. In C. R. Caldas-Coulthard and R. Iedema (Eds), *Identity Trouble: Critical Discourse and Contested Identities* (pp. 17–42). Houndmills: Palgrave Macmillan.

Lepore, L. and Brown, R. (1997). Category and stereotype activation: Is prejudice inevitable? *Journal of Personality and Social Psychology*, 72(2), 275–87.

Leung, C. (2002). *Language and Additional/Second Language Issues for School Education: A Reader for Teachers.* Reading: NALDIC.

Leung, C., Harris, R. and Rampton, B. (1997). The idealized native speaker, reified ethnicities, and classroom realities. *TESOL Quarterly*, 31(3), 543–60.

Levine, G. S. (2011). *Code Choice in the Language Classroom.* Bristol: Multilingual Matters.

Liddicoat, A. J. (2006). Learning the culture of interpersonal relationships: Students' understandings of personal address forms in French. *Intercultural Pragmatics*, 3(1), 55–80.

— (2007). Discourses of the self and other: Nihonjinron and the intercultural in Japanese language-in-education policy. *Journal of Multicultural Discourses*, 2(1), 1–15.

Lidz, C. (1991). *Practitioner's Guide to Dynamic Assessment.* New York: Guilford Press.

Lieblich, A., Tuval-Mashiach, R. and Zilber, T. (1998). *Narrative Research: Reading, Analysis, and Interpretation.* London: Sage.

Lin, A. (Ed.) (2008). *Problematizing Identity: Everyday Struggles in Language, Culture, and Education.* Mahwah, NJ: Lawrence Erlbaum Associates.

Lipiansky, E. M. (1990). Identité subjective et interaction. In C. Camilleri (Ed.), *Stratégies identitaires, Psychologie d'aujourd'hui* (pp. 173–211). Paris: PUF.

Lippi-Green, R. (2011). *English with an Accent: Language, Ideology and Discrimination in the United States* (2nd Edition). London: Routledge.

Lipson, M. (1983). The influence of religious affiliation on children's memory for text information. *Reading Research Quarterly*, 18, 448–57.

Llamas, C. and Watt, D. (2010). *Language and Identities*. Edinburgh: Edinburgh University Press.

Lyons, N. and LaBoskey, V. K. (Eds) (2002). *Narrative Inquiry in Practice: Advancing the Knowledge of Teaching*. New York: Teachers College Press.

Macaro, E. (2001). Analysing student teachers' codeswitching in foreign language classrooms: Theories and decision making. *Modern Language Journal*, 85(4), 531–48.

— (2005). Codeswitching in the L2 classroom: A communication and learning strategy. In E. Llurda (Ed.), *Non-native Language Teachers: Perceptions, Challenges and Contributions to the Profession* (pp. 63–84). New York: Springer.

MacCannell, D. (1973). Staged authenticity: Arrangements of social space in tourist settings. *American Journal of Sociology*, 79(3), 589–603.

McCarthey, S. and Moje, E. (2002). Conversations: Identity matters. *Reading Research Quarterly*, 37(2), 228–38.

McConnell, D. (2000). *Importing Diversity: Inside Japan's JET Program*. Berkeley, CA: University of California Press.

McDonough, J. and McDonough, S. (1997). *Research Methods for English Language Teachers*. London: Arnold.

MacGregor, J., Cooper, J., Smith, K. and Robinson, P. (2000). *Strategies for Energizing Large Classes: From Small Groups to Learning Communities*. San Francisco, CA: Jossey-Bass.

McHoul, A. (1978). The organization of turns at formal talk in the classroom. *Language in Society*, 7(2), 183–213.

— (1990). The organization of repair in classroom talk. *Language in Society*, 19(3), 349–77.

MacIntyre, P., Noels, K. and Moore, B. (2010). Perspectives on motivation in second language acquisition: Lessons from the Ryoanji garden. In M. Prior, Y. Watanabe and S. Lee (Eds), *Proceedings of the 2008 Second Language Research Forum* (pp. 1–9). Somerville, MA: Cascadilla.

McKay, S. (2002). *Teaching English as an International Language*. Oxford: Oxford University Press.

McKay, S. and Wong, S. (1996). Multiple discourses, multiple identities: Investment and agency in second language learning among Chinese adolescent immigrant students. *Harvard Educational Review*, 66(3), 577–608.

McKinney, C. and Norton, B. (2008). Identity in language and literacy education. In B. Spolsky and F. Hult (Eds), *The Handbook of Educational Linguistics* (pp. 192–205). London: Blackwell.

McLaren, P. (1989). *Life in Schools: An Introduction to Critical Pedagogy in the Foundations of Education*. New York: Longman.

McMahill, C. (1997). Communities of resistance: A case study of two feminist English classes in Japan. *TESOL Quarterly*, 31(3), 612–22.

McMillan, B. A. and Rivers, D. J. (2011). The practice of policy: Teacher attitudes toward 'English only'. *System*, 39(2), 251–63.

McMillan, B. A., Rivers, D. J. and Cripps, T. (2009). The L1 in the L2 classroom: University EFL teacher perceptions. In A. M. Stoke (Ed.), *JALT2008 Conference Proceedings* (pp. 768–77). Tokyo: JALT.

McVeigh, B. (2002). *Japanese Higher Education as Myth*. Armonk, NY: M. E. Sharpe.

Maher, J. C. and Yashiro, K. (1995). Multilingual Japan: An introduction. *Journal of Multilingual and Multicultural Development*, 16(1), 1–17.

Maloof, V. M., Rubin, D. and Neville Miller, A. (2006). Cultural competence and identity in cross-cultural adaptation: The role of a Vietnamese heritage language school. *International Journal of Bilingual Education and Bilingualism*, 9(2), 255–73.

Marc, E. (2005). *Psychologie de l'identité : Soi et le groupe*. Paris: Dunod.

Markee, N. and Kasper, G. (2004). Classroom talks: An introduction. *Modern Language Journal*, 88(4), 491–500.

Markus, H. R. (2006). Foreword. In C. Dunkel and J. Kerpelman (Eds), *Possible Selves: Theory, Research and Applications* (pp. xi–xiv). New York: Nova Science.

Markus, H. R. and Kunda, Z. (1986). Stability and malleability of the self-concept. *Journal of Personality and Social Psychology*, 51(4), 858–66.

Markus, H. R. and Nurius, P. (1986). Possible selves. *American Psychologist*, 41(9), 954–69.

Marra, M. and Angouri, J. (2011). Investigating the negotiation of identity: A view from the field of workplace discourse. In J. Angouri and M. Marra (Eds), *Constructing Identities at Work* (pp. 1–16). Houndmills: Palgrave Macmillan.

Marshall, C. and Rossman, G. (2010). *Designing Qualitative Research*. Thousand Oaks, CA: Sage.

Martin, E. (2001). *The Woman in the Body: A Cultural Analysis of Reproduction*. Boston, MA: Beacon Press.

Martin, J. (2004). The educational inadequacy of conceptions of self in educational psychology. *Interchange*, 35(2), 185–208.

Martin-Jones, M., Hughes, B. and Williams, A. (2009). Bilingual literacy in and for working lives on the land: Case studies of young Welsh speakers in North Wales. *International Journal of the Sociology of Language*, 195, 39–62.

Masden, K. (2013). Kumamoto General Union vs. the Prefectural University of Kumamoto: Reviewing the decision rendered by the Kumamoto District Court. In S. A. Houghton and D. J. Rivers (Eds), *Native-Speakerism in Japan: Intergroup Dynamics in Foreign Language Education* (pp. 42–59). Bristol: Multilingual Matters.

Matei, G. S. and Medgyes, P. (2003). Teaching English is a political act: A non-p.c. dialogue. In P. Rádai (Ed.), *The Status of Language Educators* (pp. 69–77). Graz: Council of Europe Publishing.

Matos, A. G. (2005). Literary texts: A passage to intercultural reading in foreign language education. *Language and Intercultural Communication*, 5(1), 57–71.

Matsumoto, Y. and Okamoto, S. (2003). The construction of the Japanese language and culture in teaching Japanese as a foreign language. *Japanese Language and Literature*, 37(1), 27–48.

Meadows, B. (2010). Taking on nationalism in the name of intercultural competence. *Proceedings of the Second Annual International Conference on Intercultural Competence*, 1, 262–80.

Meinhof, U. H. and Galasiński, D. (2005). *The Language of Belonging*. Houndmills: Palgrave Macmillan.

Mendoza-Denton, N. (2008). *Homegirls: Language and Cultural Practice among Latina Youth Gangs*. Malden, MA: Blackwell.

Mey, J. (1981). 'Right or wrong, my native speaker' Estant les régestes du noble souverain de l'empirie linguistic avec un envoy au mesme roy. In F. Coulmas (Ed.), *A Festschrift for Native Speaker* (pp. 69–84). The Hague: Mouton.

Meyerhoff, M. (2011). *Introducing Sociolinguistics* (2nd Edition). New York: Routledge.

Miller, J. (2003). *Audible Difference: ESL and Social Identity in Schools*. Clevedon: Multilingual Matters.

Miller, R. A. (1982). *Japan's Modern Myth: The Language and Beyond*. Tokyo: John Weatherhill.

Milroy, L. (1980). *Language and Social Networks*. Oxford: Blackwell.

Miyoshi, M. (2010). *Trespasses: Selected Writings*. Durham, NC: Duke University Press.

MLA (2007). *Report of the MLA Ad Hoc Committee on Foreign Languages*. Retrieved from www.mla.org/flreport

Mohan, B., Leung, C. and Davison, C. (Eds) (2002). *English as a Second Language in the Mainstream: Teaching, Learning and Identity*. London: Longman.

Mohanty, C. T. (2003). *Feminism without Borders: Decolonizing Theory, Practicing Solidarity*. Durham, NC: Duke University Press.

Moi, T. (2002). *Sexual/Textual Politics: Feminist Literary Theory*. New York: Routledge.

Mondada, L. (1999). L'accomplissement de l' « étrangéité » dans et par l'interaction : procédures de catégorisation des locuteurs. *Langages*, 134, 20–34.

Morgan, B. and Clarke, M. (2011). Identity in second language teaching and learning. In E. Hinkel (Ed.), *Handbook of Research in Second Language Teaching and Learning* (pp. 817–36). New York: Routledge.

Murphey, T., Jin, C. and Li-Chi, C. (2005). Learners' constructions of identities and imagined communities. In P. Benson and D. Nunan (Eds), *Learners' Stories: Difference and Diversity in Language Learning* (pp. 83–100). Cambridge: Cambridge University Press.

Nagatomo, D. H. (2012). *Exploring Japanese University English Teachers' Professional Identity*. Bristol: Multilingual Matters.

Nelson, C. (2009). *Sexual Identities in English Language Education: Classroom Conversations*. New York: Routledge.

Nesdale, D. and Lawson, M. J. (2011). Social groups and children's intergroup attitudes: Can school norms moderate the effects of social group norms? *Child Development*, 82(5), 1594–606.

Nicholson, L. (Ed.) (1990). *Feminism/Postmodernism*. New York: Routledge.

Nikula, T. and Huhta, A. P. (2008). Using photographs to access stories of learning English. In P. Kalaja, V. Menezes and A. M. Barcelos (Eds), *Narratives of Learning and Teaching EFL* (pp. 171–85). Houndmills: Palgrave Macmillan.

Niño-Murcia, M. and Rothman, J. (2008). *Bilingualism and Identity: Spanish at the Crossroads with Other Languages*. Amsterdam: John Benjamins.

Norton, B. (1997). Language, identity, and the ownership of English. *TESOL Quarterly*, 31(3), 409–29.

— (2000). *Identity and Language Learning: Gender, Ethnicity and Educational Change*. London: Pearson Education.

— (2001). Non-participation, imagined communities, and the language classroom. In M. Breen (Ed.), *Learner Contributions to Language Learning: New Directions in Research* (pp. 159–71). London: Pearson Education.

— (2006). Identity as a sociocultural construct in second language education. In K. Cadman and K. O'Regan (Eds), *TESOL in Context* [Special Issue], 22–33.

— (2010). Language and identity. In N. Hornberger and S. McKay (Eds), *Sociolinguistics and Language Education* (pp. 349–69). Bristol: Multilingual Matters.

Norton, B. and Gao, Y. (2008). Identity, investment, and Chinese learners of English. *Journal of Asian Pacific Communication*, 18(1), 109–20.

Norton, B. and McKinney, C. (2011). An identity approach to second language acquisition. In D. Atkinson (Ed.), *Alternative Approaches to Second Language Acquisition* (pp. 73–94). Oxford: Routledge.

Norton, B. and Toohey, K. (Eds) (2004). *Critical Pedagogies and Language Learning*. New York: Cambridge University Press.

— (2011). Identity, language learning, and social change. *Language Teaching*, 44(4), 412–46.

Norton Pierce, B. (1995). Social identity, investment and language learning. *TESOL Quarterly*, 29(1), 9–31.

Ochs, E. (1999). Indexicality and socialization. In J. Stigler, R. Shweder and G. Herdt (Eds), *Cultural Psychology: Essays on Comparative Human Development* (pp. 287–308). Cambridge: Cambridge University Press.

Ollmann, H. (1996). Creating higher level thinking with reading response. *Journal of Adolescent and Adult Literacy*, 39(7), 576–81.

Ontario Ministry of Education and Training (1999). *Ontario Curriculum for Grade 8 and 9: French as a Second Language – Core, Extended and Immersion French*. Retrieved from www.edu.gov.on.ca/eng/curriculum/secondary/fsl910curr.pdf

Ortner, S. (1972). Is female to male as nature is to culture? *Feminist Studies*, 1(2), 5–31.

Osborn, T. (2006). *Teaching World Languages for Social Justice*. Mahwah, NJ: Lawrence Erlbaum Associates.

Oxford, R. and Shearin, J. (1994). Language learning motivation: Expanding the theoretical framework. *Modern Language Journal*, 78(1), 12–28.

Paikeday, T. M. (2003). *The Native Speaker Is Dead!* Toronto, ON: Lexicography.

Park, J. (2010). Naturalization of competence and the neoliberal subject: Success stories of English language learning in the Korean conservative press. *Journal of Linguistic Anthropology*, 20(1), 22–38.

Pavlenko, A. (2001). 'In the world of the tradition I was unimagined': Negotiation of identities in cross-cultural autobiographies. *The International Journal of Bilingualism*, 5(3), 317–44.

— (2002). Poststructuralist approaches to the study of social factors in second language learning and use. In V. Cook (Ed.), *Portraits of the L2 User* (pp. 277–302). Clevedon: Multilingual Matters.

— (2005). *Emotions and Multilingualism*. Cambridge: Cambridge University Press.

— (Ed.) (2006). *Bilingual Minds: Emotional Experience, Expression and Representation*. Bristol: Multilingual Matters.

Pavlenko, A. and Blackledge, A. (Eds) (2004). *Negotiation of Identities in Multilingual Contexts*. Clevedon: Multilingual Matters.

Pavlenko, A. and Lantolf, J. P. (2000). Second language learning as participation and the (re)construction of selves. In J. P. Lantolf (Ed.), *Sociocultural Theory: Second Language Learning* (pp. 155–77). Oxford: Oxford University Press.

Pavlenko, A. and Norton, B. (2007). Imagined communities, identity, and English language learning. In J. Cummins and C. Davison (Eds), *International Handbook of English Language Teaching* (pp. 669–80). New York: Springer.

Phillipson, R. (1992). *Linguistic Imperialism*. Oxford: Oxford University Press.

Pieterse, J. (2004). *Globalization and Culture: Global Mélange*. Lanham, MD: Rowman & Littlefield.

Pittaway, D. (2004). Investment and second language acquisition. *Critical Inquiry in Language Studies*, 4(1), 203–18.

Planalp, S., De Francisco, V. L. and Rutherford, D. (1996). Varieties of cues to emotions in naturally occurring situations. *Cognition and Emotions*, 10(2), 137–53.

Polkinghorne, D. E. (1988). *Narrative Knowing and the Human Sciences*. Albany, NY: State University of New York Press.

Pomerantz, A. (1994). Agreeing and disagreeing with assessments: Some features of preferred/dispreferred turn shapes. In J. M. Atkinson and J. Heritage (Ed.), *Structures of Social Action: Studies in Conversation Analysis, Studies in Emotion and Social Interaction* (pp. 57–101). Cambridge: Cambridge University Press.

— (2005). Using participants' video stimulated comments to complement analyses of interactional practices. In H. T. Molder and J. Potter (Ed.), *Conversation and Cognition* (pp. 93–113). Cambridge: Cambridge University Press.

Pomerantz, A. and Schwartz, A. (2011). Border talk: Narratives of Spanish language encounters in the United States. *Language and Intercultural Communication*, 11(3), 176–96.

Potowski, K. (2007). *Language and Identity in a Dual Immersion School*. Bristol: Multilingual Matters.

Province of Nova Scotia (1998). *Program Policy for French Second Language Programs*. Retrieved from https://fsl.ednet.ns.ca/sites/default/files/policy-fl2.pdf

Rajagopalan, K. (2005). Non-native speaker teachers of English and their anxieties. In E. Llurda (Ed.), *Non-Native Language Teachers: Perceptions, Challenges and Contributions to the Profession* (pp. 283–303). New York: Springer.

Ramanathan, V. (2005). *The English-Vernacular Divide: Postcolonial Language Politics and Practice*. Clevedon: Multilingual Matters.

Rampton, B. (1990). 'Displacing the native speaker': Expertise, affiliation, and inheritance. *ELT Journal*, 45(2), 97–101.

— (2007). Neo-Hymesian linguistic ethnography in the United Kingdom. *Journal of Sociolinguistics*, 11(5), 584–607.

Reay, D. (2004). 'It's all becoming a habitus': Beyond the habitual use of habitus in educational research. *British Journal of Sociology of Education*, 25(4), 431–44.

Reeve, J. (2009). *Understanding Motivation and Emotion* (5th Edition). Toronto, ON: Wiley.

Reid, S. A. and Anderson, G. L. (2010). Language, social identity and stereotyping. In H. Giles, S. Reid and J. Harwood (Eds), *Dynamics of Intergroup Communication* (pp. 91–104). New York: Peter Lang.

Retzinger, S. (1991). *Violent Emotions*. London: Sage.

Reynolds, R., Taylor, M., Steffensen, M., Shirey, L. and Anderson, R. (1982). Cultural schemata and reading comprehension. *Reading Research Quarterly*, 17(3), 353–66.

Rice, E. (1980). On cultural schemata. *American Ethnologist*, 7(1), 152–71.

Ricento, T. (2005). Considerations of identity in L2 learning. In E. Hinkel (Ed.), *Handbook of Research in Second Language Teaching and Learning* (pp. 895–911). New York: Routledge.

Richards, K. (2003). *Qualitative Inquiry in TESOL*. Houndmills: Palgrave Macmillan.

— (2006). 'Being the Teacher': Identity and classroom conversation. *Applied Linguistics*, 27(1), 51–77.

Richards, J. C. and Rodgers, T. S. (1995). *Approaches and Methods in Language Teaching: A Description and Analysis*. Cambridge: Cambridge University Press.

Riley, P. (2007). *Language, Culture and Identity: An Ethnolinguistic Perspective*. London: Continuum.

Risager, K. (2007). *Language and Culture Pedagogy: From a National to a Transnational Paradigm*. Bristol: Multilingual Matters.

Rivers, D. J. (2010a). Ideologies of internationalisation and the treatment of diversity within Japanese higher education. *Journal of Higher Education Policy and Management*, 32(5), 441–54.

— (2010b). Implicating the role of Japanese national identification: National vitality, community appeal and attitudes toward English language learning in context. *Studies in Linguistics and Language Teaching*, 21, 101–22.

— (2010c). National Identification and intercultural relations in foreign language learning. *Language and Intercultural Communication*, 10(4), 318–36.

— (2011a). Evaluating the self and the other: Imagined intercultural contact within a native-speaker dependent foreign language context. *International Journal of Intercultural Relations*, 35(6), 842–52.

— (2011b). Intercultural processes in accented English. *World Englishes*, 30(3), 375–91.

— (2011c). Japanese national identification and English language learning processes. *International Journal of Intercultural Relations*, 35(2), 111–23.

— (2011d). Politics without pedagogy: Questioning linguistic exclusion. *ELT Journal*, 65(2), 103–13.

— (2011e). Strategies and struggles in the ELT classroom: Language policy, learner autonomy and innovative practice. *Language Awareness*, 20(1), 31–43.

— (2012a). Modeling the perceived value of compulsory English language education in undergraduate non-language majors of Japanese nationality. *Journal of Multilingual and Multicultural Development*, 33(3), 251–67.

— (2012b). *The Properties and Parameters of Native-Speakerism in Japan*. Invited Keynote Lecture given at the JAFAE (Japanese Association for Asian Englishes) 31st National Conference, Bunkyo Gakuin University, Tokyo, Japan.

— (2013a). Institutionalized native-speakerism: Voices of dissent and acts of resistance. In S.A. Houghton and D.J. Rivers (Eds), *Native-Speakerism in Japan: Intergroup Dynamics in Foreign Language Education* (pp. 75–91). Bristol: Multilingual Matters.

— (2013b). Labour contract law amendments: Recruitment indicative of change? *The Language Teacher*, 37(1), 68–71.

Rivers, D. J. and Ross, A. S. (forthcoming a). Idealized English Teachers: The Implicit Influence of Race in Japan. *Journal of Language, Identity & Education.*

Rivers, D. J. and Ross, A. S. (forthcoming b). Uncovering stereotypes: Intersections of race and English native-speakerhood. In S. A. Houghton, Y. Furumura, M. Lebedko and L. Song (Eds), *Developing Critical Cultural Awareness: Managing Stereotypes in Intercultural (Language) Education* (pp. 42–61). Newcastle-upon-Tyne: Cambridge Scholars Publishing.

Robinson, G. (1985). *Cross-Cultural Understanding*. New York: Prentice Hall.

Robinson, W. P. (Ed.) (1996). *Social Groups and Identities. Developing the Legacy of Henri Tajfel*. Oxford: Butterworth-Heinemann.

Rogers, C. (1951). *Client-Centred Therapy*. Boston, MA: Houghton Mifflin.

Rosaldo, R. (1993). *Culture and Truth: The Remaking of Social Analysis*. Boston, MA: Beacon Press.

Ruiz, R. (1984). Orientations in language planning. *NABE Journal*, 8(2), 15–34.

Ryan, R. M. and Deci, E. L. (2000). Self-determination theory and the facilitation of intrinsic motivation, social development, and well-being. *American Psychologist*, 55(1), 68–78.

Ryan, S. (2009). Self and identity in L2 motivation in Japan: The ideal L2 self and Japanese learners of English. In Z. Dörnyei and E. Ushioda (Eds), *Motivation, Language Identity and the L2 Self* (pp. 120–43). Bristol: Multilingual Matters.

Said, E. W. (1978). *Orientalism*. New York: Vintage Books.

— (2000). *Reflections on Exile and Other Essays*. Cambridge, MA: Harvard University Press.

Sayer, P. and Meadows, B. (2012). Teaching culture beyond nationalist boundaries: National identities, stereotyping, and culture in language education. *Intercultural Education*, 23(3), 265–79.

Scheff, T. J. (1990). *Microbiology*. London: University of Chicago Press.

Scheff, T. J. and Retzinger, S. (1991). *Emotions and Violence: Shame and Rage in Destructive Conflicts*. Lexington, MA: Lexington Press.

Schegloff, E. (1992). On talk and its institutional occasions. In P. Drew and J. Heritage (Ed.), *Talk at Work: Interaction in Institutional Settings* (pp. 101–34). Cambridge: Cambridge University Press.

Schein, L. (2000). *Minority Rules: The Miao and the Feminine in China's Cultural Politics*. Durham, NC: Duke University Press.

Schlee, G. (2004). Taking sides and constructing identities: Reflections on conflict theory. *Journal of Royal Anthropological Institute*, 10(1), 135–56.

Schwartz, S. and Sagiv, L. (1995). Identifying culture-specifics in the content and structure of values. *Journal of Cross-Cultural Psychology*, 26(1), 92–116.

Schwartz, S., Verkasalo, M., Antonovsky, A. and Sagiv, L. (1997). Value priorities and social desirability: Much substance, some style. *British Journal of Social Psychology*, 36, 3–18.

Schwieter, J. W. (2010). Developing second language writing through scaffolding in the ZPD: A magazine project for an authentic audience. *Journal of College Teaching & Learning*, 7(10), 31–45.

— (2011). Migrant Hispanic students speak up: Linguistic and cultural perspectives of low academic attainment. *Diaspora, Indigenous, and Minority Education: An International Journal*, 5(1), 33–47.

Schwieter, J. W. and Kunert, S. (2012). Short-term study abroad and cultural sessions: Issues of L2 development, identity, and socialization. In P. Chamness Miller, J. Watze and M. Mantero (Eds), *Readings in Language Studies, Vol. 3: Critical Language Studies: Focusing on Identity*. New York: International Society for Language Studies.

Scott, J. (1985). *Weapons of the Weak: Everyday forms of Peasant Resistance*. New Haven, CT: Yale University Press.

— (1990). *Domination and the Arts of Resistance: Hidden Transcripts*. New Haven, CT: Yale University Press.

— (2011). *The Art of Not Being Governed: An Anarchist History of Upland Southeast Asia*. New Haven, CT: Yale University Press.

Seedhouse, P. (2004). *The Interactional Architecture of the Language Classroom: A Conversation Analysis Perspective*. Oxford: Blackwell.

Seidlhofer, B. (2004). Research perspectives on teaching English as a Lingua Franca. *Annual Review of Applied Linguistics*, 24, 209–39.

Selting, M. (1994). Emphatic speech style – with special focus on the prosodic signalling of heightened emotive involvement in conversation. *Journal of Pragmatics*, 22, 375–408.

Shardakova, M. and Pavlenko, A. (2004). Identity options in Russian textbooks. *Journal of Language, Identity, and Education*, 3(1), 25–46.

Shoaib, A. and Dörnyei, Z. (2005). Affective in life-long learning: Exploring L2 motivation as a dynamic process. In P. Benson and D. Nunan (Eds), *Learners' Stories: Difference and Diversity in Language Learning* (pp. 22–41). Cambridge: Cambridge University Press.

Showalter, E. (1988). Feminist criticism in the wilderness. In D. Lodge (Ed.), *Modern Criticism and Theory* (pp. 331–53). London: Longman.

Silberstein, S. (2003). Imagined communities and national fantasies in the O. J. Simpson case. *Journal of Language, Identity, and Education*, 2(4), 319–30.

Silverstein, M. (2001). Whorfianism and the linguistic imagination of nationality. In P. Kroskrity (Ed.), *Regimes of Language: Ideologies, Politics, and Identities* (pp. 205–28). Santa Fe, NM: School of American Research Press.

Simon-Maeda, A. (2004). The complex construction of professional identities: Female EFL educators in Japan speak out. *TESOL Quarterly*, 38, 405–36.

Skilton-Sylvester, E. (2002). Should I stay or should I go? Investigating Cambodian women's participation and investment in adult ESL programs. *Adult Education Quarterly*, 53(1), 9–26.

Snyder, M. and Miene, P. (1994). Stereotyping of the elderly: A functional approach. *British Journal of Social Psychology*, 33(1), 63–82.

Stanley, P. (2012). *A Critical Ethnography of 'Westerners' Teaching English in China: Shanghaied in Shanghai*. London: Routledge.

Steele, C. M. (1988). The psychology of self-affirmation: Sustaining the integrity of the self. In L. Berkowitz (Ed.), *Advances in Experimental Social Psychology* (Volume 21) (pp. 261–99). London: Academic Press.

Steffensen, M., Joag-Dev, C. and Anderson, R. (1979). A cross-cultural perspective on reading comprehension. *Reading Research Quarterly*, 15(1), 10–29.

Stein, P. (2008). *Multimodal Pedagogies in Diverse Classrooms: Representation, Rights and Resources*. London: Routledge.

Stets, J. E. and Burke, P. J. (2000). Identity theory and social identity theory. *Social Psychology Quarterly*, 63(3), 224–37.

Stewart, A. (2005). Teaching Positions: A Study of Identity in English Language Teachers in Japanese Higher Education. Unpublished Ph.D. dissertation, Institute of Education, University of London.

Strauss, A. and Corbin, J. (1990). *Basics of Qualitative Research. Grounded Theory Procedures and Techniques* (2nd Edition). Newbury Park, CA: Sage.

Swaffar, J. (2006). Terminology and its discontents: Some caveats about communicative competence. *Modern Language Journal*, 90(2), 246–49.

Swain, M. (2005). The output hypothesis: Theory and research. In E. Hinkel (Ed.), *The Handbook of Research in Second Language Teaching and Learning* (pp. 471–84). Mahwah, NJ: Lawrence Erlbaum Associates.

Swain, M., Kirkpatrick, A. and Cummins, J. (2011). *How to Have a Guilt-free Life Using Cantonese in the English Class: A Handbook for the English Language Teacher in Hong Kong*. Hong Kong: Research Centre into Language Acquisition and Education in Multilingual Societies, Hong Kong Institute of Education. Retrieved from www.ied.edu.hk/rcleams/handbook/handbook.pdf

Swain, M. B. (2009). The cosmopolitan hope of tourism: Critical action and worldmaking vistas. *Tourism Geographies: An International Journal of Tourism Space, Place and Environment*, 11(4), 505–25.

Tajfel, H. (1982). Social psychology of intergroup relations. *Annual Review of Psychology*, 33, 1–39.

Tajfel, H. and Turner, J. C. (1979). An integrative theory of intergroup conflict. In W. G. Austin and S. Worchel (Eds), *The Social Psychology of Intergroup Relations* (pp. 33–47). Monterey, CA: Brooks/Cole.

Talburt, S. and Stewart, M. A. (1999). What's the subject of study abroad?: Race, gender, and «living culture». *Modern Language Journal*, 83(2), 163–75.

Teachers of English to Speakers of Other Languages [TESOL] (2003). *TESOL Position Statement on Teacher Quality in the Field of Teaching English to Speakers of Other Languages*. Retrieved from www.tesol.org/docs/pdf/374.PDF

Ten Have, P. (1999). *Doing Conversational Analysis: A Practical Guide*. London: Sage.

Thurlow, C. (2001). 'I don't have one – it's just normal.' Young teenagers' ideas about 'culture': Critical transcultural communication awareness and the exoticisation of self. In D. Killick and M. Parry (Eds), *Mapping the Territory: The Poetics and Praxis of Languages and Intercultural Communication* (pp. 111–25). Glasgow: Glasgow French & German Publications.

Toh, G. (2013). Scrutinizing the native speaker as referent, entity and project. In S. A. Houghton and D. J. Rivers (Eds), *Native-Speakerism in Japan: Intergroup Dynamics in Foreign Language Education* (pp. 183–95). Bristol: Multilingual Matters.

Toohey, K. (2000). *Learning English at School: Identity, Social Relations and Classroom Practice*. Clevedon: Multilingual Matters.

Tornberg, U. (2004). Multiculturalism – a dead end of conceptualizing difference or an open-ended approach to facilitating democratic experience in the foreign language classroom. *Utbildning & Demokrati*, 13(3), 127–43.

Tsui, A. (2007). Complexities of identity formation: A narrative inquiry of an EFL teacher. *TESOL Quarterly*, 41(4), 657–80.

Tsui, A. and Tollefson, J. (Eds) (2007). *Language Policy, Culture, and Identity in Asian Contexts*. Mahwah, NJ: Lawrence Erlbaum Associates.

Turnbull, M. and Dailey-O'Cain, J. (2009). *First Language Use in Second and Foreign Language Learning*. Bristol: Multilingual Matters.

Ushioda, E. (2001). Language learning at university: Exploring the role of motivational thinking. In Z. Dörnyei and R. Schmidt (Eds), *Motivation and Second Language Acquisition* (pp. 93–125). Honolulu, HI: University of Hawaii Press.

— (2009). A person-in-context relational view of emergent motivation, self and identity. In Z. Dörnyei and E. Ushioda (Eds), *Motivation, Language Identity and the L2 Self* (pp. 215–28). Bristol: Multilingual Matters.

— (2011). Language learning motivation, self and identity: Current theoretical perspectives. *Computer Assisted Language Learning*, 24(3), 199–210.

van den Berghe, P. L. (1987). *The Ethnic Phenomenon*. Westport, CT: Praeger.

van Hell, J., Bosman, A., Wiggers, I. and Stoit, J. (2003). Children's cultural background knowledge and story telling performance. *International Journal of Bilingualism*, 7(3), 283–303.

Vasconcelos, J. M. de (1971). *Mi planta de naranja-lima*. Buenos Aires: El Ateneo.

Vasquez, A. (1990). Les mécanismes des stratégies identitaires : une perspective diachronique. In *Stratégies identitaires* (pp. 143–171). Paris: PUF.

Vygotsky, L. (1978). *Mind in Society: The Development of Higher Psychological Processes*. Cambridge, MA: Harvard University Press.

— (1986). *Thought and Language* (A. Kozulin, Trans.). Cambridge, MA: MIT Press.

Wallace, C. (2003). *Critical Reading in Language Education*. Houndmills: Palgrave Macmillan.

Warschauer, M. (2000). The changing global economy and the future of English teaching. *TESOL Quarterly*, 34(3), 511–35.

Weedon, C. (1987). *Feminist Practice and Poststructuralist Theory*. London: Blackwell.

— (1997). *Feminist Practice and Poststructuralist Theory* (2nd Edition). London: Blackwell.

Weir, A. (1996). *Sacrificial Logics: Feminist Theory and the Critique of Identity*. New York: Routledge.

Wenger, E. (1998). *Communities of Practice: Learning, Meaning, and Identity*. Cambridge: Cambridge University Press.

— (2000). Communities of practice and social learning systems. *Organization*, 7(2), 225–45.

Whorf, B. L. (1956). *Language, Thought and Reality*, J. B. Carroll (Ed.). Cambridge, MA: MIT Press.

Widdowson, H. G. (1984). *Explorations in Applied Linguistics 2*. Oxford: Oxford University Press.

— (2000). On the limitations of linguistics applied. *Applied Linguistics*, 21(1), 3–25.

— (2004). *Text, Context, Pretext. Critical Issues in Discourse Analysis*. Oxford: Blackwell.

Williams, M. and Burden, R. L. (1997). *Psychology for Language Teachers: A Social Constructivist Approach*. Cambridge: Cambridge University Press.

Winn, L. and Rubin, D. (2001). Enacting gender identity in written discourse: Responding to gender role bidding in personal ads. *Journal of Language and Social Psychology*, 20(4), 393–418.

Woods, D. (1996). *Teacher Cognition in Language Teaching: Beliefs, Decision-Making and Classroom Practice*. Cambridge: Cambridge University Press.

Woolard, K. and Schieffelin, B. (1994). Language ideology. *Annual Review of Anthropology*, 23, 55–82.

Wortham, S. (2004). From good student to outcast: The emergence of a classroom identity. *Ethos*, 32(2), 164–87.

Worthington, C. (1999). Combatting discrimination at a Japanese university. *JPRI Working Paper 58*. Retrieved from www.jpri.org/publications/workingpapers/wp58.html

Yamazaki, M. (1986). Survival tactics for a non-Western power. *Japan Echo*, 13(3), 56–63.

Yang, M. (1996). Tradition, traveling anthropology and the discourse of modernity in China. In H. L. Moore (Ed.), *The Future of Anthropological Knowledge* (pp. 93–114). London: Routledge.

Yashima, T. (2009). International posture and the ideal L2 self in the Japanese EFL context. In Z. Dörnyei and E. Ushioda (Eds), *Motivation, Language Identity and the L2 Self* (pp. 144–63). Bristol: Multilingual Matters.

Yazedjian, A. and Boyle Kolkhorst, B. (2007). Implementing small-group activities in large lecture classes. *College Teaching*, 55(4), 164–69.

Yphantides, J. (2013). Native-speakerism through English-only policies: Teachers, students and the changing face of Japan. In S. A. Houghton and D. J. Rivers (Eds), *Native-Speakerism in Japan: Intergroup Dynamics in Foreign Language Education* (pp. 207–18). Bristol: Multilingual Matters.

Ysseldyk, R., Kimberly, M. and Anisman, H. (2010). Religiosity as identity: Toward an understanding of religion from a social identity perspective. *Personality and Social Psychology Review*, 14(1), 60–71.

Zimmerman, D. H. (1998). Identity, context and interaction. In C. Antaki and S. Widdicombe (Ed.), *Identities in Talk* (pp. 87–106). London: Sage.

Zuengler, J. (1989). Identity and IL development and use. *Applied Linguistics*, 10(1), 80–96.

Index

academic,
  freedom 45, 71, 75
  inbreeding 55
acceptance–rejection dynamics 38
active learning 140
affective lexicon 179–91
agency,
  learner 7, 11, 77–81, 84, 88, 96, 98–100, 104, 157, 159–60, 162–4, 171–2, 174–5
  teacher 43–5, 57–8, 74
alignment 73–4, 132, 135
anxiety 27, 47, 88, 98
applied linguistics 1, 2, 11, 37, 48, 127, 177
appropriation 8, 77, 80, 83, 86–9, 92–3, 95, 101
Assistant Language Teacher (ALT) 57, 63–4
authenticity 5, 36, 41, 43, 44, 52, 53, 105, 127, 135, 137, 145
auto-biographical narrative 10, 57–75
autonomy 82

body language 87, 89, 97
border crossing 122, 178
bounded space 33
British Association for Applied Linguistics (BAAL) 37
burnout 64

case study 7, 10, 106, 148, 178–81, 191, 195
censorship 58
classroom observation 13, 18
code-switching 84, 89–90, 91, 97
communities of practice 7, 100, 121–3, 127–8, 130–3, 138, 144, 192
comparing and contrasting 107, 110, 196, 211
competence,
  communicative 174
  foreign language 159
  intercultural 137, 140
  intercultural communicative 5–6, 60, 195–7
  linguistic 81–4, 87, 89, 91, 95, 97, 98, 99, 100, 121, 123–4, 126
  teacher 62
  technical 29
  transcultural 8, 79, 81, 83, 91, 95–6, 100, 101
consensus-building 89
contact experience 162, 165–6, 169, 172–5
conversation analysis 9, 13–16, 18
critical analysis 8, 196, 198, 201–2, 204–5, 208–9
  critical evaluation 196, 198, 202, 205–6, 208–9
cultural,
  capital 35, 135, 142–3, 160, 164
  differences 8, 95, 108, 110, 126, 166, 169
  diversity 126, 134, 136–7
  norms 51–2, 80, 92
  practices 93, 108, 115, 122, 186
  relativism 86, 89, 97
  understanding 10, 103, 107, 112, 119

decision making 8, 195–6, 214
dehumanization 35
deprioritizing 211
discourse,
  dominant 80, 119
  emotive 178, 181, 193
  language learner 83, 101, 133–4
  poststructuralist thought 7, 178
  public 185, 192
  transcultural 78, 99

emotions 11–12, 28, 48, 177–9, 181–2, 186, 189–93
empathy 196, 198, 211–13
employment,
  advertisements for teachers 36
  categorization 41–2

in foreign language education 33, 55
opportunities for language learners 173
opportunities for 'native speakers' 46
policies / practices 36, 55
regulation for foreigners 49
rights 71
stability / instability 53
empowerment / disempowerment 33–4, 39, 43–6, 55, 58, 68, 73–4, 185
engagement 10, 22, 25, 41, 101, 125, 128, 132, 136, 140, 154, 172–3
essentialism 122, 137
evaluation,
programme 75
standard-setting 12, 195
student competence 126
subjective 179–80

fabrications 75
focus group(s) 10, 81, 83, 86, 89, 92–101
foreigner(s) 1–2, 16, 41–2, 45–53, 63, 85–9, 184, 198, 202, 205, 209
foreignness 1–2, 16, 85
freedom,
academic 45, 58, 71, 75
to determine identity 38
in English language teaching 50
to express agency 44
language learner 77, 99, 150, 153, 164, 166, 168

gender 6, 36, 38–9, 81–3, 85, 87, 89–90, 94–101, 103–4, 106, 115–16, 118–19, 131, 141
globalization 2, 41, 78, 123, 158, 207
globalized,
market economy 101
world 5, 80, 127, 138
group(s),
learner/teacher behaviour(s) 14, 16–17, 21, 24–5, 29, 47, 61, 84–9, 96–101, 151–3
membership(s) 34, 47, 51, 137, 139, 143, 164, 174
muted 34
representation(s) 3, 95
social (identities) 2–4, 106, 119, 142, 174
sociolinguistic 132

hegemony 78, 87–9, 92, 96–9
hierarchies 34, 49, 131, 135, 197

identification(s),
ethnic 48, 52, 55, 103–4, 106, 113, 115, 118–19, 172
gender 6, 31, 36, 38, 47, 81, 83, 85, 87, 89–90, 94–6, 98–101, 103–4, 106, 115–19, 141
national 6, 33, 36, 38, 42, 48, 51, 53, 101, 104, 112, 114–15, 120–2, 124–7, 129–32, 134, 136–8, 167, 199, 203, 208, 212
race 6, 36, 38, 103, 106, 113, 119
religion 36, 103–4, 106, 108–9, 110–13, 118–20, 199
sexual 85, 100, 141
social 104, 106
identity(ies),
change 122, 197, 200, 214
construction 9, 13, 15, 18, 26, 29–30, 103–4, 119
cultural 83, 85, 91–2, 99, 100, 103–4, 193
development 1, 4–8, 11–12, 29, 33–4, 38, 55, 141, 157, 195–201, 203, 207, 210–11, 214
fixed 34, 38, 42, 51, 55, 86
formation 6, 77, 83, 99, 119
imagined 121, 129, 137, 142–3
individual 10, 15, 28, 55, 159
multiple 9, 39–40, 73, 83, 121–3, 130, 132
national 106, 114–15, 120, 122, 137
negotiation 1, 9, 11, 13, 15, 193
options 5, 6, 143–5
positioning 118, 131, 138, 154, 160
professional 10, 38, 40–5, 47–9, 54–5, 57, 60, 73
situated 9, 14
social 2–4, 6, 9–11, 42–3, 47, 55, 118, 157–8, 163–4, 166–74, 178, 192
sociolinguistic 122–3, 129–30
workplace 9, 16–17, 31, 42–3
imagination 35, 37–8, 45, 123, 132, 143, 158–61
imagined community 139, 143, 149, 152, 154, 160
immersion 57–61, 63, 67, 73

inclusion–exclusion dynamics 37, 55
inferiority complex 60
in-group / out-group 3, 6, 34–5, 47, 53, 55
interaction(s) 2, 4, 6–7, 9, 13–15, 17, 21, 27–8, 31, 33, 43, 51, 77–80, 86, 93–6, 101, 104, 126, 128, 133, 139, 146, 152, 154, 159–60, 165, 169, 174, 182, 184–6, 192
intercultural competence 5–6, 137, 207–14
Intercultural Dialogue Model 8, 12, 195–7
internationalization 41, 52
interviews 18, 100, 148–9, 151–2, 154, 157, 162, 180–1, 190
investment 11, 29, 139–40, 141–5, 148, 150, 152–5, 160, 164, 169, 173

Japan Association of College English Teachers (JACET) 36, 50
Japan Association of Language Teachers (JALT) 36, 50
Japan Exchange and Teaching (JET) Programme 44, 50, 63
joint enterprise 128, 132, 136

L1 (first language) 58, 59–63, 65–6, 67–70, 72–4, 130, 132
L2 Motivational Self System 5–6, 158–9, 197
L2 (second / foreign language) 5, 13–14, 16–18, 20, 25–6, 28–31, 60–2, 65–6, 71, 73, 130, 132, 158–9, 197
language policy,
  English only 58, 69–72
  French only 58, 61, 64–8, 74
  target language only 7, 10, 57–9, 65–6, 68–9, 72–4
learning community 139, 148, 150, 154
legitimacy 47, 124, 126, 134
lingoscapes 79
literary text 10, 103, 105
love-hate dynamics 37–8

meaning making 128, 132
moral courage 75
motivation 5, 7, 11, 31, 47, 55, 62, 84, 98, 140–2, 157–73, 175, 197
multiculturalism 121
multilingualism 121
Multiliteracies Project 144
multimembership 123, 127–8, 130
mutual engagement 128, 132, 136

name calling 47, 50
naming 47, 50, 52, 92, 94, 97
narrative inquiry 33
nationalism 124–6, 131, 138
nationalist paradigm(s) 11, 121, 125–6, 130, 134, 136–8
nativeness 15, 33
native-speaker,
  conspiracy 35–7
  criterion 6, 35–7, 50, 82
  discrimination 37
  dress-code policies 52
  employment / recruitment 36, 48–51, 53, 69
  English teachers 5, 9–10, 33–4, 39–42, 45, 48–55, 69–70, 73, 88
  fallacy 42
  halo effect 81
  hegemony 78, 87–9, 97–9
  identities 33, 41, 45, 48–9, 51, 73
  language policies / language use 68–70
  location 33, 38, 44, 46, 50–1, 54
  narratives 40–54, 57–75
  norms 127
  status label 9, 39, 85, 100
native-speakerism 42
nepotism 55
non-native language selves 77, 81, 97
non-native speaker teacher 16, 60, 63, 67, 73

Otherness 6, 7, 8, 105, 107, 110, 122, 160, 172, 186, 191, 212–13
Others of opposition 57, 74
Others of similarity 10, 57, 74
overarching culture 126

performativity 104
positioning 52–3, 103–4, 118, 131, 138, 174–5, 178, 186, 192
possible selves 5, 158–9
postmodernism 33
poststructuralism 7, 11, 128, 178, 192
power dynamics 6, 7, 38, 54, 59, 68, 71, 77–80, 88, 96, 98–100, 119, 141, 175, 178, 184–6, 191–2, 198, 205–6
pragmatics 11, 177

reading 7, 10, 61, 67, 103–7, 109–14, 117–18, 119, 145–6
repertoires,
  Japanese 132, 135–6
  legitimate 131
  linguistic 125, 132–4
  truncated 123
resistance 8, 10, 57–75, 77–8, 80–1, 83, 87–9, 92–3, 95–101

Savoir,
  apprendre/faire 196
  être 196
  savoir s'engager 196
  se transformer 196
second language acquisition 15, 61, 129, 140
Self and Other,
  analysis 7, 196, 198, 200–5, 207–10
  awareness 27, 84, 137
  categorization 8, 16, 18, 20–7, 29
  derision 18, 22–6, 29
  disclosure 8, 18, 26, 29, 31
  discrepancy 197, 211–13
  esteem 3, 46–7, 49
  evaluation 8, 205–6, 208, 210, 212–13
  image 14, 16, 94, 104
  positioning 131, 175
  present and future 204–7
  reflection 8, 159, 191–2, 198
  similarities and differences between 3, 196, 198
  threatened 47
  transcultural 96
  values 196
seniority 94–7, 101
sexuality 84–5, 90, 97, 100, 141
situated learning theory 128
small cultures 132
social identity theory 2–3, 9
social participation 168–9, 172, 174
social psychology 2, 11, 177
socially constructed 7, 115, 141, 177
sociocultural,
  contexts / environments 1, 33–55, 103, 157–9, 174, 177, 193
  majority / minority 10, 35, 38, 44–5, 48–9, 51, 55
  norms 50–2, 54
  theory/theories 139, 144
  turn 15
sociolinguistics 11, 122, 177
sojourn abroad 177, 191
sphere of subjectivity 186
standard setting 12, 195, 197, 200, 213
stereotypes 43–4, 50, 54, 107, 135, 187
storytelling 33
struggle(s) 50, 58, 73, 81, 92, 124, 131, 134, 154, 178, 186–8, 192
student-directed practice 136
study abroad 82, 191
subcultures 126

teacher-directed practice 134–6
teacher-fronted classroom 9, 13, 17–18, 26, 28, 30
Teachers of English to Speakers of Other Languages (TESOL) 37, 48, 64
team teaching 63–4
teamwork 139, 150, 152
transcultural practice 77, 79, 81, 83–4, 89, 93–4, 96–7
transculturalism 78–9, 90, 97, 100

universalism 12, 195, 197–213

values 5, 12, 34, 57, 74, 89, 94, 99, 126, 131–2, 142, 196–8, 200–13

within-self diversity 197
writing,
  creative expression 140, 150, 153–4
  feedback debriefing sessions 145
  foreign language project 140, 145, 148
  gender typicality 115–16, 120
  imagined communities 144
  L1 use 60–1, 105
  peer-editing 146
  scaffolding 144–7

xenophobia 55

year abroad 11, 177–8, 180, 182, 186–7, 191–3

zone of proximal development 144